Elementary
New Testament
Greek

Joseph R. Dongell

First Fruits Press
Wilmore, Kentucky
c2014

Elementary New Testament Greek, by Joseph R. Dongell

Published by First Fruits Press, © 2014

Digital version at http://place.asburyseminary.edu/academicbooks/6/

First Fruits Press is a digital imprint of the Asbury Theological Seminary, B.L. Fisher Library. Asbury Theological Seminary is the legal owner of the material previously published by the Pentecostal Publishing Co. and reserves the right to release new editions of this material as well as new material produced by Asbury Theological Seminary. Its publications are available for noncommercial and educational uses, such as research, teaching and private study. First Fruits Press has licensed the digital version of this work under the Creative Commons Attribution Noncommercial 3.0 United States License. To view a copy of this license, visit http://creativecommons.org/licenses/by-nc/3.0/us/.

For all other uses, contact First Fruits Press

ISBN: 9781621711490 (print), 9781621711513 (digital)

Dongell, Joseph.
    Elementary New Testament Greek / by Joseph R. Dongell.
    223 p. ; 22 x 28 cm.
    Wilmore, Ky. : First Fruits Press, c2014.
    ISBN: 9781621711490 (pbk.)
    1. Greek language, Biblical – Grammar . 2. Bible. – New Testament – Language, style.
    I. Title.
PA817 .D66 2014   487.4

Cover design by Wesley Wilcox

First Fruits Press
The Academic Open Press of Asbury Theological Seminary
859-858-2236
first.fruits@asburyseminary.edu
http://place.asburyseminary.edu/firstfruits

Asbury Theological Seminary
204 N. Lexington Ave., Wilmore, KY 40390
asburyseminary.edu
800-2ASBURY

Dedicated to my mentors in Greek

✝ Herbert Dongell,

✝ Marling Elliott,

✝ Robert W. Lyon,

and Hubert Martin

with special thanks to

Brad Johnson and Klay Harrison

Contents

Paradigms   189

Preface

The world does not another Elementary Greek Grammar! There are many fine products on the market that have proven themselves to be useful both in the classroom and for private instruction.

The need for this particular grammar arises from the peculiar shape of the MDiv curriculum at Asbury Theological Seminary. Several years ago the faculty adopted a curriculum that required one semester of Greek and one semester of Hebrew, each as preparatory for a basic exegesis course in each discipline.

It became clear after several years of trial and error that a "lexical" or "tools" approach to learning Greek and Hebrew was inadequate, no matter how skilled the instructors or how motivated the students. In today's general vacuum of grammatical training in public education across the United States, students typically enter seminary training with no knowledge of how languages work. Any training we might give them in accessing grammatical information through the use of Bible software programs will, we learned, come to naught in the absence of an understanding of just what such information actually means. We agreed that we actually needed to "teach the language itself," at least in some rudimentary fashion, if we hoped students would make sense of grammatical and linguistic issues involved biblical interpretation.

Ideally, of course, a full year's investment in each language (Greek and Hebrew) would be required as the basis for exegesis in the respective testament. But the constraints of our curriculum require that we accomplish as much as possible in each language during the course of a single semester. This puts enormous pressure upon the classroom setting, the instructor, and (obviously) the students to accomplish the critical mass of instruction allowing meaningful engagement with the original text. It is neither possible nor humane simple to compress a full year's instruction into a single semester. Difficult choices must be made in order to create a meaningful, if modest, open door into the world of exegesis.

The first 12 chapters of this grammar are designed to correspond to the first semester's instructional agenda. In these chapters we introduce all the parts of speech, explain and drill the basic elements of grammar, set forth the larger verb system (excluding the perfect system), teach the tenses of the Indicative Mood only (again, excluding the perfect system), and help students build a vocabulary of all NT words occurring 100 times or more. We also lead students into the NT itself with carefully chosen examples, while at the same time guiding them in each lesson to learn the use of the standard NT lexicon [BDAG] and an exegetical grammar [Wallace's Greek Grammar Beyond the Basics]. We are well aware of the limitations of this approach, but genuinely believe that some instruction along these lines is better than none, and that such an approach provide a foundation for students interested in moving beyond the first semester (into chapters 13-24) into a firmer grasp of the language of the NT.

Preface to the First Edition (Under Revision)

This grammar has already undergone numbers of revisions over the last 4 years, for which I must thank Mr. Brad Johnson (model language instructor) and his students for their fine-toothed combing of the text. This present publication, the first effort to combine the two semesters of elementary Greek instruction into one volume with full appendices, represents the first half of a full revision. Chapters 1-12 have been brought up the standards of the most recent suggestions. Chapters 13-24 await this latest wave of modification, with all chapters together scheduled to be in their fully revised form by February of 2015. My special thanks goes to Mr. Klay Harrison, whose expertise and enthusiasm for this labor is stamped on every page.

Publisher's Note

This textbook was designed to be the primary text for the Elementary Greek course at Asbury Theological Seminary. Therefore, you will references to other texts and assignments for our students. The books that are required for the students are:

Danker, et al (BDAG). *A Greek-English Lexicon of the New Testament and Other Early Christian Literature*. 3rd Rev. Ed. Chicago: University of Chicago Press, 2000.

Mounce, William D., ed. *Interlinear for the Rest of Us: The Reverse Interlinear for New Testament Word Studies*. Grand Rapids, Michigan: Zondervan, 2006.

Wallace, Daniel B. *The Basics of New Testament Syntax: An Intermediate Greek Grammar*. Grand Rapids: Zondervan, 2000.

or _____. *Greek Grammar Beyond the Basics*. Grand Rapids: Zondervan, 1997.

The Greek New Testament (GNT).

1: Reading Greek Aloud

Welcome to New Testament Greek! You're joining the ranks of thousands across the ages who have deepened their work with Scripture by learning the language used by writers of the New Testament (NT).

Even if there is dispute about how Greek was pronounced in Jesus' day (i.e. exactly how various letters of the alphabet actually sounded), we will reap practical benefits by fastening upon **some consistent pattern** of pronunciation. Experience has shown that it's hard to learn something we can't pronounce with confidence. Consistent pronunciation enables us to:

- memorize words more easily

- communicate with each other about Greek more effectively

- sense the connected flow and artistry of the text more readily

- There are almost **no silent letters** in Greek. Nearly every letter is to be pronounced cleanly and clearly.

- **No exotic accent** is required or encouraged. There's no need to sound ancient, or Mediterranean, or sophisticated.

- The pronunciation of Greek letters is **consistent** from word to word. No nightmares like the English "-ough-," which is pronounced differently in each of the following: cough, though, tough, bough, thought, and through.

Now it's time to get to work! Push your way through the alphabet chart carefully, repeatedly, and aloud. A solid hour spent here will get you on the right track, giving your eyes, ears and mind sufficient time to absorb the new reality of the Greek alphabet. Remember that a pathway through the woods is made only by repeatedly traveling in the same groove over time.

The Alphabet

Our primary job in this chapter is to learn how to pronounce the sounds of the letters of the alphabet as we actually find them joined together as words and sentences in the NT.

As you will soon see, there were 24 letters in the Greek alphabet in NT times. This particular set of letters (and their order) was officially adopted in Athens around 400 BC. The order of letters as we find them in this alphabet is best described as "random." Vowels and consonants are scattered about and intermingled with each other. Neither vowels nor consonants are grouped according to the nature of their sounds. But since this traditional order of letters stands as the organizing principle of Greek dictionaries, we need to memorize the standard order of letters to make good use of these tools.

Just before we engage the alphabet directly, here's some great news that makes our job easier than you would think!

	Name	Upper Case	Lower Case	Transliteration	Pronunciation	Comments
1	alpha	A	α	a	a as in **father**	The short and the long alpha are written and pronounced alike.
2	beta	B	β	b	b as in **boy**	
3	gamma	Γ	γ	g, n	g as in **girl**	Never as in **gentle**. Gamma before γ, κ, χ or ξ sounds like ng in **song.**
4	delta	Δ	δ	d	d as in **dog**	
5	epsilon	E	ε	e	e as in **pet**	
6	zeta	Z	ζ	z	ds as in **soapsuds**	But if the first letter of a word, like z in **zoo.**
7	eta	H	η	ē	ey as in **they**	
8	theta	Θ	θ	th	th as in **thin**	Never as in **this** or that.
9	iota	I	ι	i	i as in **pit** (short), or **machine** (long)	If the iota is the first letter of a word and followed immediately by vowel, then pronounced like y in **yes.**
10	kappa	K	κ	k	k as in **key**	
11	lambda	Λ	λ	l	l as in **log**	
12	mu	M	μ	m	m as in **mug**	The *name* of the letter sounds like **moo.**
13	nu	N	ν	n	n as in **night**	The *name* of the letter sounds like **new.**
14	xi	Ξ	ξ	x	x as in **box**	The *name* of the letter sounds like the xy in **boxy.**
15	omicron	O	o	o	o as in **dock**	Keep this short o and the long o (omega) distinct in pronunciation.
16	pi	Π	π	p	p as in **pest**	The *name* of the letter sounds like **pea** (not pie).
17	rho	P	ρ	r	r as in **ring**	
18	sigma	Σ	σ, ς	s	s as in **sit**	ς is found only at a word's end (final sigma); σ everywhere else.
19	tau	T	τ	t	t as in **top**	The *name* of the letter rhymes with **cow.**
20	upsilon	Y	υ	y, u	u as in **put** (short), or **dune** (long)	Transliterated as y, unless within a diphthong (see below).
21	phi	Φ	φ	ph	ph as in **phone**	The *name* of the letter sounds like **fee.**
22	chi	X	χ	ch	ch as in (the Scottish) **loch**	The *name* of the letter rhymes with **key.**
23	psi	Ψ	ψ	ps	ps as in **maps**	The *name* of the letter sounds like the psy in **Gypsy.**
24	omega	Ω	ω	ō	o as in **note**	Keep this long o and the short o (omicron) distinct in pronunciation.

Note: No English sound matches the sound of **chi**. Take the "k" in **book** and dramatically soften it, allowing air to pass softly through, just at the point we would tighten the throat to pronounce a "k".

Additional Notes about the Alphabet:

<u>Upper and Lower Case Forms</u>

Up until about 800 AD, Greek was written in what we would call "all caps." Only in the Middle Ages did scribes develop a streamlined lower case script that made writing easier and faster. Also in the earlier period scribes used no punctuation and no spaces between words.

ASYOUCANSEEONECANSTILLMAKEGOODSENSEOFATEXT
WRITTENINTHISFASHIONONEIMPORTANTBENEFITWASACO
NSI DERABLEECONOMYOFSPACETHEREBYACHIEVINGAPROPO
RTIONALREDUCTIONINTHECOSTOFPRODUCTIONSINCEWRI
TINGSURFACESINANTIQUITYWEREQUITEEXPENSIVEONLYR
ARELYWOULDCONFUSIONARISEINTHEMINDOFREADERS

The practice of primarily using *lower case* letters mixed occasionally with *upper case* letters has evolved fairly recently. Your Greek New Testament editors (whether Nestle-Aland or UBS) deploy *upper case* letters only to signal:

- a proper name
- the beginning of a quotation
- typically *NOT the beginning of a sentence*
- the beginning of a major paragraph (according to the interpretation of the modern editors)

<u>Transliteration</u>

One column in your alphabet chart supplies the English letters authorized by various scholarly bodies to represent Greek letters. If you were to submit a scholarly paper for publication to the Society of Biblical Literature, for example, the Greek words you cite must be presented in transliterated form (e.g. The Greek word δοῦλος must be expressed in English letters as **doulos**). In our process of learning Greek, we will use transliteration *very little*.

Vowels and Diphthongs

As we progress in learning Greek, the importance of understanding more about vowels will become obvious. The chart below, which organizes vowels according to "type" and "length," will prepare us to understand the shifts we will see happening between long and short vowels within the same vowel class:

	Short		Long	
"a" type	alpha	[α]	alpha	[α]
"e" type	epsilon	[ε]	eta	[η]
"o" type	omicron	[o]	omega	[ω]
"i" type	iota	[ι]	iota	[ι]
"u" type	upsilon	[υ]	upsilon	[υ]

Note:

1) You can easily distinguish between long and short vowels in the "e" and "o" classes. They are different letters altogether.

2) You will need more experience to determine whether an "a", "i" or "u" class vowel is short or long.

Combinations of Vowels (proper diphthongs)

Specific vowels can be found in **set pairs**, ending either in iota [ι] or upsilon [υ]. Each pair of vowels (below) merges together to form a single sound, and will control a single syllable (beat). Such a merger is called a **diphthong**.

vowel pairs ending in **iota** [ι]:

αι	pronounced like the **ai** in **aisle**
ει	pronounced like the **ei** in **freight**
οι	pronounced like the **oi** in **boil**
υι	pronounced like the **ui** in **suite** (like the English word **we**)

vowel pairs ending in **upsilon** [υ]:

αυ	pronounced like the **ow** in **kraut**
ευ	pronounced like the **eu** in **feud** (like the English word **you**)
ηυ	pronounced like the **eu** in **feud** (Rare. We will pronounce it just as ευ is pronounced)
ου	pronounced like the **ou** in **soup**
ωυ	pronounced like the **ou** in **soup** (Never found in the NT functioning as a diphthong. We include it here because this combination of vowels appears in the NT in the proper name **Moses**, but in the special condition explained below.)

1) Only **these particular combinations** of vowels will form diphthongs. With any other sequence of vowels, each vowel will retain its distinct sound, and each vowel will control a separate syllable (or beat).

2) On rare occasions when one of these vowel combinations is **not** to be read as a diphthong, our modern editors will set **double dots** above the second vowel. This textual marking, called a **diaeresis** [die-AIR-uh-sis], tells us to pronounce each vowel separately, thereby creating an additional syllable. (This happens most commonly with proper names.)

For example, in the Greek form of the proper name **Isaiah** [Ἡσαΐας] we will find a diaeresis over the iota [ι], breaking what normally would have been a diphthong [αι] into two separate vowel sounds [α-ι]. Now we know to treat this as a four, not a three syllable word:

Ἡ-σα-ι-ας (With the diaeresis, we must treat α and ι as separate vowels, each with its own beat.)

Ἡ-σαι-ας (Without the diaeresis, we *would have* treated α and ι as a single sound, as a diphthong.)

Similarly, in the Greek form of the proper name **Moses** [Μωϋσης] we will find a diaeresis over the upsilon [υ], breaking what normally would have been a diphthong [ωυ] into two separate vowel sounds [ω-υ]. Now we know to treat this as a three, not a two syllable word:

Μω-υ-σης (With the diaeresis, we must treat ω and υ as separate vowels, each with its own beat.)

Μωυ-σης (Without the diaeresis, we *would have* treated ω and υ as a single sound, as a diphthong.)

Combinations of Vowels (improper diphthongs)

Three vowels (α, η, ω) are sometimes found with tiny iotas [ι] written beneath them. This **iota subscript** does not change the pronunciation of the main vowel. Though these iotas can be thought of as **the only silent letters in Greek**, they are important.

ᾳ	pronounced like a simple α
ῃ	pronounced like a simple η
ῳ	pronounced like a simple ω

Consonants and Consonant Combinations

As we've already noted, the traditional alphabet has gathered the Greek letters into a random sequence with the result that the phonetic relationships between various letters have been obscured. By studying the following consonant groupings you will discern these relationships, and prepare yourself well for understanding how Greek words sometimes change their spellings under certain conditions. [Modern linguistics has developed elaborate and complex notational systems for identifying the wide range of sounds created by human beings. In this section we will be content with fairly simple, traditional terminology.]

Sibilant [σ]

> Because we "*hiss*" when pronouncing the sigma, it has been called a *sibilant* (from the Latin *sibilāre*, "to hiss").

Stops [κ, γ, χ   τ, δ, θ   π, β, φ]   Combinations [ξ,ζ,ψ]

> These consonants "*close down,*" in varying degrees, different parts of our sound-making anatomy. As you can see in the chart below, we can close down the flow of air at three different anatomical *locations*: throat, teeth, or lips. We can also *control how the air passes* through: held then released (whether explosively or gently), or continuously breathed (*aspirate*). Finally, we can control whether our *vocal chords vibrate* (*voiced* or *voiceless*).
>
> Finally, any of the nine (9) stops followed by a sigma [σ] will be rewritten as a combination letter appropriate to its class (velar, dental, or labial).

	Voiceless	Voiced	Asperate	Combination
Velar (throat)	κ	γ	χ	ξ (velar + σ = ξ)
Dental (teeth)	τ	δ	θ	ζ (dental + σ = ζ)
Labial (lips)	π	β	φ	ψ (labial + σ = ψ)

Liquids [λ, μ, ν, ρ]

> These consonants, like water, can be continually "*poured out.*"

- I lllllllllove you!
- This pie is mmmmmmarvelous!
- I'll nnnnnnever do that!
- He's a rrrrrrrat!

Additional Marks

Breathing Marks

Every Greek word beginning with a vowel or diphthong must carry either a *rough* or a *smooth* breathing mark:

- The *rough* breathing mark (ʽ) tells us to add an "*h*" sound at the beginning of the word.
- The *smooth* breathing mark (ʼ) tells us to add *nothing*.

Therefore:

- a (theoretical) Greek word ἱτ, would be pronounced like the English word "hit."
- a (theoretical) Greek word ἰτ, would be pronounced like the English word "it."

As you can see, the only difference between the two marks is the direction of their curve. Develop your own trick for remembering the distinction between these marks.

Accent Marks

Most Greek words carry *one accent* mark written above one of its vowels or diphthongs. There are three different kinds of accent marks in our texts:

The *acute*	as in	τόπος	looks like a forward-leaning slash.
The *grave*	as in	θεὸς	looks like a backward-leaning slash.
The *circumflex*	as in	τῶν	looks like an eyebrow (or in some Greek fonts like a tilde [~]).

Since it is a matter of some dispute (and of little interpretive value to know) just how ancient speakers pronounced these accents, we will handle **all three accents identically, as stress marks** (just as we stress certain syllables in English words). Notice the following English words, and the differing locations of the stress:

animal	stressed on the **third** syllable (counting from the end)	**A**-ni-mal	(antepenult)
constitution	stressed on the **second** syllable (counting from the end)	con-sti-**TU**-tion	(penult)
balloon	stressed on the **last** syllable	bal-**LOON**	(ultima)

If we listen carefully to our own English pronunciation, we will notice that we not only add **force** to a stressed syllable, but we simultaneously raise the **pitch** as well. The **TU** of "constitution" is not only pronounced with more force than other syllables, but is higher in "tone" as if being "sung" as a higher musical note. As you learn to pronounce Greek, it may be helpful to "pound and sing" as you work through a sentence: pound the desk on the accented syllable to help you add force at that very point, and "sing" that same syllable at a higher pitch.

Though most Greek words carry an accent mark, some don't. Similarly, certain English words often lose their stress and flow smoothly into the words around them. When we read John 1:1 aloud in English, "In the beginning was the Word," we usually place no stress on either article ("the"), as if the sentence were written, "In thebeginning was theWord." Notice how each article slides unstressed right into the following word without pause.

In Greek we find two opposite strategies for such pronunciation mergers:

- **Proclitics**: One set of words, the "**forward leaners**," will join themselves with the **following** word in pronunciation as if there were no space between them. [e.g. ἐν τῶν is read together as ἐντῶν]

- **Enclitics**: Another set of words, the "**backward leaners**," usually join themselves with the **preceding** word in pronunciation as if there were no space between them. [e.g. τοῦτό ἐστιν is read together as τοῦτόεστιν] Under certain circumstances you will see an enclitic with its own accent. Also, you will sometimes see that an enclitic appears to have thrown its stress backwards onto the previous word, causing it to appear with **two** accents marks (as in our example here).

For Reference Only; No Memorization Needed:

The number of Greek proclitics and enclitics is not terribly great. At some later point you might want to know just which words fill each category. The lists below will satisfy your curiosity:

- **Proclitics**: ὁ, ἡ, οἱ, αἱ, εἰ, ὡς, εἰς, ἐκ, ἐξ, ἐν, οὐ, οὐκ, οὐχ

- **Enclitics**: μέ, μοῦ, μοί, σέ, σοῦ, σοί, τις (all forms of this indefinite pronoun), πού, ποτέ, πώ, πώς, γέ, τέ, εἰμί (in all forms of the present indicative, except 2nd singular), φημί (in all forms of the present indicative, except 2nd singular). When "leaning backward," these words appear without accent marks.

Punctuation Marks

As noted above, ancient Greek manuscripts did not have punctuation marks. The editors of modern Greek texts add punctuation marks as an aide for readers. Sometimes, of course, these decisions are quite subjective and involve disputed interpretations. It is important to realize, then, that the punctuation marks we see in our modern texts don't authoritatively convey what punctuation an ancient writer might have used, had such devices been available at that time. [For famous examples of ambiguity in interpreting the implied punctuation of ancient texts, compare different English translations, and their marginal notes, at John 1:3-4 or John 14:1-2.]

Greek Mark	Appearance	Functional Equivalent	Sense
1 ,	English Comma	English Comma	Weak Break
2 ·	Raised English Period	English Colon	Strong Break
3 .	English Period	English Period	Very Strong Break
4 ;	English Semicolon	English Question Mark	Inquiry

Notice that **two** kinds of English punctuation marks **are not used** in modern Greek texts: **exclamation** marks and **quotation** marks. Their appearance in Modern English translations of the Bible involves interpretive discernment by modern editors. For example, where does the "speech" Peter begins in Galatians 2:14 really end?

Should the English "close quote" be placed after 2:15 or after 2:21? Ancient Greek manuscripts do not tell us, and English versions vary.

The Apostrophe

Just as English writers signal the dropping of a short vowel from the ***end*** of a word with an ***apostrophe*** [e.g. from ***though*** to ***tho'***], so do the editors of modern Greek texts [e.g. from κατὰ to κατ᾽].

The Diaeresis

See the explanation in the comments above about diphthongs on page 4.

The Coronis

On some occasions you will see what looks like ***an apostrophe over the middle of a word***. It merely signals that two words have been pushed together in a move called ***crasis*** [the two syllables of "crasis" rhyme with the last two syllables of "molasses"]. The coronis in no way affects the pronunciation of the newly-formed word.

In the NT, we will find crasis only when the conjunction καί (often meaning "and") is followed by any of 7 particular words [e.g. καί + ἐγώ merge to form κἀγώ]. In other words, every occasion of crasis in the NT begins with κἀ-.

Distinguishing the "Apostrophes"

Perhaps you've noticed that three different marks resemble the English apostrophe: the smooth breathing, the coronis, and the apostrophe. Distinguishing them is easy once you notice the ***positions they always take***:

Mark	Example	Position on Word	Circumstance	Frequency
Smooth Breathing	εἰς	beginning	with an initial vowel or diphthong	*very* frequently found
Coronis	κἀγώ	middle	only in κἀ- formations	rare
Apostrophe	κατ᾽	end	signaling loss of final vowel	frequently found

Syllables

We're almost ready to read Greek aloud! The last piece of the puzzle involves ***syllabification***, or ***grouping the letters*** of a word into distinct pronunciation units. In English we know to say:

> **not** ret-ired — **but** re-tired
> **not** mat-e-rnal — **but** ma-ter-nal
> **not** sickl-y — **but** sick-ly
> **not** nat-ure — **but** na-ture.

Consider the following ***guidelines*** for dividing Greek words into syllables. [In the notations below, "v" represents a vowel or diphthong. "C" represents a consonant.]

1) There will be as many syllables in a word as there are vowels (or diphthongs). For example:

Greek Word...	Broken Into Syllables
vvC	v-vC

Greek Word…	Broken Into Syllables
ἔαν	ἔ-αν (Since εα is not a diphthong, each vowel must be sounded separately.)

One consonant found between vowels (or diphthongs) will go with the *following* vowel, beginning a *new syllable*. The following notations are merely a sampling of the many possible patterns fitting this circumstance:

Greek Word…	Broken Into Syllables
vCv	v-Cv
vCvCv	v-Cv-Cv
CvCv	Cv-Cv
CvCvv	Cv-Cv-v

θάνατος would be divided as θά-να-τος.

2) **Consonant Pairs** found between vowels (or diphthongs) will be treated as follows:

Consonants pairs that are **doubled consonants** will be divided (one closing the first syllable; one opening the second).

CvCCv [Βάλλω] should be read as CvC-Cv [Βάλ-λω]

Consonants pairs that **cannot begin a word*** will be divided (one closing the first syllable; one opening the second).

CvCCv [πάντι] should be read as CvC-Cv [πάν-τι]

Consonants pairs that **can begin a word*** remain together, beginning the next syllable.

CvCvCCvCv [γινώσκετε] should be read as
Cv-Cv-CCv-Cv [γι-νώ-σκε-τε]

Note: You can look in a Greek dictionary (often called a lexicon) to see if any words begin with a given cluster. In the examples above, you will find no Greek word beginning with ντ, but many with σκ. Therefore, the latter consonantal cluster will remain together, beginning the next syllable.

3) In spite of the guidelines above, we must always **honor the components** that have contributed to the construction of a compound word. Thus for the English word "overestimate," we would never say "o-ve-**re**-sti-mate," because the "r" belongs with "over," clearly a fixed building block used to form the composite (over + estimate = overestimate). So the ξ (xi) in ἐξέρχομαι ("I am going out") should not follow the advice of #2 above, since ἐξ represents a basic building block in this compound word (ἐξ–έρχομαι, in an overly literal sense: "out (ἐξ)—I am going (ἔρχομαι)"). As your experience grows, you will easily recognize many of these

building blocks.

Digging into the New Testament Text

1) Open your Greek New Testament [GNT] and *find* **John 14:15-17.** (Even without knowing Greek, you can probably figure out where the 4th Gospel is located, and where these particular verses are situated).

    a) ***Write out and decode*** for every word the letters and markings we have studied in this chapter. For example, beginning with 14:15, the first three words would be "decoded" as follows:

    Ἐὰν — smooth breathing, epsilon (upper case), alpha, grave, nu

    ἀγαπᾶτέ — smooth breathing, alpha, gamma, alpha, pi, alpha, circumflex, tau, epsilon, acute

    με — mu, epsilon, [This word has no accent, and must be an enclitic or a proclitic.]

    b) Do you find any of the following: Crasis? Coronis? Elision? Diaeresis? Apostrophe? Upper case letters? Proclitics? Enclitics? Punctuation Marks? [Explain as needed.]

    c) c. Now ***write out*** these verses in Greek (in the normal left-to-right fashion as they appear in the GNT itself). Write largely enough to accommodate the steps below.

    d) d. S***yllabify*** all the words in these three verses by drawing ***large vertical slashes*** at the appropriate points. ***Circle*** all ***diphthongs*** you find. ***Underline*** any ***proclitic or enclitic*** together with its partnering word to show their union.

    e) e. Now work at ***pronouncing*** (reading aloud) these verses. Be patient. It will take time! Go syllable by syllable. Don't worry about speed. You are perfectly normal if you feel confused, slow, or frustrated. But soon you will be gaining real confidence with practice and repetition.

2) Open your Greek Interlinear [see "Publisher's Note" on page x] and *find* **John 14:15-17.**

    a) Notice that the Greek words in the Interlinear appear in a different order from those in the GNT. Why is the ordering of the Interlinear different? What order does it follow? (For help, see Mounce's explanation in the introduction [p. x, #2].)

    b) Notice the four "lines" of information visible as you examine this passage (**John 14:15-17**) in the Interlinear. What information does each line contain? (For help, see Mounce's explanation in his introduction [p. x, #1].)

    c) c. Move through this passage in the Interlinear until you come to the English word "Counselor." Below it on the third line you will see the Greek word spelled exactly as it appears in this passage. But on the fourth line of information you will see the number 4156. This is keyed to a Greek wordlist in appendix B of the Interlinear. Go there now.

    • How many times does this word occur in the GNT? (For help see p. 788 in the interlinear.)

    • Have all biblical references been listed here at this point? (For help see p. 788 in the interlinear.)

    d) There at entry 4156 you see the Greek word in its "first", or "dictionary" form. Instead of παράκλητον which stands in the text at John 14:16, we find παράκλητος here in the wordlist. In this circumstance the difference [between the dictionary form and what might actually appear in the text] might not seem like much, but on other occasions the difference will be remarkable. Now that we know the "dictionary form," we can look it up in the lexicon below.

3) Open your Greek Lexicon [see "Publisher's Note" on page x] and find παράκλητος. Since you are learning the Greek alphabet and the order of its letters, you should be able to find this word without too much trouble. Be sure you find ***exactly this word,*** and ***not others that are similar***.

a) First you will notice that the information supplied under παράκλητος is fairly technical, filled with abbreviations, and stuffed with bibliographical leads to other scholarly writings (often in German). You can see why this lexicon [BDAG] is the state-of-the-art tool for studying the GNT. Over the decades, it has been repeatedly revised, improved, and supplemented. It is the most authoritative source for first approaches to "word study" in NT Greek. However far you progress, you can always **grow more into** the use of this lexicon. (*Do not confuse BDAG's lower case* **kappa** *with the* **chi**.)

b) As you look through the entry, you should be able to see in **bold font** the **GNT Scripture references**. For words of **lower frequency**, BDAG will often cite **all occurrences** of such a word in the NT. Do you see the 5 references for παράκλητος in the NT?

c) Early in the entry for παράκλητος, you will see a set of English words in bold font: **one who appears in another's behalf, *mediator, intercessor, helper***. If you look closely, you will see that some of these words are italicized, while others are not. The difference between these fonts is important:

- Non-Italicized = **Definition**: A definition is an attempt to explain the logical components that make up a word's meaning. It involves some degree of analysis (taking things apart) to show the various features of "sense" and "reference" that are combined to create the notion(s) a given word might convey. E.g. Automobile = **a manufactured machine, usually with four wheels, that is self-propelled, capable of traveling significant distances, and usually capable of carrying two or more passengers. Such a vehicle is usually guided from within by a single driver.**

- Italicized = ***Glosses***: Glosses are suggested ***synonyms***, or ***substitutes*** for a given word. A Gloss does not attempt to analyze or explain, but only offers another word that might be used in its place. Glosses, at best, are useful in offering smooth translations, but not so much in offering insightful interpretations. E.g. Automobile = ***car***, ***vehicle.***

d) Look to the next page in BDAG (p. 766) and write down two or three examples of the ***definition/gloss*** distinction.

Drills and Exercises

1) **Selected Pronunciation Drills**: In the following exercise, the syllables bear no necessary resemblance to any particular Greek syllable or word, but are designed to isolate particular sounds to help us gain confidence quickly. ***Begin working horizontally***, and notice that all syllables on the horizontal row should ***rhyme***. After you gain comfort working horizontally, move to the greater challenge of ***working vertically*** with the shifting vowels. [We are using non-technical English representations, and have marked with an ***asterisk*** certain English syllables that should not be pronounced like the real English words they spell. Keep the horizontal rows rhyming, and all will be well!]

	beta	gamma	delta	zeta	theta	kappa	lambda	mu	nu	xi	pi	sigma	tau	phi	chi	psi
Short Vowels																
epsilon	βετ	γετ	δετ	ζετ	θετ	κετ	λετ	μετ	νετ	ξετ	πετ	σετ	τετ	φετ	χετ	ψετ
	bet	get	det	zet	thet	ket	let	met	net	kset	pet	set	tet	fet	chet*	pset
iota (short)	βιτ	γιτ	διτ	ζιτ	θιτ	κιτ	λιτ	μιτ	νιτ	ξιτ	πιτ	σιτ	τιτ	φιτ	χιτ	ψιτ
	bit	git	dit	zit	thit	kit	lit	mit	nit	ksit	pit	pit	tit	fit	chit*	psit
omicron	βοτ	γοτ	δοτ	ζοτ	θοτ	κοτ	λοτ	μοτ	νοτ	ξοτ	ποτ	σοτ	τοτ	φοτ	χοτ	ψοτ
	bot	got	dot	zot	thot	kot	lot	mot	not	ksot	pot	sot	tot	fot	shot	psot
Long Vowels																
alpha (long & short)	βα	γα	δα	ζα	θα	κα	λα	μα	να	ξα	πα	σα	τα	φα	χα	ψα
	bah	gah	dah	zah	thah	kah	lah	mah	nah	ksah	pah	sah	tah	fah	chah	psah
eta	βη	γη	δη	ζη	θη	κη	λη	μη	νη	ξη	πη	ση	τη	φη	χη	ψη
	bay	gay	day	zay	thay	kay	lay	may	nay	ksay	pay	say	tay	fay	chay	psay

	beta	gamma	delta	zeta	theta	kappa	lambda	mu	nu	xi	pi	sigma	tau	phi	chi	psi
iota (long)	βι	γι	δι	ζι	θι	κι	λι	μι	νι	ξι	πι	σι	τι	φι	χι	ψι
	bee	gee*	dee	zee	thee*	kee	lee	mee	nee	ksei	pee	see	tee	fee	chee	psee
omega	βω	γω	δω	ζω	θω	κω	λω	μω	νω	ξω	πω	σω	τω	φω	χω	ψω
	bō	gō	dō	zō	thō	kō	lō	mō	nō	ksō	pō	sō	fō tō	fō	chō	psō

Diphthongs

	beta	gamma	delta	zeta	theta	kappa	lambda	mu	nu	xi	pi	sigma	tau	phi	chi	psi
αι	βαι	γαι	δαι	ζαι	θαι	και	λαι	μαι	ναι	ξαι	παι	σαι	ται	φαι	χαι	ψαι
	bye	guy	die	zigh	thigh	kigh	lie	my	nigh	ksigh	pie	sigh	tie	figh	chigh	psigh
ει	βει	γει	δει	ζει	θει	κει	λει	μει	νει	ξει	πει	σει	τει	φει	χει	ψει
	bay	gay	day	zay	thay	kay	lay	may	nay	ksay	pay	say	tay	fay	chay	psay
οι	βοι	γοι	δοι	ζοι	θοι	κοι	λοι	μοι	νοι	ξοι	ποι	σοι	τοι	φοι	χοι	ψοι
	boy	goy	doy	zoy	thoy	koy	loy	moy	noy	ksoy	poy	soy	toy	foy	choy*	psoy
αυ	βαυ	γαυ	δαυ	ζαυ	θαυ	καυ	λαυ	μαυ	ναυ	ξαυ	παυ	σαυ	ταυ	φαυ	χαυ	ψαυ
	bow*	gow	dow	zow	thow	kow	low*	mow*	now*	ksow	pow	sow*	tow*	fow	show*	psow
ευ	βευ	γευ	δευ	ζευ	θευ	κευ	λευ	μευ	νευ	ξευ	πευ	σευ	τευ	φευ	χευ	ψευ
	byoo	gyoo	dyoo	zyoo	thyoo	kyoo	lyoo	myoo	nyoo	ksyoo	pyoo	syoo	tyoo	few	chyoo	psyoo
ου	βου	γου	δου	ζου	θου	κου	λου	μου	νου	ξου	που	σου	του	φου	χου	ψου
	boo	goo	doo	zoo	thoo	koo	loo	moo	new	ksoo	poo	soo	too	foo	choo*	psoo
υι	βυι	γυι	δυι	ζυι	θυι	κυι	λυι	μυι	νυι	ξυι	πυι	συι	τυι	φυι	χυι	ψυι
	bwee	bwee	dwee	zwee	thwee	kwee	lwee	mwee	nwee	kswee	pwee	swee	twee	fwee	chwee	pswee

Rho-Pi Distinction Practice

	beta	gamma	delta	zeta	theta	kappa	lambda	mu	nu	xi	pi	sigma	tau	phi	chi	psi
π (pi as final letter)	βιπ	γιπ	διπ	ζιπ	θιπ	κιπ	λιπ	μιπ	νιπ	ξιπ	πιπ	σιπ	τιπ	φιπ	χιπ	ψιπ
	bip	gip	dip	zip	thip	kip	lip	mip	nip	ksip	pip	sip	tip	fip	chip*	psip
ρ (rho as final letter)	βαρ	γαρ	δαρ	ζαρ	θαρ	καρ	λαρ	μαρ	ναρ	ξαρ	παρ	σαρ	ταρ	φαρ	χαρ	ψαρ
	bar	gar	dar	zar	thar	kar	lar	mar	nar	ksar	par	sar	tar	far	char*	psar

Rough-Smooth Distinction Practice (No Horizontal rhyming below)

Smooth	ἀν	ἐν	ἰν	ὀν	ἠν	ὠν	αἰν	εἰν	οἰν	ὐι	αὐν	οὐν	εὐν
	ahn	en	in	on	ayn	ōn	ighn	ayn	oyn	we	own*	oon	yoon
Rough	ἁν	ἑν	ἱν	ὁν	ἡν	ὡν	αἱν	εἱν	οἱν	ὑι	αὑν	οὑν	εὑν
	hahn	hen	hin	hon	hayn	hōn	highn	hayn	hoyn	hwe	hown	hoon	hyoon

2) **Alphabet Memorization**: Whenever Greek words need to be set into some sort of order (as in a dictionary), the traditional order of the alphabet is used. In order to use these tools effectively, we will need to memorize the Greek alphabet (in its order, of course!). Get to work on this task in repeated engagements (perhaps) over the period of a week. Write out (and pronounce orally) the name of the letter along with its shape. [Many find that a vertical listing is the most effective arrangement for writing and memorizing.]

2: Introduction to Verbs in the Present Active Indicative

The very heartbeat of a sentence (in any language) is the *verb*. A verb can be thought of as the *engine* of a sentence, the thing that puts a sentence *into motion*. Without a verb, words pile up into interesting phrases, but nothing will be "said":

- Thomas, on the table, the platter of roast beef…
- A little boy, a little red wagon…
- Several thousand men, from Paris…
- The cat… ⟶ in the hat!

But if a *verb is plugged in*, a pile of words comes to *life*. If a verb is plugged in, a sentence is born which *says something* to which people can react. A *claim* has been made that we can accept or reject, a *question* has been posed that we can answer, or a *command* has been issued that we can obey or disobey.

- Thomas *will set* the platter of roast beef on the table.

- A little boy *was pulling* a little red wagon.
- Several thousand men *were fleeing* from Paris.
- *Don't annoy* the cat!

A verb also functions as the *hub* of a sentence. Whether a verb appears early or late in a sentence, or is buried somewhere in the middle, the verb serves as the *organizational center* to which all other sentence parts are attached (whether directly or indirectly). In the following chapters we will see how various sentence parts are anchored into the verb.

It makes good sense, then, to begin our study of the Greek language with the verb. We'll follow tradition by using the Greek verb λύω (to destroy) to illustrate the various forms Greek verbs can take. λύω is neither particularly noteworthy theologically, nor terribly frequent in the NT. But it is short (We can save ink) and sweet (It behaves predictably).

The Forms of the Present Active Indicative of λύω

Below you can see the six forms of the verb λύω that make up a block we call the **Present Active Indicative**. Spend some time reading aloud and absorbing this chart in all of its features:

Verb Form	Syllabification		Tense	Voice	Mood	Person	Number		Resulting English Translation
λύω	λύ-ω	⟶	Present	Active	Indicative	1st	Singular	⟶	"I am destroying (something)"
λύεις	λύ-εις	⟶	Present	Active	Indicative	2nd	Singular	⟶	"You (singular) are destroying (something)"
λύει	λύ-ει	⟶	Present	Active	Indicative	3rd	Singular	⟶	"He/She/It is destroying (something)"
λύομεν	λύ-ο-μεν	⟶	Present	Active	Indicative	1st	Plural	⟶	"We are destroying (something)"
λύετε	λύ-ε-τε	⟶	Present	Active	Indicative	2nd	Plural	⟶	"You (plural) are destroying (something)"
λύουσι(ν)*	λύ-ου-σι(ν)	⟶	Present	Active	Indicative	3rd	Singular	⟶	"They are destroying (something)"

*If the word following λύουσι begins with a vowel, a "moveable" **nu** [ν] is often added to ease the flow of pronunciation.

Understanding Verb Parsing

The arrows in the chart above are meant to show that we can generate an accurate translation of a particular Greek verb only after we have **parsed** it...that is, **identified** its **Tense**, **Voice**, **Mood**, **Person**, and **Number**. Once the parsing is in mind, we can craft a translation reflecting each element of information contained within the parsing.

But what does each of these elements mean? To answer this question we need to get an overview of the **whole Greek verb system** in terms of these categories of Tense, Voice, Mood, Person and Number. If you study this section well, you will not be wasting your time! Every moment invested here in grasping a picture of the whole verb will be repaid many times in your work ahead!

[We have sequenced the following explanation (Mood, Tense, Person, Number, Voice) to ease the learning process. But when we parse Greek verbs in class or for homework, we should habitually follow the sequence we have shown above with λύω (Tense, Voice, Mood, Person, Number).]

The Meaning of the Indicative Mood

In the six forms of λύω above, you notice that all are parsed as being in the Indicative Mood. This Mood is used by speakers and writers to assert events as being **factual**. Note how all six translations assert the actions as factual, not merely as possible, imagined, hoped for, or urged.

As you see above, λύεις is translated in a **factual** way, since its form is in the Indicative Mood: *"You are destroying..."* Even if this verb were put into forms expressing other time frames (past or future), the Indicative Mood verb would still represent the event as factual:

- They will destroy... [**future** time, but still Indicative: expressing an event as **factual**]

- He destroyed... [**past** time, but still Indicative: expressing an event as **factual**]

By way of contrast, we might find λύω spelled differently to express one of three other Moods (forms which we won't be learning right now). For example we might find λύω:

- in the **Subjunctive** Mood, thereby expressing an action as **uncertain** or **hypothetical**:
  "...if you are destroying" or *"...so that you might be destroying..."*

- or in the **Optative** Mood, thereby expressing a **hope** or a **wish**:
  "...Oh that you may be destroying..."

- or in the **Imperative** Mood, thereby expressing a **command**:
  "(You must) destroy...!"

To Summarize: Verbs in the **Indicative** Mood are portraying events as **factual**.

[**Clarification**: It is important to grasp that *the Indicative Mood* **does not establish or guarantee** *factuality or truthfulness*. Just as in English, the Greek speaker/writer using the Indicative Mood may be truthful, or lying, or simply mistaken. Furthermore, a completely fictional work, like a novel, will be filled with verbs in the Indicative Mood. The Indicative Mood merely **depicts** a matter **as factual**.]

The Meaning of the Present Tense (and Tenses)

You also notice that all six verb forms of λύω above are parsed as standing in the Present Tense. What is the significance of the Greek Present tense in the Indicative Mood?

Before answering that question, let's view the larger landscape. There are **seven Tenses** in the Greek **Indicative Mood**:

1. Present Tense
2. Imperfect Tense
3. Future Tense
4. Aorist Tense
5. Perfect Tense
6. Pluperfect Tense
7. Future Perfect Tense

Though the English word "tense" suggests a focus on the "time" of an action (since the English word "tense" is related to the Latin word "tempus" meaning "time"), the Greek tenses of the Indicative mood express both Time and Aspect. The chart below will help you visualize this dual significance more readily:

	Internal Aspect ↓	External Aspect ↓	Perfect Aspect ↓
Present Time →	Present Tense	*No Greek Forms*	Perfect Tense
Past Time →	Imperfect Tense	Aorist Tense	Pluperfect Tense
Future Time →	*No Greek Forms*	Future Tense	Future Perfect Tense

By tracing the axes of this chart we can determine how *Time* and *Aspect* intersect within each *Tense* in the Indicative Mood:

		Time		Aspect
Present Tense	=	present	+	internal
Imperfect Tense	=	past	+	internal
Future Tense	=	future	+	external
Aorist Tense	=	past	+	external
Perfect Tense	=	present	+	perfect
Pluperfect Tense	=	past	+	perfect
Future Perfect Tense	=	future	+	perfect

But what do we mean by *Time*, and by *Aspect*?

Time in the Indicative Mood

Let's start with the easier one first: *Time*. All of us intuitively understand the distinction between past, present and future time. No matter what scale of time measurement we are using (seconds, minutes, hours, days, months, years, decades or centuries), we readily perceive that, *from the standpoint of a speaker or writer:*

- **past** refers to **"some time ago,"** however recent or remote that might be;

- **present** refers to **"now,"** however momentary or lengthy we consider "now" to be;

- **future** refers to **"some time ahead,"** however near or distant that might be.

[Of course these matters can become philosophically and linguistically complicated, and many events will overlap two (if not all three) of these time zones. But for the moment let's be content with the rather unreflective notion of "now-ness" as the time frame of an action expressed by a Greek verb in the Present Indicative. Look again at the 6 forms of λύω and their translations above, and you will see that each translation portrays the action as happening "**now**," from the perspective of the speaker or writer.]

Just to be clear about this, imagine λύω showing up in forms (you have not yet seen) denoting a different Time:

- It could show up in a **past time** form: "we were destroying" (Yesterday? Last year? Last month?), or
- It could show up in a **future time** form: "we will be destroying" (Later today? Next week? Next year?).

- But in the Present Tense of the Indicative Mood, we should set the action into **present time**: "we are (now) destroying" (This day? This week? This month? This year?)

Much more important than **Time** *for Biblical interpretation, though more difficult to* explain, is the matter of *Aspect*. As you saw in the table above, the *Aspect* of Greek verbs in the Present Tense is said to be *internal*. Let's step back for moment to look at the three different aspects that can be expressed by various forms of Greek verbs: *internal*, *external*, and *perfect*.

Aspect (Internal, External, Perfect) in all Moods

1) **Internal Aspect**: In expressing a given action, a Greek speaker or writer can imagine being **"down inside"** the event, sensing its **progressive, repeated, or unfolding development**. This **"within-the-event"** perspective chosen by the writer is conveyed by using specific verb forms

expressing *internal aspect*. In English this will often be expressed with a *progressive "-ing"* form.

For illustrative purposes, consider these English sentences. The underlined verbs convey in English this "inside the event" perspective, expressed through a progressive "-ing" form in each of the different time frames.

> I <u>was washing</u> my car when an ambulance sped by towards the high school.[internal, past time]
>
> Please don't call me in for supper. I <u>am washing</u> the car right now…
> [internal, present time]
>
> Yeah, you've got a big car! You <u>will</u> still <u>be washing</u> it at ten tonight!
> [internal, future time]

2) **External Aspect**: Or a Greek speaker may refer to the same event, but without interest in its internal progression or development. We can imagine ourselves somehow *suspended above the event, external to the whole of it, viewing it as a simple singularity*. Greek verbs expressing such a perspective are said to have *external aspect*.

For illustrative purposes, consider these English sentences. The underlined verbs convey this "outside the event" perspective, even though their time frames are different.

> Of course I <u>washed</u> the car yesterday! Didn't I promise to?
> [Contrast with <u>was washing</u>]
>
> Please be patient. Today we <u>wash</u> the car. Tomorrow we take it for a ride.
> [Contrast with <u>are washing</u>]
>
> It's getting late, and I'm tired. I <u>will wash</u> the car tomorrow.
> [Contrast with <u>will be washing</u>]

3) **Perfect Aspect**: Or a Greek speaker may refer to the same event, but <u>with an interest in underscoring its completeness with an on-going effect</u>. In this Aspect we can imagine ourselves *looking back at a finished event with a result continuing forward in time*. Greek verbs expressing such a perspective are said to exhibit *Perfect Aspect*. Perfect Aspect can be viewed as the *combination* of the *external* aspect (a completed event) and the *internal* aspect (a continuing effect).

Consider these English sentences:

> I'm happy to say that I <u>have washed</u> the car. Doesn't it look great!
>
> They were ordering me to wash the car, but I <u>had</u> already <u>washed</u> it.
>
> By the time you arrive in Boston, I shall <u>have washed</u> the car.

You will notice that we have used "has/have" and "had" as helping verbs in these English sentences to illustrate the Perfect Aspect in Greek verbs. But we must immediately stress that, in at least two ways, English perfect tenses are not terribly helpful in conveying the sense of Greek perfect Aspect.

1) The English perfect often conveys a sense of immediacy: "I have washed the car" often suggests to us that "I have <u>just now finished</u> washing the car." But the Greek Perfect aspect doesn't necessarily convey such an idea.

2) The English perfect does not make it sufficiently clear that a result continues beyond the finished action. To most English ears, "God has forgiven my sins" is basically equivalent to "God forgave my sins." That is, the English perfect ("has forgiven") is often just another way of referring to a past event *without clearly implying an ongoing effect*.

The upshot of this is twofold:

1) If we want to express the full sense of the Greek Perfect Aspect, we must resort to English paraphrases. Unfortunately, those paraphrases will often be bulky and awkward, unfit for (for example) the public reading of Scripture. But careful Bible instruction (whether in church or the academy) must often resort to such.

2) If we want to avoid bulky and awkward paraphrases when translating Greek verbs with Perfect Aspect, we may use English perfects (forms using have, has, or had), *so long as we realize that this is a* convention, *a "trick" we agree upon for convenience.*

To see this at work, let's look at four examples from the NT. We have underlined the English perfects used conventionally to represent actual Perfects in the Greek text.

> Matthew 4:4 It has been written, 'Man shall not live by bread alone…'
>
> John 1:34 I have seen and have borne witness that this man is the Son of God.
>
> Romans 5:5 "…the love of God has been poured out in our hearts…"
>
> Acts 5:28 "You have filled Jerusalem with your teaching."

The Paraphrases below are designed to take into account the full sense of the Greek Perfect aspect (together with various factors supplied from context, theology, and semantics), and might read as follows:

> Matthew 4:4 Scripture was written in antiquity, but still remains valid in the present (to Jesus), 'Man shall not live by bread alone…'
>
> John 1:34 What I once saw still transfixes me, and what I once testified still rings in your ears, that this man is the Son of God.
>
> Romans 5:5 The love of God was poured out into our hearts, so that even now (at the time of Paul's writing) our hearts remain full of love…
>
> Acts 5:5 You filled Jerusalem with your teaching, and even now the city remains saturated with it.

To summarize: In the Greek verb, the seven tenses of the Indicative mood stand in the intersections of three "times" (past, present, and future) and three "aspects" (internal, external, and perfect). The Greek Present Tense stands in the intersection of:

- Present Time and

- Internal Aspect.

Two Vital Notes Regarding Aspect:

1) We need to make it clear that verbal Aspect is a perspective chosen by speaker or writer, not a property of an action itself. Take, for example, the event of the resurrection of Jesus. What sort of an event was it? Was it a simple event, perhaps accomplished in a single moment? Or was there a process to it, with progressive stages? Or was it an event having enduring consequences? *If expressed as a verb, in what Aspect should the resurrection of Jesus be placed* (internal, external, perfect)?

But such questions are misguided. The genius of the verbal Aspect is not that it somehow depicts the nature of events themselves, but that it offers speakers and writers important options for how they depict, express, or envision those events. We can all agree that the resurrection of Jesus stands as a single, unrepeatable, unchangeable event in history. Yet NT writers were free to choose any verbal Aspect they wished when speaking of the resurrection, depending on their communicative purposes. As a mental exercise, imagine finding these three sentences in the NT:

> "As God was raising Jesus, the disciples sat huddled in fear and despair." [assume a Greek verb with internal aspect]
>
> "God raised Jesus and seated him far above all powers." [assume a Greek verb with external aspect]
>
> "God has raised Jesus from the dead, giving us the victory!" [assume a Greek verb with perfect aspect]

Please note carefully that three different verbal Aspects have been used to speak of the one and only event of the resurrection, without changing the nature of the event itself. In the first sentence, the event is "stretched out", so to speak, allowing us to envision the ongoing mindset of the disciples at the moment of resurrection. In the second sentence, our imaginary author wishes to treat the event simply, without reference to its internal development, *even if God had raised Jesus gradually over the period of a month*! In the third sentence, our imaginary author likely wishes to stress the ongoing benefits of the resurrection, *though the authors of the first two sentences would not necessarily have denied such benefits*! Again, verbal Aspect allows us to discern the chosen perspective of a writer on a given event, not the nature of those events themselves.

2) Despite its importance, verbal aspect doesn't actually tell us very much about how to picture an event "in reality". Consider these examples:

> Just as I <u>was firing</u> my rifle, I realized that my target was not a deer but a burlap rag flapping in the wind.
>
> As Wilson <u>was racing</u> down the sideline, I realized that no one could stop him from returning that kickoff for a score.
>
> As the oak <u>was growing</u> upward toward the sky, a partly fallen elm was nudging it little by little toward the house.
>
> Since pirates <u>were attacking</u> British ships more frequently, the Royal Navy increased its patrol in those waters.
>
> Though I <u>was visiting</u> her every time I could, she still decided that I had abandoned her.
>
> Over the years, I <u>was giving</u> campaign donations to the Democrats, but voting Republican!
>
> As the glaciers <u>were receding</u>, rough rocky landscapes with dramatic waterfalls were revealed.

Assume that all of these underlined verbs in these sentences represent the internal aspect of corresponding Greek verbs. As you looked over each sentence, you constructed a "picture" of the action. One action took place within a <u>split second</u> (1). One action took place over the span of perhaps <u>ten seconds</u> (2). Other actions took place over <u>several years'</u> time (3, 4, 5, 6). The action in 3 progresses <u>seamlessly</u>, while actions 4, 5 and 6 progress through a series of <u>distinct events</u>. The distinct

events within 4 and 5 were apparently <u>unpredictable</u>, while the events of 6 likely <u>followed the calendar</u> of political campaigns. In 7, the action took place over many long <u>centuries</u>.

<u>The point is this</u>: Each of these events is presented by a verb form expressing internal Aspect, as shown by the "was/were blank-ing" English forms. But as we read these sentences, we all created mental pictures of the actions by adding <u>other factors</u> to the equation: our general understanding of word meaning (to fire, to race, to grow, to visit, to recede, etc.), contextual clues (i.e. information supplied within these sentences), and our general knowledge of how the world works (e.g., glaciers are slow, guns fire in an instant). In other words, the <u>forms</u> of these verbs suggested only the general matter of authorial perspective (internal, external, perfect), while a host of other factors supplied something of a "fuller picture" of the event. This "fuller picture" we call Aktionsart. But remember: The verb form itself tells us only about Aspect (authorial perspective), while a combination of other factors tell us about Aktionsart (how to picture the event in the real world).

Therefore, when interpreting the Greek New Testament, we must not jump from identifying a verb's Aspect to describing its Aktionsart. We can't say, for example, "The form of this verb expresses external aspect; therefore we know that this event happened in a single, simple, undivided moment of time." Yes, the Aspect of a verb, as determined by its form, may be external. But the contours and shape of the actual event (the Aktionsart) cannot be determined by the parsing of a verb.

The Meaning of Person (1st, 2nd, and 3rd)

As you have noticed, the six forms of λύω supplied above are shown as expressing 1st, 2nd or 3rd Persons. This variation relates to the relationship between speakers and hearers.

- Verbs in the **First Person** depict acts done by the <u>Speaker or Writer.</u>
  I (for the singular); **We** (for the plural)
- Verbs in the **Second Person** depict acts done by the <u>Listeners or Readers being addressed</u>.
  You (for the singular); **You** [y'all] (for the plural)
- Verbs in the **Third Person** depict acts done by some <u>Third Party or Parties spoken or written about</u>.
  He, or **She**, or **It** (for the singular); **They** (for the plural)

The Meaning of Number (Singular, Plural)

As you have noticed, the first three forms of λύω are identified as singular, and are grouped together because they depict an action performed by one actor (I, you, or he/she/it). The second three forms of λύω are identified as plural, and are grouped together because they depict an action performed by **multiple** actors (we, you, or they).

Notice that the gender of these persons is not identified by these verb forms. "We," for example, could stand for men, women, or a mixed group. Because English insists on expressing the singular of third person in a gender-specific way, we must keep alive the ambiguity of the Greek form, and remember to keep our gender options open with a form like λύει: "he, or she, or it is destroying." Of course in actual speech or writing, the context will almost always clarify gender identity.

To put these matters of person and number together in the Present Indicative of λύω, study the following:

λύω = I am destroying

    [The speaker, a single individual (of unspecified gender), is destroying]

λύεις = You are destroying

    [The one being addressed, a single individual (of unspecified gender), is destroying]

λύει = He, she or it is destroying

    [Someone or something spoken about, a single entity (of unspecified gender), is destroying]

λύομεν = We are destroying

    [The speakers, more than one individual (of unspecified gender), are destroying]

λύετε = You [y'all] are destroying

    [The ones being addressed, more than one individual (of unspecified gender), are destroying]

λύουσι(ν) = They are destroying

    [People or things spoken about, more than a single entity (of unspecified gender), are destroying]

The Meaning of Voice (Active, Middle, Passive)

As you have noticed, the six forms of λύω supplied above are identified as standing in the Active Voice:

1) **Active Voice** You might have noticed that every form of λύω we have studied was translated to show that the persons involved (I, you, he/she/it, we, y'all, they) are the ones who **perform or carry out** the action in question.

2) **Passive Voice** By way of contrast, you will one day learn forms of λύω that stand in the **Passive Voice**. These forms will *reverse the polarity of action*, and should be translated to show that **the persons involved** (I, you, he/she/it, we, y'all, they) **are acted upon by someone or something else**:

Translation of the **Present** Passive **Indicative** for λύω [no forms to learn now]

- I am being destroyed
- You are being destroyed
- He/she/it is being destroyed

- We are being destroyed
- Y'all are being destroyed
- They are being destroyed

3) **Middle Voice** Finally, you will one day learn forms of λύω that stand in the **Middle Voice**. These forms will imply that *the persons involved* (I, you, he/she/it, we, y'all, they) *are performing* the action, but will also emphasize that *these persons are somehow more intimately involved in the action* than usual. This foggy notion must be teased out circumstance by circumstance, with a fair amount of interpretive wiggle room remaining. To illustrate some of these interpretive possibilities, imagine finding our verb λύω in an indisputably *Middle form*. How might we translate it to convey a *middle sense*?

> We <u>destroyed</u> (ourselves).
> [A middle verb can imply that the action was reflexive: self-inflicted.]
>
> We <u>destroyed</u> our health.
> [A middle verb can imply that the action was performed upon some intimate part of the body.]
>
> We (ourselves) <u>destroyed</u> the counterfeit money.
> [A middle verb can imply that the action was performed directly, not through an intermediary.]

<u>But the forms of λύω that we are learning in this chapter are all Active in Voice: The persons involved are performing the activity of destroying upon some (yet unnamed) victim.</u>

Parsing Options

Now we can view the options available to us in each category when we *parse verbs*. We have set into **bold** font each option that has been activated in the Present Active Indicative forms of λύω that we are studying in this chapter.

Tense	Voice	Mood	Person	Number
Present	**Active**	**Indicative**	**1st**	**Singular**
Imperfect	Middle	Subjunctive	**2nd**	**Plural**
Future	Passive	Optative	**3rd**	
Aorist		Imperative		
Perfect				
Pluperfect				
Future Perfect				

Each Indicative Tense is comprised of:

Time	+	Aspect
Present		Internal
Past		External
Future		Perfect

Anatomy of the Forms of the Present Active Indicative of λύω

"Base" and "Endings"

Look again at the forms of λύω in the Present Active Indicative:

		Tense	Voice	Mood	Person	Number	
1s)	λύω	Present	Active	Indicative	1st	Singular	"I am destroying (something)"
2s)	λύεις	Present	Active	Indicative	2nd	Singular	"You (singular) are destroying (something)"
3s)	λύει	Present	Active	Indicative	3rd	Singular	"He/She/It is destroying (something)"
1p)	λύομεν	Present	Active	Indicative	1st	Plural	"We are destroying (something)"
2p)	λύετε	Present	Active	Indicative	2nd	Plural	"You (plural) are destroying (something)"
3p)	λύουσι(ν)	Present	Active	Indicative	3rd	Plural	"They are destroying (something)"

You have probably guessed by now that these forms of λύω are comprised of a stable "base" to which are added various "endings." Even without deciding to do so, your mind's eye probably deconstructed these forms into components as follow:

			"base"		"ending"
1s)	λύω	=	λύ	+	ω
2s)	λύεις	=	λύ	+	εις
3s)	λύει	=	λύ	+	ει
1p)	λύομεν	=	λύ	+	ομεν
2p)	λύετε	=	λύ	+	ετε
3p)	λύουσι(ν)	=	λύ	+	ουσι(ν)

And since the translations of these forms differ only in <u>person and number</u> (I, you, he, he/she/it, we, you, they), you likely guessed that these endings are telling us <u>person and number</u>. *And so it is!* And if you master these endings (ω εις ει ομεν ετε ουσι), you will be well on your way to recognizing and translating the great majority of Greek verbs whenever they appear in the Present Active Indicative.

Verbs with Roots ending in Short Vowels (Contract Verbs)

Though the endings appear simple enough, they actually are comprised of two separate components: a **_connecting vowel_** (which varies between o and ε), and a **_personal ending_**. Right now this degree of analysis might seem a bit theoretical and unnecessary, but soon you will find this explanation helpful for understanding other formations. So, examine the following breakdown:

		Base		Ending					Theoretical Form		Final Form
				Connecting Vowel		Personal Ending					
1)	1s	λυ	+	o	+	(μι)	combines as	[λυ–ομι]	which "reacts" to form		λύ–ω
2)	2s	λυ	+	ε	+	σι	combines as	[λυ–εσι]	which "reacts" to form		λύ–εις
3)	3s	λυ	+	ε	+	τι	combines as	[λυ–ετι]	which "reacts" to form		λύ–ει
5)	1p	λυ	+	o	+	μεν	combines as	[λυ–ομεν]	which "reacts" to form		λύ–ομεν
6)	2p	λυ	+	ε	+	τε	combines as	[λυ–ετε]	which "reacts" to form		λύ–ετε
7)	3p	λυ	+	o	+	ντι	combines as	[λυ–οντι]	which "reacts" to form		λύ–ουσι(ν)

The exact "chemistry" producing the finished form is not fully understood, even by scholars examining these matters closely. Read through the following explanations, _not so much to master them_, but to _get a feel_ for the chemistry. [The numbers below correspond to the numbering of the forms above.]

1) For verbs that use connecting vowels (o or ε), the personal ending (μι) is not used. To compensate for this loss, the connecting vowel omicron (o) is lengthened to an omega (ω).

2) The sigma (σ) drops out between vowels, as it often does, and a final sigma (ς) is added. Note that this reduces the number of syllables, and forms a diphthong in the process (ει).

3) Under these conditions, the tau (τ) is transformed into a sigma (σ). The newly formed sigma (σ), finding itself between two vowels, disappears. Great news! Nothing happens!

4) Great news! Nothing happens!

5) Under these conditions, a tau (τ) will be transformed into a sigma (σ). A nu (ν) before a sigma (σ) under these conditions is lost, and the omicron (o) is lengthened to a diphthong (ου) to compensate for the loss of the nu (ν).

Verbs with Roots Ending in Short Vowels (Contract Verbs)

We mentioned earlier that λύω behaves nicely, and serves well as a pattern for learning many hundreds of other "nice" Greek verbs. But other verbs rock the boat a little, and "tweak" the appearance of the endings just a bit. Below in the first column you will see the familiar forms of λύω. In the second, third and fourth columns you will see three types of "tweaking" that go on in other verbs. Look over these forms, *reading from left to right*, before reading the explanation that follows:

	to destroy	to honor	to make	to show	Translation
		τιμα—	ποιε—	δηλο—	
1s	λύω	τιμῶ	ποιῶ	δηλῶ	I am —ing
2s	λύεις	τιμᾷς	ποιεῖς	δηλοῖς	You are —ing
3s	λύει	τιμᾷ	ποιεῖ	δηλοῖ	He/She/It is —ing
1p	λύομεν	τιμῶμεν	ποιοῦμεν	δηλοῦμεν	We are —ing
2p	λύετε	τιμᾶτε	ποιεῖτε	δηλοῦτε	You are —ing
3p	λύουσι(ν)	τιμῶσι(ν)	ποιοῦσι(ν)	δηλοῦσι(ν)	They are —ing

I hope you have noticed that, despite the "wrinkle" that takes place in these new verbs, the endings you have seen with λύω are still visible when you look closely:

1) In 1st singular, *the omega is quite visible*, though the accent has changed.

2) In 2nd singular, *the iota-sigma still ends all forms*, though the iota is subscripted in one form (τιμᾷς), and the accent has changed.

3) In 3rd singular, *the iota still ends all forms*, though it has been subscripted (ᾷ) in the alpha-contract forms, or has combined to form other diphthongs, and the accent has changed.

4) In 1st person plural, *the μεν remains unchanged*, though the preceding vowel and accent might have changed.

5) In 2nd plural, *the τε remains unchanged*, though the preceding vowel and accent have changed.

6) In 3rd plural, *the σι remains unchanged*, though the preceding vowel and accent might have changed.

In other words, if you know the endings for λύω in the Present Active Indicative, *you should be able to recognize and translate those verbs that "tweak" the connecting vowels*. But it will be helpful to see some explanation of what has happened in these forms, *though it is not really necessary to memorize the exact steps taken*.

- The "base" of τιμῶ is τιμα– to which are added the various personal endings. But because *alpha* is a highly reactive vowel, it will always contract with the following vowel or diphthong of the endings.

Uncontracted (theoretical) Endings:	άω	άεις	άει	άομεν	άετε	άουσι
Contracted (real-life) Endings:	ῶ	ᾷς	ᾷ	ῶμεν	ᾶτε	ῶσι

The "base" of ποιῶ is ποιε– to which are added the various personal endings. But because *epsilon* is a highly reactive vowel, it will always contract with the following vowel or diphthong of the endings.

Uncontracted (theoretical) Endings:	έω	έεις	έει	έομεν	έετε	έουσι
Contracted (real-life) Endings:	ῶ	εῖς	εῖ	οῦμεν	εῖτε	οῦσι

The "base" of δηλῶ is δηλο– to which are added the various personal endings. But because *omicron* is a highly reactive vowel, it will always contract with the following vowel or diphthong of the endings.

Uncontracted (theoretical) Endings:	όω	όεις	όει	όομεν	όετε	όουσι
Contracted (real-life) Endings:	ῶ	οῖς	οῖ	οῦμεν	οῦτε	οῦσι

Verbs Without Connecting Vowels (μι Verbs)

But another family of verbs exists…we'll call them the RED family for now. How do these two families differ? Essentially in one small detail: In the Present Indicative, the BLUE family **uses a connecting vowel** (CV) between the "base" and the personal endings, while the RED family **doesn't**.

BLUE family verb formation: "base" + connecting vowel + personal ending

RED familiy verb formation: "base" + [No C.V.!] + personal ending

	Blue Family								Red Family						
	Base		CV		Pers.End		Final Form			Base		CV		Pers.End		Final Form
1	λυ	+	ο	+	(μι)	=	λύω		1	διδω	+	—	+	μι	=	δίδωμι
2	λυ	+	ε	+	σι	=	λύεις		2	διδω	+	—	+	σι	=	δίδως
3	λυ	+	ε	+	τι	=	λύει		3	διδω	+	—	+	τι	=	δίδωσι(ν)
4	λυ	+	ο	+	μεν	=	λύομεν		4	διδω	+	—	+	μεν	=	δίδομεν
5	λυ	+	ε	+	τε	=	λύετε		5	διδω	+	—	+	τε	=	δίδοτε
6	λυ	+	ο	+	ντι	=	λύουσι(ν)		6	διδω	+	—	+	ντι	=	διδόασι(ν)

We have already observed the "chemistry" that creates the final form of λύω out of its combination of elements. Now consider the comments below regarding the formation of final forms of δίδωμι. These need not be memorized, but should be carefully read.

1) Since RED family verbs do not use connecting vowels (ο or ε), the personal ending (μι) is *used, not discarded* as in the BLUE FAMILY verbs.

2) While it appears that the iota (ι) has simply been eliminated, it is not clear just what step or series of steps has taken place.

3) Under the influence of Attic Greek, the tau (τ) is changed in this circumstance to a sigma (σ). A moveable "nu" is possibly added.

4) Great news! Nothing happens!

5) Great news! Nothing happens!

6) The 3rd plural personal ending for RED family verbs (αντι) differs slightly from that of BLUE (ντι). In the case of the REDs, the tau (τ) shifts to become a sigma (σ), the nu (ν) drops out, and the alpha is lengthened (it had been short) to compensate for the loss.

Final Note

You have noticed the variation between omega (ω) and omicron (o) in the final vowel of the "base." This is a regular and predictable pattern you will see in similar verbs (the long vowel in the singular, the short form in the plural). Remember, this vowel is part of the "base," and should not be confused with the Connecting Vowel used in BLUE family verbs.

Standard Nomenclature

Traditionally the BLUE family of verbs is known as the ***Omega Conjugation***, while RED family verbs are known as the μι Conjugation. These labels are obviously drawn from the appearance of the 1st person singular form in the Present Active Indicative. From now on we will use the traditional nomenclature.

Overview and Summary

Now we can set several verbs in parallel columns to view the whole formation of the Present Active Indicative. We will add several more μι verbs to this chart, just to show a few more important examples of its type.

	Omega Conjugation				Mi Conjugation				
	No Contraction	Alpha Contraction	Epsilon Contract	Omicron Contract	"o" stem	"e" stem	"a" stem	"nu" stem	
	to destroy	*to honor*	*to make*	*to show*	*to give*	*to place/put*	*to stand*	*to show*	Translation
1s	λύω	τιμῶ	ποιῶ	δηλῶ	δίδωμι	τίθημι	ἵστημι	δείκνυμι	I am —ing
2s	λύεις	τιμᾷς	ποιεῖς	δηλοῖς	δίδως	τίθης	ἵστης	δείκνυεις*	You are —ing
3s	λύει	τιμᾷ	ποιεῖ	δηλοῖ	δίδωσι(ν)	τίθησι(ν)	ἵστησι(ν)	δείκνυσι(ν)	He/She/It is —ing
1p	λύομεν	τιμῶμεν	ποιοῦμεν	δηλοῦμεν	δίδομεν	τίθεμεν	ἵσταμεν	δείκνυμεν	We are —ing
2p	λύετε	τιμᾶτε	ποιεῖτε	δηλοῦτε	δίδοτε	τίθετε	ἵστατε	δείκνυτε	You are —ing
3p	λύουσι(ν)	τιμῶσι(ν)	ποιοῦσι(ν)	δηλοῦσι(ν)	διδόασι(ν)	τιθέασι(ν)	ἱστᾶσι(ν)	δεικνύασι(ν)	They are —ing

*With this particular verb, the 2nd singular form happens to imitate the 2nd singular of λύω (λύεις).

Notes

MI verbs with ε and α as the final vowel of the "base" will show the same movement from long vowel (η) to short (ε or α) as they move from singular to plural (compare with δίδωμι which shifts from long ω to short o). Even MI verbs with bases ending in "nu" make the same shift, though it is less obvious (the long upsilon shifts to a short upsilon).

Digging into the New Testament Text

1) **_Find_ I Thess 5:16-24** in your GNT. (If you need help finding I Thessalonians, look in the table of contents for Πρὸς Θεσσαλονικεῖς ά for the page/location). <u>Read aloud 5:20-21 until smooth</u>. Be ready to read these verses aloud in class.

2) Open your Greek Interlinear and **_find_ I Thess 5:16-24**. Since we've studied various **moods** of the verb, we're going to look at this stretch of text to see what moods the verbs are in. As you look at this text in the Interlinear, you will notice that the **third line** of information contains the **parsings** of all Greek words. All (finite) verbs are identified with parsing codes that begin with the **English letter "v,"** easily signaling to us that the Greek word immediately above it is a **"verb."**

How many verbs do you find in 5:16-24?

The entire parsing code of a verb, you will notice, has three clusters of information. The first verb you see in 5:16, for example, is parsed as: **v.pam.2p**

Decoded, these particular letters and numbers represent the following information:

Verb | **P**resent-**A**ctive-I**m**perative | **2**nd person-**p**lural

In other words, the **_third letter_** in the **_middle grouping_** tells us what **mood** the verb is in [**v.pam.2p**]. Mounce's code for the four moods is as follows:

i	=	**I**ndicative mood	(expressing factuality)
s	=	**S**ubjunctive mood	(expressing possibility)
m	=	I**m**perative mood	(expressing command)
o	=	**O**ptative mood	(expressing wish)

Now go through 5:16-24 again. <u>What mood is each verb in? Do you see how the basic sense of the mood is communicated in the English translation? As you reflect on this, what comes to mind about the message of 5:16-24</u>?

3) In the Interlinear, find in 5:23 the English expression "through and through." You will notice that this expression is the NIV's attempt to translate the single Greek word ὁλοτελεῖς. On the fourth line beneath it you see its wordlist code: 3911. Go back to Appendix B, and note the "dictionary form" there provided. Then look up **_exactly this dictionary form in BDAG_**.

What definition is offered in BDAG?

What glosses are offered?

How often does this word appear in the NT?

4) Go to pages 192-194 in Wallace's Intermediate Grammar, *The Basics of NT Syntax* [pages 442–448 if you are using Wallace's *Greek Grammar Beyond the Basics*] [see "Publisher's Note" on page x]. The table of contents on p. 192 [442] gives a listing of the various senses or values that each mood can express. Notice that the Imperative and Optative moods have few variations in sense. Now turn to p. 194 [447] to see the relative frequency of usage. What does this chart of frequencies tell you about how typical or a-typical our text is (I Thess. 5:16-24) in terms of verb mood?

Now go to pp. 210-212 [485–493] and look more closely at the different ways the Imperative mood can be used. Out of the four options of Command, Prohibition, Request, and Conditional, the imperatives in 5:16-24 are probably Commands (that is, strong urgings from a superior to inferiors).

5) Reflect on our use of tools. We move from the GNT, to the Interlinear, to the Lexicon, and finally to the Grammar. Over time we will continue gaining skill and ease in this process.

Chapter Two Vocabulary

Our goal throughout the first 12 chapters of this course is to acquaint you with words that are found **100 times or more** in the GNT. We will be presenting them in meaningful groups, as far as possible, to make memorization easier. In this first lesson we will retain our focus on verbs, with the only exception being the conjunction καί.

We will also be introducing the idea of **verb roots**, but without explanation at this point. For now it is enough merely to see the roots as they appear in brackets below, and to be aware that down underneath each verb is a basic point of origin, the root, from which all other forms are generated. You will notice that some verbs in the Present Active Indicative look exactly like their roots, while other verbs appear to have modified their roots considerably. Again, for now we just want to get accustomed to **the idea of the root**. Please note that each word in the vocabulary list will follow the general pattern of λύω in the table on page 27, unless the word appears explicitly in that table.

λύω	[λυ]	*I destroy*
τιμάω*	[τιμα]	*I honor*
ποιέω*	[ποιε]	*I make, do*
δηλόω*	[δηλο]	*I show, explain*
δίδωμι	[δο]	*I give*
τίθημι	[θε]	*I put, place, lay*
ἵστημι	[στα]	*I set, place, stand*
δείκνυμι	[δεικ]	*I show, explain*

βλέπω	[βλεπ]	*I see*
κηρύσσω	[κηρυγ]	*I preach, proclaim*
λέγω	[λεγ]	*I say*
ἀποστέλλω	[ἀποστελ]	*I send (out, away)*
λαμβάνω	[λαβ]	*I take, or receive*
γινώσκω	[γνω]	*I know*
ἀκούω	[ἀκου]	*I hear, obey*
γράφω	[γραφ]	*I write*

καί	*and*	[conjunction]

*The asterisked forms above are shown in **un**contracted form for the sake of vocabulary acquisition. In "real" Greek text, these forms would appear only in contracted form (i.e. τιμῶ, ποιῶ, δηλῶ). In a lexicon, these forms will appear in **un**contracted form. (i.e. τιμάω, ποιέω, δηλόω).

Exercises

I. Short Answer

Doing exercises is a vital part of learning. Only through repetition and practice will we develop confidence in Greek. The answers are located at the end of this exercise. Go back over these questions and answers until it "flows"!

1) What does the <u>Indicative Mood</u> signify?

2) What does the <u>Subjunctive Mood</u> signify?

3) What does the <u>Optative Mood</u> signify?

4) What does the <u>Imperative Mood</u> signify?

5) What does the <u>Active Voice</u> signify?

6) What does the <u>Passive Voice</u> signify?

7) What does the <u>Middle Voice</u> signify?

8) How many <u>Tenses</u> are there in the <u>Indicative Mood</u>?

9) Each Tense of the Indicative Mood conveys what <u>two distinct kinds of information</u>?

10) What <u>Three Times</u> may verbs in the Indicative Mood possibly express?

11) From <u>whose perspective</u> are these Times "measured"?

12) What <u>three Aspects</u> may verbs in the Indicative Mood express?

13) What is the significance of the <u>Internal aspect</u>?

14) What is the significance of the <u>External aspect</u>?

15) What is the significance of the <u>Perfect Aspect</u>?

16) What <u>Time and Aspect</u> are signified by the <u>Present tense of the Indicative Mood</u>?

17) What is <u>Aktionsart</u>, and how does it differ from <u>Aspect</u>?

18) What does the <u>Person</u> of a verb signify?

Solutions to Exercise I

1) That the speaker or writer is portraying something as *factual*.
2) That the speaker or writer is portraying something as *hypothetical or uncertain*.
3) That the speaker or writer is expressing a *wish or a hope*.
4) That the speaker or writer is expressing a *command or directive*.
5) That the Person(s) implied in the verb ending is *doing the action*.
6) That the Person(s) implied in the verb ending is *being acted upon*.
7) That the Person(s) implied in the verb ending is *doing the action, and somehow more intimately involved*.
8) *Seven* (You need not name them.)
9) The *Time* of a verb, and; The *Aspect* of a verb.
10) *Past, present, future*.
11) From the perspective of the *speaker or writer*.
12) *Internal, external, and perfect*
13) A speaker or writer is *down within* the event, expressing it as somehow *progressing or developing*.
14) A speaker or writer is *above* the event, viewing it *as a whole, without reference to its progression or development*.
15) A speaker or writer views an event from the vantage point of its *completion*, and conceives of an *ongoing result flowing forward from a completed event*.
16) Time: *present*, Aspect: *internal*
17) <u>Aspect</u> is more *general*, and is the *perspective* chosen by the speaker or writer when expressing an event. We determine Aspect by *parsing the verb form*. <u>Aktionsart</u> is the *fuller picture* we may develop of an event as we (readers) might imagine it happening *in reality*. We develop that picture by gathering pieces of *information from various sources* (from word meaning, from general experience, from context, from theology, etc.).
18) Person identifies how the "doer" of the verb action relates to conversational coordinates: 1st person refers to the one(s) *speaking or writing*; (I, we); 2nd person refers to the one(s) *being addressed* (you, y'all); 3rd person refers to the one(s) *being talked about* (he, she, it, they).

II. Memorizing the Endings for λύω

It is necessary to commit this set of endings to memory, since they will pave the way to recognizing many other verbs and variations. In vertical columns, write out the endings until you have mastered them. Always be pronouncing them aloud to sear them into your memory.

1s   λύω   –ω   _____ _____ _____ _____ _____ _____ _____

2s   λύεις   –εις _____ _____ _____ _____ _____ _____ _____

3s   λύει   –ει   _____ _____ _____ _____ _____ _____ _____

1p   λύομεν –ομεν _____ _____ _____ _____ _____ _____ _____

2p   λύετε   –ετε _____ _____ _____ _____ _____ _____ _____

3p   λύουσι –ουσι _____ _____ _____ _____ _____ _____ _____

III. Parse and Translate

Let's start with λύω, and work to establish good habits of **parsing**. It may feel repetitive right now, but we need to plant these patterns in our mind. The answers are located at the end of this exercise. Read and say everything aloud! Work at this until it flows smoothly.

1) λύω

2) λύουσι

3) λύομεν

4) λύει

5) λύετε

6) λύεις

7) λύομεν

8) λύω

9) λύει

10) λύετε

11) λύεις

12) λύουσι

Solutions to Exercise III

1) Present Active Indicative, first person singular, from λύω: "I am destroying…"
2) Present Active Indicative, third person plural, from λύω: "They are destroying…"
3) Present Active Indicative, first person plural, from λύω: "We are destroying…"
4) Present Active Indicative, third person singular, from λύω: "he/she/it is destroying…"
5) Present Active Indicative, second person plural, from λύω: "Y'all are destroying…"
6) Present Active Indicative, second person singular, from λύω: "You are destroying…"
7) Present Active Indicative, first person plural, from λύω: "We are destroying…"
8) Present Active Indicative, first person singular, from λύω: "I am destroying…"
9) Present Active Indicative, third person singular, from λύω: "He/she/it is destroying…"
10) Present Active Indicative, second person plural, from λύω: "Y'all are destroying…"
11) Present Active Indicative, second person singular, from λύω: "You are destroying…"
12) Present Active Indicative, third person plural, from λύω: "They are destroying…"

IV. *Parse and Translate*

Let's shift now to the **contract** verbs. Review the forms presented in the chapter above. *Remember that all of the personal endings used fo*r λύω *are visible in contract verbs, even if slightly distorted.* The answers are located at the end of this exercise. Read and say everything aloud! Work at this until it flows smoothly.

1) ιμῶ

2) ποιεῖς

3) ηλοῖ

4) τιμῶμεν

5) ποιεῖτε

6) δηλοῦσι

7) τιμᾷς

8) ποιεῖ

9) δηλοῦμεν

10) τιμᾶτε

11) ποιοῦσι

12) δηλῶ

13) τιμᾷ

14) ποιοῦμεν

15) δηλοῦτε

16) τιμῶσι

17) ποιῶ

18) δηλοῖς

Solutions to Exercise IV

1) Present Active Indicative, first person singular, from τιμάω: "I am honoring…"
2) Present Active Indicative, second person singular, from ποιέω: "You are making…"
3) Present Active Indicative, third person singular, from δηλόω: "He/she/it is showing…"
4) Present Active Indicative, first person plural, from τιμάω: "We are honoring…"
5) Present Active Indicative, second person plural, from ποιέω: "Y'all are making…"
6) Present Active Indicative, third person plural, from δηλόω: "They are showing…"
7) Present Active Indicative, second person singular, from τιμάω: "You are honoring…"
8) Present Active Indicative, third person singular, from ποιέω: "He/she/it is making…"
9) Present Active Indicative, first person plural, from δηλόω: "We are showing…"
10) Present Active Indicative, second person plural, from τιμάω: "Y'all are honoring…"
11) Present Active Indicative, third person plural, from ποιέω: "They are making…"
12) Present Active Indicative, first person singular, from δηλόω: "I am showing…"
13) Present Active Indicative, third person singular, from τιμάω: "He/she/it is honoring…"
14) Present Active Indicative, first person plural, from ποιέω: "We are making…"
15) Present Active Indicative, second person plural, from δηλόω: "Y'all are showing…"
16) Present Active Indicative, third person plural, from τιμάω: "They are honoring…"
17) Present Active Indicative, first person singular, from ποιέω: "I am making…"
18) Present Active Indicative, second person singular, from δηλόω: "You are showing…"

V. Parse and Translate

Let's shift now to **MI** verbs. Review the forms presented in the chapter above. *Remember that there is significant overlap in the Omega and MI family verb ending. Only the lack of a variable Connecting Vowel between base and personal endings creates the different look.* The answers are located at the end of this exercise. Read and say everything aloud! Work at this until it flows smoothly.

1) δίδως

2) τίθετε

3) ἵστησι

4) δεικνύασι

5) δίδοτε

6) τίθησι

7) ἱστᾶσι

8) δείκνυμι

9) δίδομεν

10) τίθης

11) ἵστατε

12) δείκνυσι

13) διδόασι

14) τίθημι

15) ἵστης

16) δείκνυτε

17) δίδωσι

18) τιθέασι

19) ἵσταμεν

20) δείκνυς

Solutions to Exercise V

1) Present Active Indicative, second person singular, from δίδωμι: "You are giving…"
2) Present Active Indicative, second person plural, from τίθημι: "Y'all are placing…"
3) Present Active Indicative, third person singular, from ἵστημι: "He/she/it is standing…"
4) Present Active Indicative, third person plural, from δείκνυμι: "They are showing…"
5) Present Active Indicative, second person plural, from δίδωμι: "Y'all are giving…"
6) Present Active Indicative, third person singular, from τίθημι: "He/she/it is placing…"
7) Present Active Indicative, third person plural, from ἵστημι: "They are standing…"
8) Present Active Indicative, first person singular, from δείκνυμι: "I am showing…"
9) Present Active Indicative, first person plural, from δίδωμι: "We are giving…"
10) Present Active Indicative, second person singular, from τίθημι: "You are placing…"
11) Present Active Indicative, second person plural, from ἵστημι: "Y'all are standing…"
12) Present Active Indicative, third person singular, from δείκνυμι: "He/she/it is showing…"
13) Present Active Indicative, third person plural, from δίδωμι: "They are giving…"
14) Present Active Indicative, first person singular, from τίθημι: "I am placing…"
15) Present Active Indicative, second person singular, from ἵστημι: "You are standing…"
16) Present Active Indicative, second person plural, from δείκνυμι: "Y'all are showing…"
17) Present Active Indicative, third person singular, from δίδωμι: "He/she/it is giving…"
18) Present Active Indicative, third person plural, from τίθημι: "They are placing…"
19) Present Active Indicative, first person plural, from ἵστημι: "We are standing…"
20) Present Active Indicative, second person singular, from δείκνυμι: "You are showing…"

VI. Mixed Translation

Translate each of these compound sentences. They join together all the different types of verbs we have studied. Write out in Greek at least two of these sentences.

1) λύω καὶ δίδως καὶ τιμῶ καὶ βλέπουσι.

2) λύεις καὶ τίθετε καὶ ποιεῖς καὶ κηρύσσομεν.

3) λύει καὶ ἵστησι καὶ δηλοῖ καὶ λέγω.

4) λύομεν καὶ δεικνύασι καὶ τιμῶμεν καὶ ἀποστέλλεις.

5) λύετε καὶ δίδοτε καὶ δηλοῦσι καὶ λαμβάνομεν.

6) λύουσι καὶ τίθησι καὶ τιμᾷ καὶ γινώσκω.

7) λύει καὶ ἵστασι καὶ δηλοῖς καὶ ἀκούετε.

8) λύομεν καὶ δείκνυμι καὶ δηλοῦσι καὶ γράφεις.

9) λύετε καὶ δίδομεν καὶ ποιῶ καὶ λαμβάνουσι.

10) λύουσι καὶ τίθης καὶ τιμᾶτε καὶ κηρύσσομεν.

3: Nouns and Their Cases

Building a Simple Sentence in Greek

In the last chapter we devoted ourselves to *verbs* in general (the ideas of tense, voice, mood, person, number), and to mastering the *Present Active Indicative* forms for all types of verbs. You also remember that a verb is the **heartbeat** of a sentence, the **engine** putting things in motion, the **organizational hub** around which everything is organized.

Let's take one of the verbs we studied last chapter ($\delta i\delta\omega\mu\iota$) and randomly choose the 3rd plural ($\delta i\delta\acute{o}\alpha\sigma\iota$ = "They are giving…") to illustrate how we can attach various items to a verb to build a fuller sentence *in English*:

We might want to specify *who the givers are*:	<u>Angels</u> are giving…
We might want to identify just *what they give*:	Angels are giving <u>crowns</u>…
We might want to clarify *the quality or nature* of what they give:	Angels are giving crowns <u>of gold</u>…
We might want to identify *those to whom* these things are being given:	Angels are giving crowns of gold <u>to children</u>.
We might want to address someone directly when declaring the whole sentence:	<u>Oh Teacher</u>, angels are giving crowns of gold to children!

In our native languages, each of us adds these elements without wondering how to do so. Without realizing it, we have absorbed the "rules" our language uses for organizing verbal traffic so we can understand each other.

In **English**, one "rule" for how to add these items and build sentences is that **word order** is crucial for distinguishing the **Do-er** from the **Patient** (the one to whom something happens). Consider these two sentences:

- Tom carried Jane.
- Jane carried Tom.

These sentences have exactly the same words, but **word order alone** tells us that different **roles** are played by Tom and Jane. In the first sentence we know that Tom will exert energy, and that in the second sentence Jane will exert energy. In simple English sentences like these, the "Doer" must **precede** the verb, while the "Patient" must **follow** the verb. That's just the "rule" we all follow, whether or not we think about it.

Let's Imagine

But imagine a language that found a way around depending on word order for making sense. What if we could "tag" our words to show the roles being played? For this imaginary game, let "<u>L</u>" stand for "Listener," "<u>D</u>" for "Doer," "<u>P</u>" for Patient, "<u>R</u>" for "Receiver," and "<u>Q</u>" for "Quality." We will double underline our verb, just keep an eye on the hub of the sentence. Now let's take the English sentence we created earlier, and tag the various roles within it:

> O Teacher[L], angels[D] are giving crowns[P] of gold[Q] to apostles[R]!

If we and our audience understood the game, we could abandon our dependence on word order, and offer sentences with many different word sequences without sacrificing clarity! In the examples below, the **superscripts alone identify the roles** being played, *no matter where* these words might actually occur in the sentence.

Angels[D]	crowns[P]	gold[Q]	apostles[R]	teacher[L]	are giving	=	
Crowns[P]	gold[Q]	angels[D]	teacher[L]	apostles[R]	are giving.	=	
Crowns[P]	gold[Q]	teacher[L]	angels[D]	apostles[R]	are giving.	=	
Crowns[P]	gold[Q]	teacher[L]	apostles[R]	angels[D]	are giving.	=	O Teacher, angels are giving crowns of gold to apostles!
Crowns[P]	gold[Q]	apostles[R]	teacher[L]	are giving	angels[D].	=	
Angels[D]	apostles[R]	crowns[P]	gold[Q]	are giving	teacher[L].	=	
Teacher[L]	angels[D]	apostles[R]	are giving	crowns[P]	gold[Q].	=	

Greek is such a language! While not completely ignoring word order, Greek tags its words far more extensively than does English. The languages using extensive tagging strategies for communicating meaning are called **inflected** languages.

So how does Greek tag its words? Rather than using superscripted tags, **Greek attaches various endings** to many of its words to signal just what **roles** they might play in a given sentence. Learning to read and understand Greek will require us to know all of the tagging strategies used by Greek. One such pattern of tags can be seen attached below to the word ἄγγελος (angel). Notice the various endings that have been attached to the basic stem of the word (ἄγγελ--): (Pronounce all elements in the following chart *aloud,* in rows from left to right. This will help seal the sequence of <u>form</u>, <u>case</u>, <u>number</u>, <u>gender</u> in the mind.)

Greek Forms	Identification		
	Case	Number	Gender
ἄγγελος	nominative	singular	masculine
ἀγγέλου	genitive	singular	masculine
ἀγγέλῳ	dative	singular	masculine
ἄγγελον	accusative	singular	masculine
ἄγγελε	vocative	singular	masculine
ἄγγελοι	nominative	plural	masculine
ἀγγέλων	genitive	plural	masculine
ἀγγέλοις	dative	plural	masculine
ἀγγέλους	accusative	plural	masculine
ἄγγελοι	vocative	plural	masculine

Now let's take a look at the information supplied by these endings to the reader:

An Introduction to Cases

Notice that 5 different *cases* are signaled by these endings. Think of these cases as the *roles* played in the sentence above [O Teacher, angels are giving crowns of gold to children]. At the moment, we'll study only the *most prominent* and *most frequent roles* suggested by the cases:

The Nominative Case:

Words in the nominative case will be identifying more particularly the person(s) already implied by the verb. You remember that the forms of λύω in the last chapter already identify "Doers" *in a general way* (I, you, he/she/it, we, y'all, they). Usually the speakers and listeners (first and second persons: I, you, we, ya'll) already know who they are, and need no further identification or description. But persons or things that are *spoken about* (third persons: he/she/it, they) typically need further identification through the use of nominatives (*unless the general context makes it clear*).

		Greek Expression	Translation
ambiguous	➜	δίδωσι	He/she/it is giving…
clearer	➜	ἄγγελος δίδωσι	*An angel* is giving… or…
		δίδωσι ἄγγελος	*An angel* is giving…
ambiguous	➜	διδόασι	They are giving…
clearer	➜	ἄγγελοι διδόασι	*Angels* are giving… or…
		διδόασι ἄγγελοι	*Angels* are giving…

Additional Notes about the Nominative:

1) You should now see how Greek can be more flexible than English in word order. Observe that the Greek words ἄγγελος and ἄγγελοι can appear before or after the verb without creating confusion because they have been "tagged" as nominatives, as the "Doer(s)" in these sentences.

2) You also should notice that English does not allow redundancy, a "doubling up", when translating third person verbs (he/she/it, they) which are further clarified by a nominative:

ἄγγελος δίδωσι	NOT An angel *he* is giving…BUT *An angel* is giving…
ἄγγελοι διδόασι	NOT Angels *they* are giving…BUT *Angels* are giving…

But if it is a *first or second person* (of the verb) that is being clarified by a Greek nominative, English needs to retain (in translation) the first or second person pronoun for the sake of clarity:

ἄγγελοι δίδομεν	*We* angels are giving…
ἄγγελοι δίδοτε	*You* angels are giving…

The Accusative Case:

Something found in the accusative case usually functions as the *Patient undergoing something*. To put it another way, we might say that *Something or Someone 'got blank-ed'* in a sentence. But just how much the Patient was affected or changed by the event… *can only be determined by the content of the sentence (and the discourse) as a whole.* Consider the following examples of "Patients" in these English sentences:

English Sentence with a *coyote* as the *Patient*

- Mr. Wilson shot and killed *a coyote* in the grocery store.
- Mr. Thompson trapped *a coyote* in the grocery store.
- Ms. Prince fed *a coyote* in the grocery store.
- Mr. Lance sheltered *a coyote* in the grocery store.
- Ms. Brock raised *a coyote* in the grocery store.
- Mr. Smith saw *a coyote* in the grocery store.
- Mr. Earle smelled *a coyote* in the grocery store.
- Mrs. Grant touched *a coyote* in the grocery store.
- Mr. Crooks petted *a coyote* in the grocery store.
- Mrs. Jackson imagined seeing *a coyote* in the grocery store.
- Mr. Alexander remembered *a coyote* in the grocery store.

- Mrs. Davis <u>pondered</u> *a coyote* in the grocery store.
- Ms. Allen <u>made</u> *a coyote* out of cardboard in the grocery store.
- Mr. Pickwick <u>incinerated</u> *a coyote* in the grocery store.

You can see that...*even though all of these sentences fit into the same grammatical pattern of "Somebody 'blanked' a coyote"*... it is **impossible** to invent **one label** to cover **all the roles** played by the coyote. In one example a coyote comes into existence, while in another it goes out of existence (pretty ultimate stuff, from the point of view of the coyote!). In some examples the coyote undergoes change, while in others nothing actually happens to change the coyote. In some examples the changes are mild, in others, they are drastic. In some examples the coyote feels something, while in others it feels nothing. In some examples the coyote willingly participates, while in others desperately avoids participation. In some examples, no tangible coyote even exists!

Now you can see the **difficulty** of finding an **appropriate label** to cover all of these circumstances. Any label we might try (like Patient, Experiencer, Undergoer, Object, or Receiver of Action) might describe the role of the coyote in some sentences, but not all. The good news is that somehow we can intuitively recognize that "coyote" fills the slot in this empty sentence: "Someone blank-ed a coyote", and that each sentence above uses this same pattern. Put another way, we know **what 'got blank-ed'** in each sentence above. A *coyote* "got blanked"!

In the experimental sentence we have been using (O Teacher, angels are giving crowns of gold to apostles!), something 'got blanked'. What 'got blanked'? **Crowns!** So we should expect to find this word in the Greek **accusative case**. The Greek word for crown is στέφανος, and it uses the same pattern of endings as does ἄγγελος. The accusative plural form, then, would be στεφάνους. We can now expand our sentence accordingly, and at the same time demonstrate how "tagging" this word as an accusative allows us to vary the word order considerably without jeopardizing the meaning of the sentence. (Read each sentence and its translation *aloud* to feel the full effect.)

Greek Sentence	English Translation
ἄγγελοι διδόασι στεφάνους	Angels are giving *crowns*
ἄγγελοι στεφάνους διδόασι	Angels are giving *crowns*
διδόασι ἄγγελοι στεφάνους	Angels are giving *crowns*
διδόασι στεφάνους ἄγγελοι	Angels are giving *crowns*
στεφάνους ἄγγελοι διδόασι	Angels are giving *crowns*
στεφάνους διδόασι ἄγγελοι	Angels are giving *crowns*

The Genitive Case

In our experimental sentences above, "crowns" are described as being "of gold." Because we know what a crown is, and know that gold is a precious metal used to form various artifacts, we discern that "of" is an English way of linking an "artifact" to the "material" out of which it is made. Similar expressions might be:

- a house *of* cards
- a cloud *of* dust
- a tower *of* rock
- a block *of* steel

But as we discovered with the accusative case, languages are amazingly complex and resourceful. For example, the English word "of" can link two nouns bound together in a wide variety of logical relationships:

a tower of rock	the 'of' links *tower* to the **material** out of which it is made.
a man of wisdom	the 'of' links *man* to the **character** or quality he exhibits.
a barrel of water	the 'of' links *barrel* to the **contents** it holds.
the love of country	the 'of' links *love* to the **object** which is loved.
the love of a mother	the 'of' links *love* to the **actor** who does the loving.
a river of life	the 'of' links *river* to the **effect** it can deliver.
a woman of Scotland	the 'of' links *woman* to her **origin**.
the farm of Mr. Jones	the 'of' links *farm* to its **owner**.
a piece of pie	the 'of' links *piece* to the **whole** from which it was taken.
....and so on...	

Right now it is not important to learn these relationships. *Actually, we already know them so well that we constantly use them in ordinary conversation without thinking!* What is important to know is that the **genitive case** *in Greek* covers much the same ground as the word *of* does in English. For now, we can use *of* as a way of connecting (in English translation) a pair of Greek nouns, when a second noun stands in the genitive case and is meant to qualify in some way the first noun of the pair.

We are now able to add the **genitive** to our experimental sentence, specifying the **material** out of which the crowns are made. One of the Greek words for "gold" is χρυσός, the genitive singular being χρυσοῦ.

> ἄγγελοι διδόασι στεφάνους χρυσοῦ
> Angels are giving crowns *of gold*

Notes about the Genitive

1) Notice that Greek needs no word like "of" to connect "crowns" to "gold." The fact that "gold" stands in the genitive case adequately signals the "of-ness" of "gold." The inflected ending (the tags) of the word shows its function.

2) Though we have said several times that the Greek language, being an inflected (tagged) language, has great freedom in word order, Greek is not completely indifferent to word order. For example, **a genitive will typically follow the noun it is modifying**. So as we jumble the word order below, note that we will **maintain a word-order bond** between στεφάνους and χρυσοῦ. (Read aloud the Greek and English to feel the full effect of word order variations.)

ἄγγελοι διδόασι <u>στεφάνους χρυσοῦ</u>	Angels are giving crowns of gold
ἄγγελοι <u>στεφάνους χρυσοῦ</u> διδόασι	Angels are giving crowns of gold
διδόασι ἄγγελοι <u>στεφάνους χρυσοῦ</u>	Angels are giving crowns of gold
διδόασι <u>στεφάνους χρυσοῦ</u> ἄγγελοι	Angels are giving crowns of gold
<u>στεφάνους χρυσοῦ</u> ἄγγελοι διδόασι	Angels are giving crowns of gold
<u>στεφάνους χρυσοῦ</u> διδόασι ἄγγελοι	Angels are giving crowns of gold

3) In Greek, just as in English, it is not always clear just what sort of relationship a speaker or writer has in mind when using "of" or the genitive case. Famously, the phrase "<u>The love of God</u>" is capable of different interpretations:

- taking the genitive as **actor** (God is doing the loving);
- taking the genitive as **object** (God is the one who is loved);
- taking the genitive as **source** (Love, like a fluid perhaps, flows out from God…);
- taking the genitive as **character** (God's kind of love…).

Learning about these sorts of options in the Greek language and how different interpretations can legitimately be generated from a single Greek expression is *a primary reason* for studying New Testament Greek. *It is of little value just to be able to reproduce the translations we find readily available in modern English Versions.* To be able to say that ἀγάπη θεοῦ can be translated as "the love of God" *doesn't advance our understanding of the Bible much at all, and certainly cannot justify the investment of the time and energy required for learning Greek.* But knowing, for example, that the genitive relationship in Greek might represent 15 or 20 different interpretive possibilities *makes all the difference, and deepens our engagement with and understanding of the Scripture immensely!*

Fortunately, not every genitive in the GNT would make sense translated 20 different ways! That level of ambiguity showing up every third or fourth word would have made communication impossible. Most of the time, the sense of the genitive is obvious, as in "crowns of gold". Much of the time, using the English word "of" will provide an adequate translation, even if we need to do more work at a later point to tease out just what "of" might mean in a given situation.

The Dative Case

The dative case in Greek, like the genitive, is a big tent housing many roles. The simplest and most common role is traditionally called the **Indirect Object**, which we can define for the moment as **the person(s) receiving something that is given, sent, brought or spoken.** English examples are easy to generate and recognize:

- I gave a book <u>to my son</u> for Christmas.
- She sent a box of cookies <u>to the prisoner</u> last week.
- They sang praises <u>to God</u> for hours on end.
- We brought a puppy home <u>to our daughter</u>.

Notice that Indirect Objects can occur *only with certain verbs* (to give, send, bring, speak, etc.). This will make it easier to identify an Indirect Object in a sentence. Also, do not imagine that every appearance of the word "to" signals an Indirect Object in English. The following English sentences DO NOT have indirect objects, though they feature an English "to":

- Come, let's go <u>to the store</u>.
- I love <u>to dance</u> <u>to big band music</u>.
- The game ended, 7 <u>to 4</u>.

Again, we can have an Indirect Object *only with certain verbs*, and *only when a person* (or persons) *is receiving something*. Greek will happily set such *receivers* in the *dative* case.

Back to our example sentence. We are now ready to add the dative, specifying the Indirect Object, *the persons to whom the crowns were given*. The Greek word for "apostle" is ἀπόστολος, the dative plural being ἀποστόλοις. Examine now the finished product:

> ἄγγελοι διδόασι στεφάνους χρυσοῦ ἀποστόλοις
> Angels are giving crowns of gold *to apostles*.

You know what's coming next! Because Greek is an inflected language, and has tagged ἀπόστολος to show its role in the sentence as an Indirect Object, we should be able to make sense of our sentence *whatever the order of words might be*! (Read aloud the Greek and English to feel the full effect.)

ἄγγελοι διδόασι στεφάνους χρυσοῦ <u>ἀποστόλοις</u>	Angels are giving crowns of gold *to apostles*.
ἄγγελοι <u>ἀποστόλοις</u> διδόασι στεφάνους χρυσοῦ	Angels are giving crowns of gold *to apostles*.
ἄγγελοι διδόασι <u>ἀποστόλοις</u> στεφάνους χρυσοῦ	Angels are giving crowns of gold *to apostles*.

…and so on! It is now too awkward to present all possible variations in word order.

The Vocative Case

On rare occasion, speakers and writers address their audiences directly through stand-alone expressions. In English, such **direct addresses** are often signaled by "Oh/O" and by commas setting the whole expression off from the rest of the sentence. An expression of direct address can be found anywhere in the sentence.

> My soul longs for your deliverance, *Oh God*.
>
> This, *my friends*, has been a banner year for the company.

In Greek, such expressions of direct address are set in the *vocative case*. On occasion, the vocative is accompanied by an "Oh/O" (in Greek, ὦ). Though ancient Greek writers rarely used punctuation marks of any sort, the modern editors of the GNT use commas to isolate vocatives, just as we find in English texts.

Let's add to our Greek example sentence the vocative "Oh teacher", illustrating at the same time the use of commas by modern editors of the GNT.

<u>διδάσκαλε</u>, ἄγγελοι διδόασι στεφάνους χρυσοῦ ἀποστόλοις

ἄγγελοι, <u>διδάσκαλε</u>, διδόασι στεφάνους χρυσοῦ ἀποστόλοις

ἄγγελοι διδόασι, <u>διδάσκαλε</u>, στεφάνους χρυσοῦ ἀποστόλοις

ἄγγελοι διδόασι στεφάνους χρυσοῦ, <u>διδάσκαλε</u>, ἀποστόλοις

ἄγγελοι διδόασι στεφάνους χρυσοῦ ἀποστόλοις, <u>διδάσκαλε</u>

Each of these sentences could be translated:

"O Teacher, angels are giving crowns of gold to apostles."

Additional Note about the Vocative:

You have seen in the forms provided for ἄγγελος that *in the plural* the nominative and the vocative share *the same form* (ἄγγελοι). While this can lead to some confusion, the presence of commas in the GNT could help you recognize the difference.

But if you are really sharp, you should say, "Well, the commas are supplied by modern editors! How do we know they are right?" Good point! *And that is just the kind of question good students ask!* Such a plural form would need to be "tried out" in a sentence as a nominative, then as a vocative. In all likelihood, the context would make it perfectly clear which works best. If context doesn't make it clear....well, *that's why you are learning Greek! Now you understand why English versions may differ among themselves, why scholars may disagree on a given point, and what the full range of interpretive options might really be, which no English version can set before the reader!* We are not working this hard just to be able to produce a "translation" of the Greek. Dozens of English versions do that quite well! We are working to be able, among other things, to look *beneath* translations, to understand how Greek works so as to see what interpretive decisions have been made by translators *without our even knowing it*!

The Number of Nouns

As the chart at the beginning of this chapter shows us, the various endings of the Greek noun ἄγγελος locate this noun in one of two "numbers", *singular* or *plural*. This is just as simple as it seems: **singular** refers to "one" angel, and **plural** refers to "more than one."

In the example sentence we have been using, you have already noticed that we had to place each Greek noun into either a singular or a plural form. [ἄγγελοι is a nominative *plural*; στεφάνους is an accusative *plural*; χρυσοῦ is a genitive *singular*; ἀποστόλοις is a dative *plural*; διδάσκαλε is a vocative *singular*.]

If we wish, we can modify our sentence to switch the number for each noun. Notice how the Greek forms change from the first sentence, which is our "original":

ἄγγελοι διδόασι στεφάνους χρυσοῦ ἀποστόλοις	Angels are giving crowns of gold to apostles.
ἄγγελοι διδόασι στεφάνους χρυσοῦ <u>ἀποστόλῳ</u>	Angels are giving crowns of gold *to an apostle.*
ἄγγελοι διδόασι <u>στέφανον</u> χρυσοῦ ἀποστόλῳ	Angels are giving *a crown* of gold to an apostle.
<u>ἄγγελος</u> δίδωσι στέφανον χρυσοῦ ἀποστόλῳ	*An angel* is giving a crown of gold to an apostle.

Important Note about Number:

You might have noticed in this last sentence that we changed more than just the number of the noun for "angel". We also changed our verb from third person *plural* (διδόασι) to third person *singular* (δίδωσι). *This is a required move!* The reason for this should be obvious after a moment's reflection. If the nominative is clarifying the identity of the person signaled by the verb, then these two elements (the nominative noun and the person of the verb) *must agree in number*. In traditional grammatical instruction this is called **Subject-Verb Agreement**.

While English is not as inflected as Greek, we can still see places where subject-verb agreement becomes visible in our choice of English words or their spelling.

Original.	But shifting the *subject*…	also requires a shift in the *verb number*
I am sleeping	*You* am sleeping	You *are* sleeping…
He is eating…	*They* is eating…	They *are* eating…
He runs quickly…	*We* runs quickly…	We *run* quickly…

The Forms of Nouns of the 2nd Declension

You have already met the various forms of the masculine noun ἄγγελος, seeing how they express the *five cases* and *two numbers* in which that word can appear. You have noticed that the other nouns we have met (στέφανος; χρυσός; ἀπόστολος; διδάσκαλος) use the same set of endings employed by ἄγγελος.

Now we need to expand our awareness of the family of endings at work with ἄγγελος. In the second column below, we will meet a noun (βίβλος = "book") representing family members that are *feminine* in gender. In the third column below, we will meet a noun (δῶρον = "gift") representing family members that are *neuter* in gender. Carefully read this chart *aloud*.

Number	Case	Masculine Nouns	Feminine Nouns	Neuter Nouns
Singular	nominative	ἄγγελος	βίβλος	δῶρον
	genitive	ἀγγέλου	βίβλου	δώρου
	dative	ἀγγέλῳ	βίβλῳ	δώρῳ
	accusative	ἄγγελον	βίβλον	δῶρον
	vocative	ἄγγελε	βίβλε	δῶρον
Plural	nominative	ἄγγελοι	βίβλοι	δῶρα
	genitive	ἀγγέλων	βίβλων	δώρων
	dative	ἀγγέλοις	βίβλοις	δώροις
	accusative	ἀγγέλους	βίβλους	δῶρα
	vocative	ἄγγελοι	βίβλοι	δῶρα

1) As you look across the chart horizontally, you see that the genitives and datives are identical between all three columns.

2) You also notice that the masculine and feminine forms are exactly alike throughout. No differences!

3) You notice that in the neuter singular, the nominative and vocative appear to have taken the form of the accusative, making these three forms identical (ον).

4) You notice that in the neuter plural, the nominative, vocative, and accusative all share the same ending (α).

5) Now you can see the value of knowing (or finding out) what gender a noun is. If you see the ending (ον), and know that the noun is masculine, then it must be accusative singular. But if you know the noun is neuter, then it could be nominative, vocative, or accusative. So how will we know which case it is? By context. By trying out all options to see which option best fits both the "grammatical machinery" and "sense" of the sentence.

6) And finally, the name which tradition has given to this whole family of endings is "**The Second Declension**." From now on, we will refer to this family of endings by its traditional name. In later lessons we will learn the other declensions (the **First** and the **Third**).

its power to deliver real insight into how most sentences work (in both Greek and English).

So let's display our experimental sentence on a framework inspired by the Reed-Kellogg approach:

Diagramming Simple Sentences

We have actually learned quite a bit by this point! We now know how a great many sentences in Greek actually work: how the **verb** is the *organizational hub* around which everything else is organized, and how **nouns** in *various cases* (nominative, genitive, dative, accusative, vocative) can collect around the verb or around each other. But a picture is worth a thousand words! How might this appear if represented graphically?

In the 1870's, two grammarians [Alonzo Reed, Brainerd Kellogg] developed a strategy for visually depicting the grammatical structures of English sentences. The so-called *Reed-Kellogg* approach soon won out over competing schemes, and became a standard part of American education until perhaps the 1970's.

As the scientific study of language (Linguistics) surged forward in the 1950's, it became clear that traditional approaches like the Reed-Kellogg system were inadequate for capturing all the complexities of grammar. New approaches, such as "tree diagramming", were developed for advanced linguistic analysis.

But the Reed-Kellogg approach remains extremely useful for most grammatical analysis, even if it fails on various technical and theoretical points. A similar situation holds between so-called Newtonian and Einsteinian physics. Newton's view of time and space has been superseded by the discovery that time and space are variable, and that the speed of travel distorts time as one approaches the speed of light. The fixed and stable world of Newton is gone forever.

But most of us will never travel anywhere near the speed of light, relative to the objects of our world. So, despite being technically antiquated, Newtonian-styled calculations of time and space work just fine for everything most of us will ever do, while also matching nicely our intuitive sense of how the world around us works. *Similarly, the technical obsolescence of Reed-Kellogg approach does not diminish*

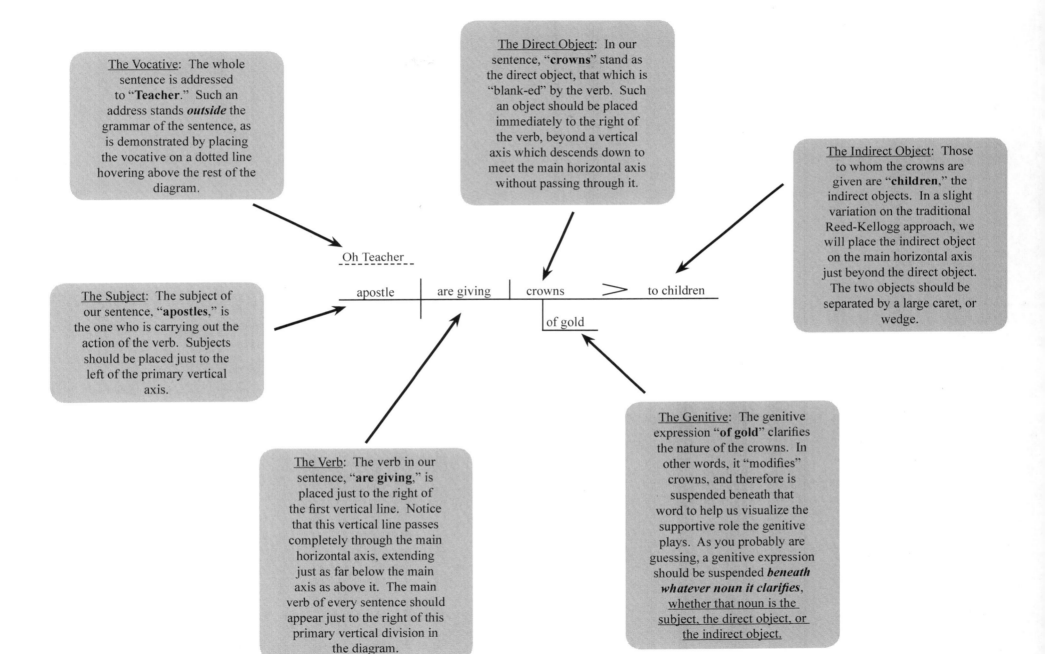

The Vocative: The whole sentence is addressed to "**Teacher**." Such an address stands *outside* the grammar of the sentence, as is demonstrated by placing the vocative on a dotted line hovering above the rest of the diagram.

The Direct Object: In our sentence, "**crowns**" stand as the direct object, that which is "blank-ed" by the verb. Such an object should be placed immediately to the right of the verb, beyond a vertical axis which descends down to meet the main horizontal axis without passing through it.

The Indirect Object: Those to whom the crowns are given are "**children**," the indirect objects. In a slight variation on the traditional Reed-Kellogg approach, we will place the indirect object on the main horizontal axis just beyond the direct object. The two objects should be separated by a large caret, or wedge.

The Subject: The subject of our sentence, "**apostles**," is the one who is carrying out the action of the verb. Subjects should be placed just to the left of the primary vertical axis.

The Verb: The verb in our sentence, "**are giving**," is placed just to the right of the first vertical line. Notice that this vertical line passes completely through the main horizontal axis, extending just as far below the main axis as above it. The main verb of every sentence should appear just to the right of this primary vertical division in the diagram.

The Genitive: The genitive expression "**of gold**" clarifies the nature of the crowns. In other words, it "modifies" crowns, and therefore is suspended beneath that word to help us visualize the supportive role the genitive plays. As you probably are guessing, a genitive expression should be suspended *beneath whatever noun it clarifies*, whether that noun is the subject, the direct object, or the indirect object.

Oh Teacher

apostle | are giving | crowns > to children

of gold

New Testament Exploration

Matthew 26:18 He said, "Go into the city to a certain man and say to him, ὁ διδάσκαλος λέγει· 'My time is near. I will observe the Passover with my disciples at your house.'"

Mark 4:38 And he was in the stern, sleeping on a cushion. They woke him up καὶ λέγουσιν αὐτῷ· διδάσκαλε, don't you care that we are about to die?"

Digging Deeper into the New Testament Text

1) **Find** **Romans 5:1-5** in your GNT. Read aloud 5:5 until smooth. Be ready to read these verses aloud in class.

2) Open your Greek Interlinear and **find** **Romans 5:1-5**. Since we've studied various **cases** of the noun, we're going to look at one particular case issue in these verses. As you look at this text in the Interlinear, you will notice that the **third line** of information contains the **parsings** of all Greek words. All nouns are identified with parsing codes that begin with the **English letter "n,"** easily signaling to us that the Greek word immediately above it is a **"noun."**

How many nouns do you find in 5:1-5?

The entire parsing code of a noun, you will notice, has two clusters of information. The first noun you see in 5:1, for example, is parsed as: **n.gsf**

Decoded, these particular letters and numbers represent the following information:

Noun | **G**enitive-**S**ingular-**F**eminine

In other words, the **first letter** in the **second grouping** tells us what **case** the noun is in [**n.gsf**]. Mounce's code for nouns is:

Case	Number	Gender
n= nominative	s = singular	m = masculine

g = genitive   p = plural   f = feminine

d = dative   n = neuter

a = accustive

v = vocative

Now go through 5:1-5 again. Underline: What case is each noun in? [At this point we don't need to know or translate these nouns.]

3) Go in Wallace's Intermediate Grammar *The Basics of NT Syntax* to pages 41-64 [*Greek Grammar Beyond the Basics*, pages 72–136]. The table of contents on p. 41 [72] gives a listing of the various senses or values that the **genitive** case can express. Obviously, this can go far beyond the senses carried by the English word *of*. We aren't going to memorize these usages, but merely expose ourselves to the range of the genitive.

The main "Verbal Genitive" options will occupy our attention here: the **subjective** genitive and the **objective** genitive. On pp. 57-59 [113–119] you see a fuller discussion of these particular senses. You can see from the diagram on p. 58 [118] that our very expression "the love of God" can be analyzed in two different ways: according to the subjective sense, and then according to the objective sense. According to the **subjective** sense (imagining "love" to be the verb in a sentence diagram), we could take "God" to be **subject** of such a sentence. According to the **objective** sense (imagining "love" to be the verb in a sentence diagram), we could take "God" to be **object** of such a sentence. We're left with two very different notions of what the Apostle Paul is saying. Do believers now sense a swelling love for God (objective), or do they sense a swelling love that God has (subjective) for them?

Two leading scholars take two different pathways here. James D. G. Dunn (with the majority) chooses the **subjective** as making best sense in this passage. N. T. Wright takes the **objective** reading, believing that the OT backdrop of Deuteronomy 6:4-5 (with its call to love the Lord with all one's heart) should swing our discernment. [Notice that the NIV translation seems to push the reader strongly toward the **subjective** side here. If we read only the NIV, we would likely not be aware of the possibility of a different notion that the Greek grammar here makes possible.]

4) IV. In the Interlinear, find in 5:5 the English expression "has poured out." You will notice that this expression is the NIV's attempt to translate the single Greek word ἐκκέχυται. On the fourth line beneath it you see its

wordlist code: 1773. Go back to Appendix B, and note the "dictionary form" there provided. Then look up *exactly this dictionary form in BDAG*.

- What definitions are offered in BDAG? Which one does BDAG suggest for the occurrence in 5:5?

- What additional insight does BDAG offer about the typical use of this word?

- The parsing code for this verb suggests that it is a <u>Perfect Passive</u> of the Indicative mood. From our work in Chapter Two, what significance might there be for the Perfect Passive here?

Chapter Three Vocabulary

<u>Masculine Nouns of the Second Declension</u>: (This list contains several of the **22** 2nd declension *masculine* nouns used 100x or more.)

ἄγγελος	angel
ἀπόστολος	apostle
διδάσκαλος	teacher
θάνατος	death
λόγος	word
ὄχλος	crowd
στέφανος	crown
χρυσός	gold

<u>Feminine Nouns of the Second Declension</u>: (This list includes all 2nd declension *feminine* nouns used 100x or more.)

βίβλος	book
ὁδός	road
ἔρημος	wilderness

<u>Neuter Nouns of the Second Declension</u>: (This list includes all 2nd declension **neuter** nouns used 100x or more.)

δῶρον	*gift*
εὐαγγέλιον	*gospel*
παιδίον	*child*
τέκνον	*child*
ἔργον	*work*

<u>Conjunctions</u>:

καί	*and* (from Chapter Two)
ἀλλά	*but* (in a strong contrastive sense)

Exercises

I. Short Answer

1) What is an <u>inflected language</u>?

2) What does the <u>Nominative case</u> often identify?

3) What does the <u>Genitive case</u> often identify?

4) What does the <u>Dative case</u> often signify?

5) What does the <u>Accusative case</u> often signify?

6) What does the <u>Vocative case</u> often signify?

<u>Solutions to Exercise I</u>

1) A language that relies more on *word tagging* than on word order to communicate the *roles* played in a sentence.
2) The person or thing *performing an action*.
3) The person or thing in an *"of-relationship"* with (usually) a preceding noun.
4) The person *to whom something is given, brought, or spoken*.
5) The person or thing *acted upon*.
6) The person directly addressed by the speaker of the sentence.

II. Memorizing the Endings for λόγος

It is necessary to commit this set of endings to memory, since they will pave the way to recognizing many nouns and other parts of speech (kinds of words). In vertical columns, write out the endings until you have mastered them. Always be pronouncing them aloud to sear them into your memory.

Nom.	λόγος	−ος
Gen.	λόγου	−ου
Dat.	λόγῳ	−ῳ
Acc.	λόγον	−ον
Voc.	λόγε	−ε

Nom.	λόγοι	−οι
Gen.	λόγων	−ων
Dat.	λόγοις	−οις
Acc.	λόγους	−ους
Voc.	λόγοι	−οι

III. Memorizing the Endings for τέκνον

It is necessary to commit this set of endings to memory, since they will pave the way to recognizing many nouns and other parts of speech (kinds of words). In vertical columns, write out the endings until you have mastered them. Always be pronouncing them aloud to sear them into your memory.

Nom.	τέκνον	−ον								
Gen.	τέκνου	−ου								
Dat.	τέκνῳ	−ῳ								
Acc.	τέκνον	−ον								
Voc.	τέκνον	−ον								
Nom.	τέκνα	−α								
Gen.	τέκνων	−ων								
Dat.	τέκνοις	−οις								
Acc.	τέκνα	−α								
Voc.	λόγοι	−α								

IV. Parse

For each of the following nouns of the second declension, identify the *case*, *number*, and *gender* (always in that order). Be sure to identify *every possible* parsing for a given word. Remember that the *gender* of each noun is *fixed*: though a given noun will shift in case and number, it will remain true to its own gender. [Note: *It is not really possible to translate these words meaningfully, since their case function can only be expressed in the context of a sentence. This exercise focuses solely on accurately identifying the information suggested by the ending.*]

1) ἄγγελος

2) βίβλους

3) δῶρα

4) ἀγγέλου

5) δῶρον

6) βίβλον

7) ἀγγέλων

8) βίβλοις

9) ἄγγελοι

10) ἀγγέλοις

11) δώρῳ

12) βίβλων

13) ἄγγελε

14) δώρων

15) βίβλος

16) δώρου   .

V. Parse, Diagram and Translate

Take each of these sentences through the same steps: **1)** write out at least two of these sentences in Greek, **2)** parse the verb, **3)** parse each noun, **4)** set the words (in English if you wish) into their appropriate positions on a sentence diagram, **5)** offer a translation based on the information you have generated.

1) ὄχλοι διδόασι διδασκάλοις στεφάνους χρυσοῦ.

2) τέκνα λόγους θανάτου παιδίοις γράφουσι.

3) διδάσκαλος ἀποστόλοις δῶρα τέκνων δηλοῖ.

4) βίβλον λόγων ὄχλοις ἀπόστολοι ἀποστέλλουσι.

5) διδασκάλοις ἄγγελοι κηρύσσουσι λόγους ἀποστόλων.

6) ἔργα θανάτου λύομεν, ἀλλὰ δηλοῦσι λόγους εὐαγγελίου.

7) ὁδὸν χρυσοῦ βλέπω, ἀλλ᾿ ἀκούετε διδάσκαλον θανάτου.

8) κηρύσσετε ὁδὸν ἔργων, καὶ βίβλον λόγων δηλοῖς.

9) ποιεῖ στέφανον χρυσοῦ ἀπόστολος, ἀλλὰ λύουσι δῶρα ἀποστόλων ἄγγελοι.

10) ὄχλον διδασκάλων θανάτου τιμῶσι, ἀλλὰ τιμῶ ὄχλον ἀποστόλων.

4: The (Definite) Article

In the last chapter we learned how to analyze and translate simple Greek sentences. We learned how **nouns** play various roles, depending on their cases, as thy orbit around the (grammatical) hub of the sentence: the **verb**.

But what awkward and artificial sentences we've been working with! ["Oh Teacher, angels are giving crowns of gold to children."] We can't fault any word we've used in them. Each word is perfectly legitimate in its own right. But something feels downright childish about them. Something is **missing** that would give these sentences a more realistic feel. What is it?

It's the little word **the**. Somehow we know that these sentences, if we met them in the real world, would likely have several "the's":

> Oh Teacher, **the** <u>angels</u> are giving **the** <u>crowns</u> of gold to **the** children.

In English we call "the" the **definite article**, and it's by far the **most frequently used word** in English and in Greek. On average, **one of every seven words** in the GNT is the **article**. So by getting our minds wrapped around the article, we're taking a huge step forward in learning NT Greek! But why might this be, and what sort of work does this tiny word do?

The Logic and Use of the (Definite) Article

First, a warning. The Greek and the English definite articles **often** function in the **same way**. So when we see a Greek article in the GNT, we will often end up using an English definite article (**the**) to translate it. But the Greek article **often** functions **differently** from the English definite article. **The two are not simply interchangeable in every instance!** But since we are only getting started in Greek, we will go ahead and translate the Greek article as **the**, and learn other subtleties later.

But what does **the** mean? In English as in Greek, the definite article very frequently **identifies and distinguishes some particular individual** (or group of individuals) from others. For example, if I asked, "Did you park **the** car in **the** garage?" I am signaling to you that I am curious about a **particular** car, not any car, and not just cars in general; and that I have in mind a **particular** garage, not just any garage. If I said, "Did you pick up **the** children?" I am signaling to you that I have **particular** children in mind.

But now the explanation becomes more fascinating! How can the one little word **the** identify a **particular car**, and then turn right around and identify a **particular garage**, and then **particular children**? Certainly the English letters **t-h-e** contain no information about color, size, shape, age, location (etc.) which would point me to this car as opposed to that one, and to that garage as opposed to another! So how does **the** work its magic?

As you might have guessed, **the** itself contains no information identifying the right car or the right garage. But it does tell us that **we** listeners or readers **should somehow already know** which car and which garage are in question. In other words, when I ask, "Did you park **the** car in **the** garage?" you should begin saying to yourself, "*Somehow I should already know what car and what garage he is talking about.*" If it helps, think of the article as a **wink of the eye** telling us that we **already** have resources for identifying just which item the speaker has in mind.

So, why did our manufactured sentences sound so awkward without any **the's**? Because real conversation and real writing moves forward, from sentence to sentence, by adding *only small bits of new information to a larger body of old information.* In other words, the rate at which new information is communicated is rather low. Much of each new sentence we encounter appeals to *old information already shared between speaker and listener.* Therefore most sentences will be peppered with articles "winking" to us to identify items we already know about!

But how do we know which particular individual "The" is pointing to?

1) ...because something was **just mentioned** (Anaphoric) [In English and Greek]

We can use an article to identify something the *second* time it is mentioned, because we learned of it in an *earlier* mentioning.

> Mom gave me a Christmas ornament she had made years ago. **The** ornament was blue with silver sparkles.
>
> [Once we meet *an* ornament, we can subsequently refer to it as *the* ornament.]

2) ...because an **explanation immediately follows** (Kataphoric) [In English and Greek]

We can use an article to identify something if it is immediately identified or explained.

> Mom gave me **the** ornament which she had been saving for many years.

3) ...because of **shared circumstances, customs, and culture** (Circumstantial) [In English and Greek]

We can often use an article to identify something if we know what *context* we're in.

> Whenever you enter a *church*, always take note of where **the** pulpit is located.
>
> [Since each church *customarily* has a pulpit, we will expect to see one upon entering any church. Notice, there was no prior mention of "pulpit". It is the circumstance of being in a typical church which allows us to specify its pulpit, even if no particular church is in view!]a

4) ...because something is **unique** (Monadic) [In English and Greek]

We can use an article to identify something if (surprise!?) only *one such thing* exists!

> **The** earth, **the** moon, and **the** sun fulfill their orbits with exquisite precision!

5) ...because something is the **best or worst** in quality or character (Par Excellence) [In English and Greek]

We can use the article to identify something if it is easily distinguished either because it is the very best or the very worst of its peers.

> Please don't ever again mention **the** play. I hope to blot it from my mind for good!
>
> [Spoken by one Mets fan to another about the fielding error which cost them the World Series. It was the *worst play ever* in the history of that sports franchise.]

6. ...because something is **celebrated, infamous, or familiar** (Well-Known) [In English and Greek]

We can use the article to identify something if it is already well-known.

> So this is **the** place!
>
> [Spoken by a visitor to Dallas, Texas, when viewing the location of the assassination of President John F. Kennedy. This place is not the only place in the world (monadic), nor is it necessarily the very best or worst place (Par Excellence). But it is very well-known.]

The Forms of the (Definite) Article

Since the article must be able to match itself to a noun found in any case, number, or gender, it makes sense that the article must be capable of full flexibility, of being able to express itself in *any case, number or gender*.

Number	Case	Masculine	Feminine	Neuter
		Gender		
Singular	Nominative	ὁ	ἡ	τό
	Genitive	τοῦ	τῆς	τοῦ
	Dative	τῷ	τῇ	τῷ
	Accusative	τόν	τήν	τό
Plural	Nominative	οἱ	αἱ	τά
	Genitive	τῶν	τῶν	τῶν
	Dative	τοῖς	ταῖς	τοῖς
	Accusative	τούς	τάς	τά

1) All forms begin with *tau* (τ) except nominative masculines, and nominative feminines.

2) These four forms *without tau* (τ) have two other distinctive features:

   a) each has a *rough* breathing mark (a breathed "h" sound)

   b) each lacks an accent (they are *proclitics*, flowing into the pronunciation of the next word)

3) In terms of accent, all genitives and datives have the *circumflex*.

4) The masculine and neuter forms are similar to the second declension endings for nouns you have already learned.

5) At this point, the entire set of *feminine forms* need to be memorized as a *new venture*.

The Article Linked (in agreement) with Nouns

We have re-produced the second declension forms we learned in the previous chapter, and have coupled each noun with the appropriate form of the article. This is how Greek will express "the angel(s)", or "the book(s)", or "the gift(s)". Study this well:

Number	Case	Masculine Article + Noun	Feminine Article + Noun	Neuter Article + Noun
Singular	nominative	ὁ ἄγγελος	ἡ βίβλος	τὸ δῶρον
	genitive	τοῦ ἀγγέλου	τῆς βίβλου	τοῦ δώρου
	dative	τῷ ἀγγέλῳ	τῇ βίβλῳ	τῷ δώρῳ
	accusative	τὸν ἄγγελον	τὴν βίβλον	τὸ δῶρον
Plural	nominative	οἱ ἄγγελοι	αἱ βίβλοι	τὰ δῶρα
	genitive	τῶν ἀγγέλων	τῶν βίβλων	τῶν δώρων
	dative	τοῖς ἀγγέλοις	ταῖς βίβλοις	τοῖς δώροις
	accusative	τοὺς ἀγγέλους	τὰς βίβλους	τὰ δῶρα

Key Clarifications:

1) The Greek article enjoys standing *in front of* its partner noun, as in English. (The accent of many articles has shifted from the *Acute* (forward leaning) to *Grave* (backward leaning) because of the following word, in accordance with rules not yet taught.)

2) **CRUCIAL CONCEPT**: Greek *nouns* are (almost always) *fixed in gender*. E.g., a masculine noun will always be masculine. But because an *article* ought to be able to be **linked with any noun** at any time, the *article* must be completely *flexible*, able to express itself in any *case*, *number* or *gender* in which the controlling noun happens to stand.

3) **CRUCIAL CONCEPT**: The Greek article must agree with its partner noun in *information*, *not necessarily in spelling*. Note the genitive singular feminine example above: τῆς βίβλου. The article and its partner noun are not spelled similarly, but they perfectly agree with each other in *information*: They both are *genitive*, *singular*, and *feminine*. While several pairings above *do* agree in spelling, this should be seen as a *lucky circumstance, and not as a necessary feature* of how agreement works.

An Overview of the Ten Parts of Speech

To this point we have studied *four (4) different kinds* of words: verbs, nouns, conjunctions, and the article. Greek may be analyzed as having a *total of ten (10)* different kinds of words. Every single Greek word you encounter in the GNT will fit into one of these word classes! We'll take a look at all of them now to get the big picture in view, though you won't yet be responsible for all of them. [The "Typical Roles" described below are very general, but are useful to us here at the outset.]

	Part of Speech	Typical Role	English Example	Interlinear Code (in Mounce)	
1)	verb	sets in motion an action or state	I *saw* the president.	v	(**v**erb)
2)	noun	person, place, "thing"	I saw the **president**.	n	(**n**oun)
3)	article	particularizes a noun	I saw *the* president.	d	(**d**efinite article)
4)	adverb	modifies a verb	I saw the president *yesterday*.	adv	(**adv**erb)
5)	adjective	modifies a noun	I saw the **former** president yesterday.	a	(**a**djective)
6)	conjunction	adds things together	I saw the president **and** the first lady.	cj	(**c**on**j**unction)
7)	pronoun	replaces a noun	I saw **them** yesterday.	r	(p**r**onoun)
8)	preposition	relates a noun to the sentence	I saw them **in** the deli yesterday.	p	(**p**reposition)
9)	interjection	attention-getting device	**Hey**! I saw them yesterday!	j	(inter**j**ection)
10)	particle	adds tone or nuance to a sentence	I *indeed* saw them yesterday.	pl	(**p**artic**l**e)

New Testament Exploration

John 3:10–11   Jesus answered and said to him, "σὺ εἶ ὁ διδάσκαλος τοῦ Ἰσραὴλ καὶ ταῦτα οὐ γινώσκεις; Truly, truly, I say to you, we speak about what we know and testify about what we have seen, yet you all do not receive our testimony. (σὺ εἶ = *you are*; Ἰσραὴλ = *Israel*; ταῦτα = *these things*; οὐ = *not*)

Digging Deeper into the New Testament Text

1) Find **II Corinthians 5:16-21** in your GNT. <u>Read aloud 5:16-17 until smooth</u>. Be ready to read these verses aloud in class. Continue looking at these verses to notice several <u>adverbs</u>, two <u>conjunctions</u>, a <u>verb</u>, and an <u>interjection</u> that you can already recognize. What are they?

Still in your GNT, broaden your scope to 5:16-21. Scan through all of these verses. <u>How many articles</u> have you found? For each of them, write out <u>all possible parsings</u> according to the forms of the article already given to you in this chapter.

2) Now open your Greek <u>Interlinear</u> to **II Corinthians 5:16-21**. From our discussion above, you know that the Interlinear code for the article is the English letter *d* (for **D**efinite Article). Scan across the parsing line (the third line of the Interlinear) to <u>find all articles</u>. Did your own search of the GNT match the results of your Interlinear search?

Now you can see that the Interlinear offers ***not all possible parsings*** for the article, but only the ***parsing that fits*** its use in this sentence, according to the noun with which it is used. Examine **5:19**, and <u>find three (3) articles</u>. Do you see that they match in case, number, and gender with their respective nouns? [They also happen to match in spelling.]

Still in your Interlinear, do a ***Parts of Speech Inventory***, following the codes provided on line three (3) of the Interlinear. Simply work sequentially through **5:16-19**, listing the code and the part of speech. For example:

5:16 cj (conjunction), p (preposition), d (definite article), adv (adverb)…

[**Note**: Mounce has used two additional codes to represent two specialized forms of the verb: a <u>verbal noun</u> (***infinitive***) is coded as **f**, and a <u>verbal adjective</u> (***participle***) is coded as **pt**. Technically, these are verbs, and do not represent new parts of speech. We, along with Mounce, will call them the ***infinitive*** and the ***participle***, but will remember that they are ***verbs***. Now you know all of Mounce's coding.]

3) In the Interlinear, find in 5:17 the English word "creation." You will notice that this expression is the NIV's translation of the Greek word κτίσις. On the fourth line beneath it you see its wordlist code: 3232. Go back to Appendix B, and note the "dictionary form" there provided. Then look up ***exactly this dictionary form in BDAG***.

   a) What definitions are offered in BDAG? Which one does BDAG suggest for the occurrence in 5:17?

   b) How do the NIV translation, and the suggested BDAG translation of 5:17 differ?

4) Go in Wallace's Intermediate Grammar *The Basics of NT Syntax* to pages 93-128 [*Greek Grammar Beyond the Basics*, pages 206–290]. The table of contents on p. 93 [206] gives a listing of the various senses treated in Part I, while p.114 [255] gives an overview of Part II. It's amazing what a little word like "the" can do in Greek! <u>Simply leaf through these pages for now</u>. If you have a chance at a later point in your academic studies to venture into Advanced Greek, you will be exploring (among other things) the subtle but important insights that come when the Greek article is mastered.

Chapter Four Vocabulary

Adverbs: (This list contains most adverbs used 100x or more.)

πῶς	*how?*
ἔτι	*still, even now*
ποῦ	*where?*
οὐκέτι	*no longer*
πάλιν	*again*
εὐθύς	*immediately* (also appearing as εὐθέως)
πάντοτε	*always*
νῦν	*now*
καλῶς	*well, rightly, fittingly*
ὧδε	*here (in this place)*
κακῶς	*poorly, badly, wickedly*
ἐκεῖ	*there (in that place)*

Particles:

οὐ, οὐκ, οὐχ	*not* (οὐκ when a vowel follows, οὐχ when a rough breathing vowel follows)

Interjections:

ἰδού or ἴδε	*Look! Notice! See!*

Exercises

I. Short Answer

1) What does the <u>definite article typically do</u>?

2) <u>How</u> does the listener/reader understand <u>which particular item</u>(s) is singled out?

3) <u>In what ways</u> might a listener/reader have <u>prior knowledge</u> of an item(s)?

4) Why does the <u>article</u> have forms to represent every <u>case, number and gender</u>?

5) Will an article agree in <u>spelling</u> with the noun it modifies?

6) <u>Name</u>, describe common <u>function</u> of, and <u>identify the Interlinear symbol</u> for each of the <u>10 Parts of Speech</u>.

<u>Solutions to Exercise I</u>

1) It signals that the speaker/writer is ***singling out something particular***.
2) The listener/reader will have ***prior knowledge*** of it.
3) [See the list of explanations in the lesson above.]
4) It must be able to modify ***any noun,*** however that noun might appear.
5) Not necessarily. But it must agree in ***information*** [case, number, gender].

II. Memorize the Article

There is no part of speech more important to commit to memory than the article. As noted before, about every 7th word in the GNT (on average) is the article. It often serves as a grammatical signpost suggesting to us just how the parts of the sentence fit together. Use your own paper to write out its forms, and continually pronounce aloud as you write.

	Singular			Plural		
	Masculine	Feminine	Neuter	Masculine	Feminine	Neuter
Nominative	ὁ	ἡ	τό	οἱ	αἱ	τά
Genitive	τοῦ	τῆς	τοῦ	τῶν	τῶν	τῶν
Dative	τῷ	τῇ	τῷ	τοῖς	ταῖς	τοῖς
Accusative	τόν	τήν	τό	τούς	τάς	τά

III. Add Articles:

For each of the following nouns of the second declension, add the appropriate article to agree with it in information: in case, number and gender.

1. _____ ἄγγελος 2. _____ βίβλους 3. _____ δῶρα 4. _____ ἀγγέλου

5. _____ δῶρον 6. _____ βίβλον 7. _____ ἀγγέλων 8. _____ βίβλοις

9. _____ ἄγγελοι 10. _____ ἀγγέλοις 11. _____ δώρῳ 12. _____ βίβλων

13. _____ ἀγγέλους 14. _____ δῶρον 15. _____ βίβλος 16. _____ δώρου

17. _____ ἀγγέλῳ 18. _____ ἀγγέλων 19. _____ βίβλῳ 20. _____ δώρῳ

IV. Add Articles, notice adverbs, and (re-)Translate

You will recognize these sentences from Chapter Three. Now we are ready to add **articles** to many of these nouns. We have also sprinkled in some of the **adverbs** we have learned in this chapter. Write out in Greek at least two of these sentences.

1) νῦν _____ ὄχλοι διδόασι _____ διδασκάλοις στεφάνους χρυσοῦ.

2) ἰδοὺ _____ τέκνα _____ λόγους θανάτου _____ παιδίοις πάλιν γράφουσι.

3) _____ διδάσκαλοι _____ ἀποστόλοις _____ δῶρα _____ τέκνων δηλοῦσι πάντοτε.

4) _____ βίβλον λόγων _____ ὄχλοις _____ ἀπόστολοι ὧδε ἀποστέλλουσι.

5) _____ διδασκάλοις _____ ἄγγελοι κηρύσσουσι _____ λόγους _____ ἀποστόλων ἐκεῖ.

6) ἰδοὺ _____ ἔργα θανάτου οὐ λύομεν, ἀλλὰ δηλοῦσι _____ λόγους _____ εὐαγγελίου.

7) _____ ὁδὸν χρυσοῦ βλέπω, ἀλλ' οὐκ ἀκούετε _____ διδάσκαλον θανάτου.

8) οὐκέτι κηρύσσετε _____ ὁδὸν ἔργων, καὶ _____ βίβλον λόγων οὐκέτι δηλοῖς.

9) ἰδοὺ ποιεῖ _____ στέφανον χρυσοῦ _____ ἀπόστολος καλῶς, ἀλλὰ κακῶς λύουσι _____ δῶρα _____ ἀποστόλων _____ ἄγγελοι.

10) εὐθὺς _____ ὄχλον _____ διδασκάλων θανάτου τιμῶσιν, ἀλλὰ τιμῶ _____ ὄχλον _____ ἀποστόλων.

5: Adjectives, The Verb "to Be" and Nouns of the 1st Declension

Not Just Any Apostle!

In our own speech we often **describe** the things we're talking about: the **holy** apostle, or the **good** apostle, or the **first** apostle, or the **last** apostle, or the **other** apostle, or the **dead** apostle, and so on.

Words that do the work of modifying or describing nouns are known as **Adjectives**, another of the ten **parts of speech** (types of words) we are encountering in Greek. [We've already learned of verbs, nouns, articles, conjunctions, and adverbs.] In Mounce's Interlinear code, an **adjective** is signaled by an "**a**."

		Masculine	Feminine	Neuter
Singular	nominative	καλός	καλή	καλόν
	genitive	καλοῦ	καλῆς	καλοῦ
	dative	καλῷ	καλῇ	καλῷ
	accusative	καλόν	καλήν	καλόν
Plural	nominative	καλοί	καλαί	καλά
	genitive	καλῶν	καλῶν	καλῶν
	dative	καλοῖς	καλαῖς	καλοῖς
	accusative	καλούς	καλάς	καλά

The Agreement of Adjectives with Their Governing Nouns

Since an adjective modifies (and so serves) a noun, it only seems reasonable that an adjective **must agree** with the noun it is modifying in case, number, and in gender. In other words, **all three components** of parsing information (**case, number, gender**) must match. Carefully note that this does not mean that the endings of an adjective must match its partnered noun in **spelling**; only that they match in **information**!

Because an adjective (like the article) must be able to agree with a noun of any gender as it is found in any case or number, the adjective must have endings enabling it to cover the full range of cases, numbers and genders. Below is the adjective καλός (καλός, ή, όν, *good, noble, fine, excellent*) shown in its full range of possible forms.

The Positions of the Adjective

We have made it clear that Greek word order is **highly flexible**, open to many variations without essential change in sentence meaning. But Greek is **not totally indifferent** to word order. In the matter of how an adjective stands in relation to the noun it modifies, Greek has specific preferences. Consider the following sentence involving articular nouns without adjectives:

ὁ ἄγγελος τὴν βίβλον τοῖς τέκνοις δίδωσι

(The angel is giving the book to the children.)

Now, let's modify each of the nouns with the adjective we have just learned (καλός). Notice how the adjective is placed ***between the article and its noun***, in an ***article-adjective-noun*** sequence:

[ὁ καλὸς ἄγγελος] [τὴν καλὴν βίβλον] [τοῖς καλοῖς τέκνοις] δίδωσι

(English Translation: The ***good*** angel is giving the ***good*** book to the ***good*** children.)

But the same idea can be expressed in Greek with a ***second pattern***, the ***article-noun-article-adjective*** sequence. As you can see below, the adjective is placed ***after*** the noun, but with the ***article repeated*** just before the adjective:

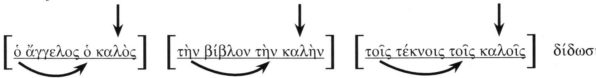

[ὁ ἄγγελος ὁ καλὸς] [τὴν βίβλον τὴν καλὴν] [τοῖς τέκνοις τοῖς καλοῖς] δίδωσι

(English Translation: The ***good*** angel is giving the ***good*** book to the ***good*** children.)

These ***two patterns*** of word order relating an adjective to its (articular) noun are called ***Attributive Positions***.

But notice what happens when the adjective is ***not preceded*** by the article [***article-noun-adjective***, or ***adjective-article-noun***]:

Either... ὁ ἄγγελος καλὸς ...or... καλὸς ὁ ἄγγελος

These sequences (in the ***nominative*** case) create an ***Independent Declaration***: The angel ***is good***. Even though we see no Greek word for "is" in these sequences, these arrangements call on us to "supply" the idea of "being" (whether in the present, past, or future, as context may require). These patterns of word order are called ***Predicate Positions***, since they make predications (actual declarations).

Along with ***Attributive*** and ***Predicate*** positions is the third and last position we'll consider: the ***Substantive Position***. Consider these English lines:

The ***righteous*** always help the ***poor***;

The ***wicked*** always abuse the ***poor***.

The words *righteous*, *wicked*, and *poor* happen to be adjectives, since they normally are used to modify nouns:

>   …the ***righteous*** businessman…

>   …the ***wicked*** businessman…

>   …the ***poor*** businessman…

But if we think about it, we can actually sense that the lines offered above actually entice us to "supply" or "understand" unwritten, implied nouns:

>   The ***righteous*** (persons) always help the ***poor*** (persons);

>   The ***wicked*** (persons) always abuse the ***poor*** (persons).

In other words, adjectives (in both English and in Greek) can actually ***function like nouns*** under certain circumstances. In Greek, such a role for adjectives is usually signaled by the ***Substantive Position***, ***article-adjective-(no noun)***. Let's consider our original example sentence, first as we have seen it before, and then with two of its adjectives set into ***Substantive Position***:

> ὁ καλὸς ἄγγελος τὴν καλὴν βίβλον τοῖς καλοῖς τέκνοις δίδωσι

>   The good angel is giving the good book to the good children.

> ὁ καλὸς τὴν καλὴν βίβλον τοῖς καλοῖς δίδωσι

>   The good (one) is giving the good book to the good (ones).

You can imagine how important the ***surrounding context*** will be when you encounter an adjective in ***Substantive Position***. Just what noun we should "understand" can usually be discerned from the context:

>   I saw seven hats on the shelf. I decided to buy the blue (one).
>   [obviously a hat]

>   I saw seven books on the shelf. I decided to buy the blue (one).
>   [obviously a book]

>   I saw seven scarves on the shelf. I decided to buy the blue (one).
>   [obviously a scarf]

If the adjective (in Substantive Position) is replacing a noun easily identified in the immediate context (or a noun easily supplied by conventional wisdom), then the adjective will likely match the gender of that noun. But more typically, the gender of a substantival adjective will suggest these (rather common-sense) values:

		Translational "helping" Words
Masculine:	male person(s) [or male and/or female if generic]	"man" "men" "one" or "ones"
ὁ καλὸς	….the good man…(male)	
ὁ καλὸς	….the good one… (generic)	
οἱ καλοὶ	….the good men… (male)	
οἱ καλοὶ	….the good ones… (generic)	
Feminine:	female person(s)	"woman" "women"
ἡ καλὴ	….the good woman…	
αἱ καλαὶ	….the good women…	
Neuter:	non-person(s)	"thing" or "things
τὸ καλὸν	….the good thing…	
τὰ καλὰ	….the good things…	

Summary of the Positions of the Adjective

Name	Pattern		Example	Translation
Attributive Positions	article-**adjective**-noun	(internal)	ὁ καλὸς ἄγγελος	The good angel…
	article-noun-article-**adjective**	(external)	ὁ ἄγγελος ὁ καλὸς	The good angel…
Predicate Positions	article-noun-**adjective**	(following)	ὁ ἄγγελος καλὸς	The angel is good.
	adjective-article-noun	(preceding)	καλὸς ὁ ἄγγελος	The angel is good.
Substantive Position	article-**adjective**		ὁ καλὸς	The good (one)…

The Verb "to be" (εἰμί) in the Present Indicative

Perhaps *the most common verb* in any language is the verb expressing "*being*." The English verb of being takes a variety of forms: *am, is, are, was, were, be, being, been*. We have just learned that a Greek adjective in Predicate Position can imply the verb of being. Now it is time explicitly to meet the Greek verb of being (εἰμί) in its *Present Indicative* paradigm:

εἰμί	I am	ἐσμέν	we are
εἶ	you (singular) are	ἐστέ	you (y'all) are
ἐστί (ν)	he/she/it is	εἰσί(ν)	they are

Predicate Nouns and Adjectives

As you can already imagine, verbs of "being" beg to be *completed* (in idea) either by a *noun* or by an *adjective*:

Completed by a *Noun*	Completed by an *Adjective*
I am an *apostle*.	I am *happy*.
You are an *apostle*.	You are *happy*.
He/she/it is an *apostle*.	He/she/it is *happy*.
We are *apostles*.	We are *happy*.
Y'all are *apostles*.	Y'all are *happy*.
They are *apostles*.	They are *happy*.

But in Greek, *in what case* should such a noun or adjective appear? You are accustomed to looking for an *Accusative Direct Object* to complete the idea of the verbs we have met so far. Those verbs are *Transitive* verbs, which can be thought of as "transmitting" some form of *energy or action* to (or at) their objects. But to say, "I *am* an apostle" involves *no* transfer of *energy or action* from "I" to "apostle." In fact, the best way of picturing the relationship between "I" and "apostle" is by the mathematical *Equation* sign: "I = apostle." In other words, verbs of *being* essentially function as verbs of *Equation*. In grammatical lingo, such verbs are called *Linking* verbs, or *Copulative* verbs. Now we can anticipate the answer to our opening question: Equation verbs (under most circumstances) will be *completed by the Nominative Case* because they have set up *equations* with their *Nominative Subjects*.

Transitive Verbs	*Equation/Linking/Copulative Verbs*
Subject ⟶ Direct Object	Subject ═══ Predicate
(Nominative) **(Accusative)**	(Nominative) **(Nominative)**
I love (⟶) **an apostle.**	I am (=) **an apostle.**
You love (⟶) **a teacher.**	You are (=) **a teacher.**
They love (⟶) **plumbers.**	They are (=) **plumbers.**
	I am (=) **happy.**
	You are (=) **sad.**
	They are (=) **wealthy.**

Word Order for Predicate Nouns and Adjectives

In Greek, the sequence in which <u>Subject</u>, <u>Verb</u>, and <u>Predicate Nominative</u> (noun or adjective) may appear is open to all ***variations***. But it is important to realize that the ***underlying grammar*** (the logic of the grammar) ***does not change***. [At this beginning phase of our work, it is probably best to translate all of these variations identically, though the actual context in the GNT could suggest that some emphasis is being placed on a given word when set at the *beginning* or at the *end* of its clause.]

Possible Sequences	Examples	Translation
Subject—Verb—**Predicate**	οἱ ἄγγελοί εἰσι <u>καλοί</u>	The angels are <u>good</u>.
Subject—**Predicate**—Verb	οἱ ἄγγελοι <u>καλοί</u> εἰσι	The angels are <u>good</u>.
Verb—Subject—**Predicate**	εἰσὶν οἱ ἄγγελοι <u>καλοί</u>	The angels are <u>good</u>.
Verb—**Predicate**—Subject	εἰσὶ <u>καλοί</u> οἱ ἄγγελοι	The angels are <u>good</u>.
Predicate—Subject—Verb	<u>καλοὶ</u> οἱ ἄγγελοί εἰσι	The angels are <u>good</u>.
Predicate—Verb—Subject	<u>καλοί</u> εἰσιν οἱ ἄγγελοι	The angels are <u>good</u>.

Diagramming Adjectives and Predicate Nominatives

Attributive adjectives will be placed <u>beneath</u> the nouns they modify.

The apostle (subject) | is (verb) \ weary (predicate adjective)

holy (adjective)

Substantive adjectives will be placed <u>beneath</u> the (bracketed) implied nouns they modify (e.g. one(s), thing(s)).

The ["ones"] (subject) | give (verb) | gifts (object)

good (adjective)

Predicate nominatives (whether nouns or adjectives) will be placed <u>to the right</u> of the verb of being, separated by a slanted line. (We will keep articles with their nouns.) When the subject is known only by the person of the verb, we will enter that implied pronoun (I, you, he/she/it, we, you, they) in brackets in the subject slot.

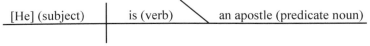

[He] (subject) | is (verb) \ an apostle (predicate noun)

Nouns of the First Declension (καρδία, φωνή, δόξα)

It's time to add the First Declension to our repertoire. Read aloud through the forms of these three nouns:

Number	Case	Feminine Article + Noun	Feminine Article + Noun	Feminine Article + Noun
Singular	nominative	ἡ καρδία	ἡ φωνή	ἡ δόξα
	genitive	τῆς καρδίας	τῆς φωνῆς	τῆς δόξης
	dative	τῇ καρδίᾳ	τῇ φωνῇ	τῇ δόξῃ
	accusative	τὴν καρδίαν	τὴν φωνήν	τὴν δόξαν
Plural	nominative	αἱ καρδίαι	αἱ φωναί	αἱ δόξαι
	genitive	τῶν καρδιῶν	τῶν φωνῶν	τῶν δοξῶν
	dative	ταῖς καρδίαις	ταῖς φωναῖς	ταῖς δόξαις
	accusative	τὰς καρδίας	τὰς φωνάς	τὰς δόξας

You will notice these features at work:

1) All nouns using these patterns are feminine in gender.

2) All endings bear great resemblance to the article, which you have already learned.

3) In the plural, these different words all use the same endings, and match the appearance of the article.

4) In the singular, these different words all use the same consonants in their endings (ς, ν), matching the article.

5) In the singular, these words differ in their endings only in vowel pattern:

καρδία	φωνή	δόξα
uses "pure alpha"	uses "pure eta"	mixes alpha and eta
	(like the article)	

New Testament Exploration

John 10:14–15   Εγώ εἰμι ὁ ποιμὴν ὁ καλὸς καὶ γινώσκω τὰ ἐμὰ καὶ γινώσκουσί με τὰ ἐμά, just as the Father knows me and I know the Father—and I lay lay down my life on behalf of the sheep. (Εγώ = *I*; ποιμὴν = *shepherd*; τὰ ἐμὰ = *my own* [Nom. or Acc. Neuter]; με = *me* [Acc.])

Digging Deeper into the New Testament Text

1) Find **Matthew 5:3-8** in your GNT. Read these verses aloud in Greek until smooth. Be ready to read these verses aloud in class.

   a) Find all adjectives, and parse them the best you can.

   b) Can you spot four (4) nouns of the 1st declension you have learned in this lesson? Where are they?

2) Now open your Greek Interlinear to **Matthew 5:3-8**. From our discussion above, you know that the Interlinear code for the adjective is the English letter *a* (for **A**djective). Scan across the parsing line (the third line of the Interlinear) to find all adjectives. How many have you found?

Notice that 5:3, 5, and 7 each begin with the same structure. Do you see the adjective--article—adjective construction? Essentially this involves *two different positions* of the adjective operating *together*: the second and third words in each of these verses (article-adjective) stand in the **substantive** position: [the poor (ones); the meek (ones); the merciful (ones)]. The first word (the adjective "blessed") in each of these verses stands in *predicate* position: [the poor (ones) *are* blessed; the meek (ones) *are* blessed; the merciful (ones) *are* blessed]. You can see from the layout of the Interlinear that there is no verb in the Greek for "is." The English "is" has been "supplied" from the predicate position of the adjective "blessed." [Is it possible to argue that the supplied verb should be set into the future tense? See the future tenses in the rest of the Beatitudes!] Even though most English translations follow the Greek word order [Blessed are the...], be sure you understand that "blessed" is not the subject, but the predicate adjective.

3)   In the Interlinear, find in 5:3, 4, 5, 6, 7, 8 (and beyond) the English adjective "blessed." You will notice that this expression is the NIV's translation of the Greek adjective μακάριοι. On the fourth line beneath it you see its wordlist code: 3421. Go back to Appendix B, and note the "dictionary form" there provided. Then look up *exactly this dictionary form in BDAG*.

   a)   What two definitions are offered in BDAG? Read carefully the explanations provided.

   b)   What possible alternative translation does BDAG offer for Matthew 5:3 and following?

4)   Go in Wallace's Intermediate Grammar *The Basics of NT Syntax* to pages 129-139 [*Greek Grammar Beyond the Basics*, pages 291–314]. The table of contents on p. 129 [291] gives a view of the many technical matters that can be involved in dealing exhaustively with adjectives. Simply leaf through these pages for now. There is no need to understand what you see. If you have a chance at a later point in your academic studies to venture into Advanced Greek, you will be exploring (among other things) the subtle but important insights that come when the Greek adjective is mastered.

On p. 139 [313], see the paragraph treating II Tim 3:16. Notice the following English layout of the two options being discussed. Notice that in the *absence of articles* (which serve as clear signposts when present), it is not perfectly clear whether the adjective "inspired" is to be seen as in *attributive* or (along with "profitable") as in *predicate* position. When you think about it, an important difference between the two ways of reading emerges. In the *first option* below (predicate position), the claim is actually made that all scripture is inspired. In the **second option** below (attributive

position), the door is open for one to conclude that not all scripture is inspired, though all that is inspired is characterized as useful. [In other words, the second option leaves the door open for a category uninspired scripture.] How does Wallace argue that the first option is more likely grammatically? First Option

Every scripture is *inspired* and profitable...

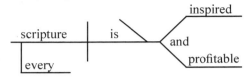

Second Option

Every *inspired* scripture is also profitable...

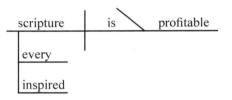

Chapter Five Vocabulary

Adjectives: (This list contains most adjectives used 100x or more.)

NSM	NSF	NSN		
καλός,	-ή,	-όν	good	
ἀγαθός,	-ή,	-όν	good	
ἄλλος,	-η,	-ο	other	[Notice the unusual ending!]
ἕτερος,	-α,	-ον	other	
πρῶτος,	-η,	-ον	first	
ἔσχατος,	-η,	-ον	last	
ἅγιος,	-ία,	-ον	holy	[The iota is included to show accent shift]
νεκρός,	-ά,	-όν	dead	
ἴδιος,	-ία,	-ον	one's own	
μόνος,	-η, -	ον	only	
ὅλος,	-η,	-ον	whole	

First Declension Nouns: (This list includes those used 100x or more. The two proper names are less frequent.) The words below are presented in standard lexical format for nouns: *nominative singular*; then *genitive singular ending*, then *article*. With this information in hand, you know exactly *which set of endings* a word uses, along with the *gender* of that noun (signaled by the article).

ἀγάπη,	ης,	ἡ	love
δικαιοσύνη,	ης,	ἡ	righteousness
καρδία,	ας,	ἡ	heart
ἀλήθεια,	ας,	ἡ	truth
εἰρήνη,	ης,	ἡ	peace
οἰκία,	ας,	ἡ	house
ἁμαρτία,	ας,	ἡ	sin
ἐκκλησία,	ας,	ἡ	church
φωνή,	ῆς,	ἡ	voice
βασιλεία,	ας,	ἡ	kingdom
ἐξουσία,	ας,	ἡ	authority
ψυχή,	ῆς,	ἡ	soul
γῆ,	ῆς,	ἡ	earth
ζωή,	ῆς,	ἡ	life
ὥρα,	ας,	ἡ	hour
δόξα,	ης,	ἡ	glory
ἡμέρα,	ας,	ἡ	day
Μαρία,	ας,	ἡ	Mary
Μάρθα,	ας,	ἡ	Martha

Note: Many of these first declension nouns are ***abstract***, referring to concepts or intangible things (e.g., righteousness, peace, life, glory, truth). In Greek, these nouns often appear with the article, though the article is not typically translated into English. [For example, ἡ ἀλήθεια can simply be translated as "***truth***."] On occasion, however, the Greek article can be considered "live," since the writer could be intending to make reference…not simply to the abstract notion of "truth" in general…but to that particular body of truth comprising, say, the Christian gospel. If the context so leads us, we may translate ἡ ἀλήθεια as "***the truth***."

Exercises

I. Short Answer

1) What does an <u>adjective typically do</u>?

2) <u>How</u> must an adjective <u>agree</u> with the noun it modifies?

3) Describe the <u>sequences</u> and <u>names</u> of each of the <u>positions</u> an adjective may be found in.

4) What <u>sense</u> is communicated by each <u>position</u> of the adjective?

5) <u>What kind of verb</u> is εἰμί?

6) <u>What</u> case commonly <u>completes</u> a verb of being, and why?

<u>Solutions to Exercise I</u>

1) It *modifies a noun.*
2) It must agree with its governing noun in *all three* parsing dimensions: *case, number, and gender.*
3) It may be in the *attributive position:* article—**adjective**—noun; or article—noun—article--**adjective**. It may be in the *predicate position:* article—noun—**adjective**; or **adjective**—article—noun. It may be in the *substantive position:* article—**adjective**.
4) *Attributive position:.* The adjective simply modifies a noun right where it stands […the good apostle…]. *Predicate position:* A complete affirmation is made [The apostle *is* (was, will be) good.]. *Substantive position*: The adjective assumes an implied noun […the good (*one*)…].
5) εἰμί is a verb of "being," usually forming a kind of *equation* [I am (=) an apostle; I am (=) good.]
6) The *nominative* case usually completes a verb of being, since it (in a sense) *equates* the predicate to the *subject* (which is usually in the *nominative*).

II. Memorize the First Declension

Memorize this declension. The feminine forms of the article, which you have already memorized, should help you greatly. Use your own paper to write out its forms, and continually pronounce aloud as you write.

	Singular				Plural
	Feminine			Masculine	
Stem Ending In	εα, ια, ρα	α[1]	η		
Nominative	−α	−α	−η	−ης	−αι
Genitive	−ας	−ης	−ης	−ου	−ων
Dative	−ᾳ	−ῃ	−ῃ	−ῳ	−αις
Accusative	−αν	−αν	−ην	−ν	−ας
Vocative	−α	−α	−η	−α	−αι

[1]Stem ending in α and the preceding letter is not ε, ι, or ρ.

III. Exercise with Predicate Adjectives (with and without εἰμί)

Work through each of the short sentences provided. Work repeatedly through these until you begin to feel comfortable working with and recognizing the predicate adjective, whether with or without the copulative verb.

1) ἐσμὲν καλοί

2) ὁ λόγος καλός

3) ἐστὲ ἅγιοι

4) τὸ παιδίον καλὸν

5) ἐσχάτοι εἰσί

6) ἁγίαι αἱ ἐκκλησίαι

7) ἀγαθός εἰμι

8) νεκρὰ ἡ ἐκκλησία

9) πρώτη εἶ

10) οἱ λόγοι ἀγαθοί

11) εἰσὶ(ν) νεκροί

12) πρῶτα τὰ παιδία

Solutions to Exercise III

1) ἐσμὲν καλοί - We are good.
2) ὁ λόγος καλός - The word is good.
3) ἐστὲ ἅγιοι - Y'all are holy.
4) τὸ παιδίον καλὸν - The child is good.
5) ἔσχατοι εἰσί - They are last.
6) ἁγίαι αἱ ἐκκλησίαι - The churches are holy.
7) ἀγαθός εἰμι - I (masc) am good.
8) νεκρὰ ἡ ἐκκλησία - The church is dead.
9) πρώτη εἶ - You (fem.) are first.
10) οἱ λόγοι ἀγαθοί - The words are good.
11) εἰσὶ(ν) νεκροί - They are dead.
12) πρῶτα τὰ παιδία - The children are first.

IV. Synthetic Sentences (with attributive and substantive adjectives)

The sentences below gather together most of what we have learned so far, including vocabulary. For each sentence: 1) parse each verb, including a "basic" translation of it, as if it stood alone without the rest of the sentence; 2) identify the case, number and gender of every noun; 3) explain the usage of the case of the noun (e.g. subject, direct object, indirect object, or genitive "of"); 4) for each adjective, explain how it agrees with a noun it modifies, and what position it is in; 5) provide a smooth English translation…in normal English word order; 6) diagram each sentence (in English, if you wish); 7) write out in Greek at least two sentences.

1) γράφεις καλῶς τοὺς λόγους τῆς ἐξουσίας τοῖς ἀγαθοῖς.

2) στεφάνους χρυσοῦ τοῖς ἀγαθοῖς τέκνοις οὐκέτι ποιῶ.

3) τοῖς ἑτέροις τὰς βίβλους τῆς ἀγάπης νῦν ἀποστέλλομεν.

4) τὴν δόξαν τῆς ἁγίας ἐκκλησίας ὁ ὄχλος ὧδε βλέπει.

5) ἔτι δίδοτε τοῖς νεκροῖς τὴν ζωὴν τῆς δικαιοσύνης.

6) εὐθὺς αἱ ψυχαὶ αἱ ἄλλαι τὴν δόξαν τῆς μόνης βασιλείας λαμβάνουσι.

7) ὁ πρῶτος ἀπόστολος τοῖς ἑτέροις τὰς ἁμαρτίας τῆς ἰδίας καρδίας οὐ δηλοῖ.

8) τὰ ἔσχατα παιδία ἐκεῖ τὰς φωνὰς τοῦ θανάτου ἄκουσι.

9) ὁ ἀπόστολος ὁ πρῶτος τὴν ἀλήθειαν τῆς εἰρήνης πάντοτε λέγει.

10) τὸ ἀγαθὸν εὐαγγέλιον τῆς δόξης πάλιν κηρύσσει ὁ ἄγγελος ὁ ἔσχατος.

6: Prepositions

Enriching the Simple Sentence in Greek

In the last chapter we added the **adjective** to our understanding of how Greek sentences work. We had already studied the Present Active Indicative for all types of **verbs**, and had learned how **nouns** function in their cases to fill various roles in the sentence. We then learned how **articles** help point out and particularize nouns. At the same time, we encountered **adverbs** and **interjections**. Now we want to add another piece of the puzzle, studying **_certain kinds of phrases_** having unrivaled flexibility and variety. Both English and Greek use these phrases with great frequency. Consider the following account of "Thomas and the House."

"Tom and that House"

Tom had heard _about_ the house _from_ his sister Rachael. _According_ to her, an exquisite Victorian mansion sat _on_ a hilltop overlooking the river _near_ the old water works. As Tom drove _along_ the avenue, he glanced again _at_ the map Rachael had sketched. Sure enough. There it was. _Beside_ it was parked a vintage Deusenberg still _in_ working order. As if _under_ a spell, Tom slipped _out_ of his car and _through_ the open gate. He paused _for_ a moment _beside_ an ornate birdbath that must have been crafted _over_ a century ago. _After_ a few delicious moments of gazing upwards, he pressed on _past_ the welcome mat, _up_ the steps, _across_ the porch, and _toward_ the front door. A dreamy aroma, inviting yet mysterious, wafted _out of_ the house. He knocked, and knocked again…and again, but no one answered. The door was ajar. Should he enter? _Against_ his better judgment, Tom pushed open the door, and stepped right _into_ the front hallway. Just then he sensed a presence _behind_ him, and felt a hand rest _upon_ his left shoulder. His legs sagged, as if he were _under_ a heavy load. Just then….

You Get the Idea

Well, there's no need to go much further with the story! I'm sure everything will turn out just fine for Tom. In the meantime, you've noticed a number of _underlined phrases_, each beginning with some sort of _directional, temporal or relational word_. Such keywords are called **prepositions**, and the phrases in which they appear are called **prepositional phrases**. Even if you haven't heard such terminology until now, you already know how to use these kinds of phrases quite well in your native language.

In the GNT

Your Greek New Testament is loaded with prepositional phrases, many carrying **_heavy theological freight_**: _by_ faith, _through_ grace, _according to_ the Scriptures, _in_ Christ, _under_ condemnation, _for_ our sins, and so on. By the time we're finished with this lesson, you will have a general understanding of **_all 17 prepositions_** used in the GNT, and some idea of how to handle them when you meet them.

Building the Prepositional Phrase

You noticed that the English **prepositional phrases** in our story were built essentially of two elements: a **preposition** and an accompanying **noun** (or pronoun standing for a noun). We call such a noun (or pronoun) **the object** of the preposition.

Preposition	+	Object (Noun or Pronoun)
about…		house
according...		her
on…		hilltop
towards…		address
at…		map
beside…		it
etc...		

The same approach generally holds true in Greek as well, but with one important difference. You might have guessed it! Because Greek is a highly inflected language, Greek **nouns** that are coupled with prepositions must appear in **specific** cases depending on which preposition is used, and perhaps on which sense that prepositional phrase carries in that particular context.

To illustrate, let's set the Greek noun ὄχλος (" crowd") into three different phrases to show that some Greek prepositions have a strict preference for one particular case that should follow:

"in the crowd"	ἐν τῷ ὄχλῳ	(The Greek Preposition ἐν is always teamed with a *dative*.)
"from the crowd"	ἐκ τοῦ ὄχλου	(The Greek Preposition ἐκ is always teamed with a *genitive*.)
"into the crowd"	εἰς τὸν ὄχλον	(The Greek Preposition εἰς is always teamed with an *accusative*.)

Or we can show that other Greek prepositions may be coupled with *different cases* to express *different senses*:

"through the crowd"	διὰ τοῦ ὄχλου	(διά with the *genitive* suggests *"through-ness."*)
"because of the crowd"	διὰ τὸν ὄχλον	(διά with the *accusative* suggests *cause*.)

The 17 Greek Prepositional Phrases

Now let's take a look at *all 17 proper prepositions* found in the GNT, arranged by the cases that may follow them. In brackets notice the number of times this preposition appears in the GNT (bold numbers mark high frequency). Take the time to *read aloud* through this whole display *patiently and repeatedly*, giving your mind a chance to absorb not only the parts but the whole layout.

Prepositions (9) Allowing Only *One Case* to Follow:

ἀντί	[13]	takes the *genitive*	*instead of, for*	ἀντὶ τοῦ ὄχλου	instead of the crowd
ἀπό	[646]	takes the *genitive*	*from, away from*	ἀπὸ τοῦ ὄχλου	away from the crowd
ἐκ	[915]	takes the *genitive*	*from, out from*	ἐκ τοῦ ὄχλου	out of the crowd
πρό	[47]	takes the *genitive*	*before*	πρὸ τοῦ ὄχλου	before the crowd
ἐν	[2752]	takes the *dative*	*in, among*	ἐν τῷ ὄχλῳ	in the crowd
σύν	[128]	takes the *dative*	*along with*	σὺν τῷ ὄχλῳ	along with the crowd
ἀνά	[13]	takes the *accusative*	*in the midst of*	ἀνὰ τὸν ὄχλον	in the midst of the crowd
εἰς	[1767]	takes the *accusative*	*to, into*	εἰς τὸν ὄχλον	into the crowd
πρός	[700]	takes the *accusative*	*to, toward*	πρὸς τὸν ὄχλον	toward the crowd

Prepositions (6) Allowing *Two Cases* to Follow: (always either the genitive or the accusative)

διά	[666]	takes the *genitive*	*through*	διὰ τοῦ ὄχλου	through the crowd
		takes the *accusative*	*because of*	διὰ τὸν ὄχλον	because of the crowd
κατά	[471]	takes the *genitive*	*against*	κατὰ τοῦ ὄχλου	against the crowd
		takes the *accusative*	*according to*	κατὰ τὸν ὄχλον	according to the crowd
μετά	[467]	takes the *genitive*	*with*	μετὰ τοῦ ὄχλου	with the crowd
		takes the *accusative*	*after, behind*	μετὰ τὸν ὄχλον	behind the crowd
περί	[331]	takes the *genitive*	*concerning*	περὶ τοῦ ὄχλου	concerning the crowd
		takes the *accusative*	*around*	περὶ τὸν ὄχλον	around the crowd
ὑπέρ	[149]	takes the *genitive*	*in behalf of*	ὑπὲρ τοῦ ὄχλου	in behalf of the crowd
		takes the *accusative*	*over*	ὑπὲρ τὸν ὄχλον	over the crowd
ὑπό	[217]	takes the *genitive*	*by*	ὑπὸ τοῦ ὄχλου	by the crowd
		takes the *accusative*	*underneath*	ὑπὸ τὸν ὄχλον	underneath the crowd

ἐπί	[878]	takes the *genitive*	**on, near, toward**	ἐπὶ τοῦ ὄχλου	near the crowd
		takes the *dative*	**on, near, toward**	ἐπὶ τῷ ὄχλῳ	near the crowd
		takes the *accusative*	**on, near, toward**	ἐπὶ τὸν ὄχλον	near the crowd
παρά	[191]	takes the *genitive*	***out from***	παρὰ τοῦ ὄχλου	out from the crowd
		takes the *dative*	***beside***	παρὰ τῷ ὄχλῳ	beside the crowd
		takes the *accusative*	***along side***	παρὰ τὸν ὄχλον	alongside the crowd

Some Changes in the Appearance of Prepositions

Fortunately, Greek prepositions themselves don't need to change their own spellings to show case, number or gender. They are not inflected. *They are exactly what they are!* But several prepositions are slightly modified to **ease the pronunciation of the following word**. English uses a similar shift to ease the pronunciation of words following the indefinite article:

The indefinite article when followed by a **consonant**:	I gave my teacher *a* cake for Christmas.
The indefinite article when followed by a **vowel**:	I gave my teacher *an* apple for Christmas.

Similarly, Greek prepositions **ending in a vowel** are sensitive to a following vowel, especially vowels with rough breathing. Notice the various appearances possible for some prepositions as their final vowel has elided, and (perhaps) the exposed consonant has been aspirated. Below are all 17 Greek prepositions and the various changes that may take place. You will likely be able to recognize them even when they have undergone a touch of cosmetic surgery.

Dictionary Form		Possible Variations	Dictionary Form		Possible Variations
ἀντι	→	ἀντ᾽ ἀνθ᾽	διά	→	δι᾽
ἀπό	→	ἀπ᾽ ἀφ᾽	κατά	→	κατ᾽ καθ᾽
ἐκ	→	ἐξ	μετά	→	μετ᾽ μεθ᾽
πρό	·······	No change	περί	·······	No change
ἐν	·······	No change	ὑπέρ	·······	No change
σύν	·······	No change	ὑπό	→	ὑπ᾽ ὑφ᾽
ἀνα	→	ἀν᾽			
εἰς	·······	No change	ἐπί	→	ἐπ᾽ ἐφ᾽
πρός	·······	No change	παρά	→	παρ᾽

General Categories of Prepositional Meanings:

In general, all of the *"glosses"* (suggested translation values) supplied above for prepositions will fit into one of *three categories*. It may be helpful to consider which of these categories is at work as you are working out your translations.

temporal:	e.g. before, after, while, since…
spatial:	e.g. under, over, upon, against, beside, in, into, out of, away from…
conceptual:	e.g. although, because, instead of, according to, concerning, in behalf of…

The Meaning of Prepositions (Simple Glosses, Complex Possibilities)

The "meaning" we have offered above for each preposition should be thought of merely as a *practical "handle"* for picking up and learning the *most common sense* for that preposition. For example, when you encounter the most frequently appearing preposition in the NT (ἐν), it will quite often work to translate it as "**in**." This is *not* the "root" meaning, or the "literal" meaning, or the "basic" meaning, or the "essential" meaning. (I've put all those terms in quotes because they have too often been used illegitimately.) We should attach no special theological or philosophical weight to "in" just because it is the most frequently used gloss for ἐν.

When we press on into careful exegetical work, we cannot be content with simple equations like ἐν = "in." What should we do? If "in" works smoothly according to the sense of the sentence and surrounding passage, then well and good, especially if the sentence deals with simple, tangible matters [Peter was living "in" Galilee]. But if any ambiguity could be involved, or if any theological issue might be at stake, the best recourse will be to *plunge into BDAG*, which will itemize all possible senses that ἐν might take, and will offer a rich supply of glosses (translation options) to consider.

For just a taste of this, let's consider what BDAG offers as possible glosses for ἐν. Though we've learned that its "handle" is "*in*," BDAG sprinkles the following possible

glosses among the various larger senses it suggests for this preposition: *in, on, near, among, before, with, in the case of, on account of, consisting of, amounting to, when, while, and during*. You will realize that these represent very different senses, and could steer us in very different interpretative directions for a given passage.

Adjectival and Adverbial Roles of Prepositions

Prepositional phrases are *usually adverbial* in nature. In other words, they typically clarify and elaborate upon the activity specified by the *verb*. Nearly any verbal action can be further defined in terms of place, time, or conceptual notion:

John baptized Jesus in the Jordan river, before the death of Herod, for the forgiveness of sins.

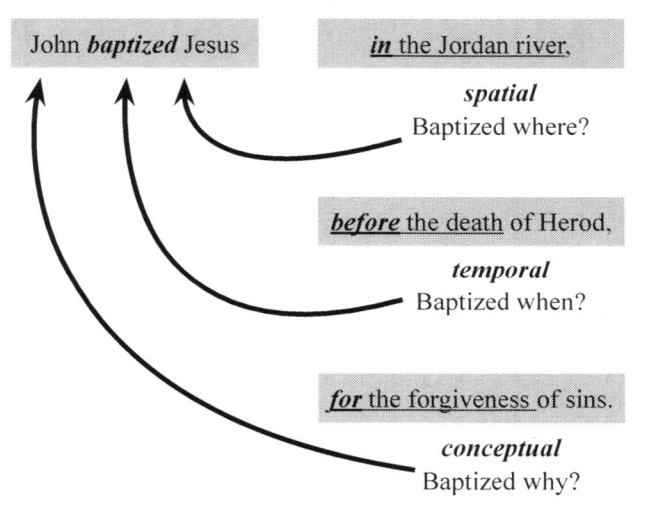

John *baptized* Jesus

in the Jordan river,

spatial
Baptized where?

before the death of Herod,

temporal
Baptized when?

for the forgiveness of sins.

conceptual
Baptized why?

But while most prepositional phrases are adverbial (modifying verbs), some are *adjectival* (modifying *nouns*). This is most clearly signaled by the prepositional phrase standing in *attributive position*, just as if the *whole prepositional phrase* were an *adjective*:

Internal Attributive Position

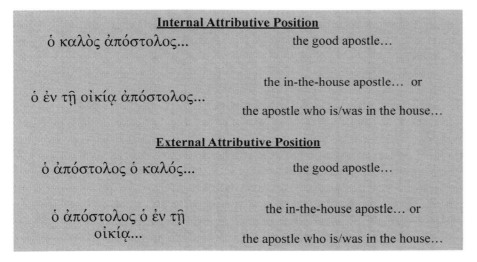

As you might have expected, an adjectival prepositional phrase can also be found in *substantive position*, as if the whole phrase were functioning like a simple adjective:

Substantive Position

ὁ καλὸς...   the good (one)...

ὁ ἐν τῇ οἰκίᾳ...   the in-the-house (one)... or

                                    the one who is/was in the house...

This means that a prepositional phrase can be *diagrammed* by setting it beneath that portion of the sentence which it modifies: *beneath the verb* (if adverbial, as usual), or *beneath any given noun* it might on occasion modify (if adjectival).

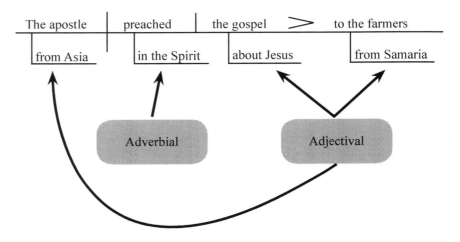

Prefixed Prepositions

As you grow in your study of Greek, you will discover that a great many verbs have prepositions *prefixed* to them. *All 17* prepositions you are learning in this chapter can be attached to verbs in this way. [Those prepositions never attaching themselves to verbs are called "improper" prepositions. We will not be studying them.]

Though only a few of the verbs in our core vocabulary (words used 100 times or more in the GNT) have prepositions prefixed to them, it will be helpful to lay a foundation at this point explaining how those prepositions could *affect the meaning* of a given verb. Thankfully, English can be helpful to us here again.

Transparent (obvious) Change

Here the typical meaning of the preposition is simply added to the verb in a way that allows us to see what each of the two components has contributed to the resulting meaning.

English Example	Greek Example	
I pay	ἔρχομαι	I go
I **repay**	ἐξέρχομαι	I go <u>out</u>
(**re-** modifies the sense in an obvious way)	(ἐξ is a form of ἐκ, meaning "out")	

2. **Intensity Change**: Here the preposition doesn't really carry its own meaning into the verb, but rather intensifies the action of the verb (perhaps by implying completeness, repetition, or vigor). In English, a preposition (perhaps now classified as an adverb) will follow the verb.

English Example	Greek Example	
The house is burning	λύω	I destroy
The house is burning **up**	καταλύω	I <u>totally</u> annihilate
(*Totality* is the issue, not the *direction* of burning.)	(If the context bears this out.)	

3. **Untrackable Change**: Sometimes the preposition significantly alters the sense of the simple verb in a surprising direction not easily gathered from the sense of the preposition. While we may conjecture how the prefixed preposition could have generated the new outcome, it is better to treat the compound as a unique entity, not as a development from the simple verb. To "understand" has nothing to do with "standing under" anything, and "reading" has nothing to do with "knowing something again." Highly imaginative explanations to the contrary will likely have no basis in linguistic or historical fact.

English Example	Greek Example	
I stand	γινώσκω	I know
I **under**stand	ἀναγινώσκω	I read

4. **No Discernable Change**: Sometimes the prefixed preposition has not changed the meaning of the simple verb at all. While exegetes are often tempted to "find" special nuances and secret meanings for Greek words, there are occasions when such temptations ought to be resisted. If neither the context nor solid lexical study suggests that a prefix has in fact altered the sense of the simple verb, then we should translate the simple and the compounded forms alike. Such variations of form (but not of sense) in the GNT are often best explained as "stylistic variation."

English Example	Greek Example	
I exaggerated	ζάω	I come to life
I **over** exaggerated	ἀναζάω	I come to life
(Exaggeration already involves one in pressing over the limits of truth)	(The compound form does not necessarily mean that one comes to life "again.")	

Summary of Interpretive Advice

As we've already suggested, it is best to consider **BDAG** as our ***best resource*** as we encounter prepositions in the GNT. BDAG will alert us to all possible senses a preposition may have, and will often register opinions regarding specific texts with particular difficulties. In other words, it is important to know that prepositions can be used by ancient authors with a ***precision*** we must not miss.

On the other hand as we grow in our experience, we will discover a need to avoid quick, dogmatic conclusions when interpreting GNT prepositions. We will encounter certain phenomena that should qualify our quest for precision. We will learn:

- that some prepositions can at times overlap other prepositions in meaning; and

- that some prepositions do not always change their meaning when the case following them changes.

In other words, a writer may shift from one preposition to another, or from one case to another (with the same preposition) only to create ***stylistic variation***, not a clear or precise shift in meaning. Such variation avoids monotony, making the language itself more interesting, attractive and memorable.

Phil. 1:15–16 Some, indeed, because of both envy and strife, τινὲς δὲ καὶ δι᾽ εὐδοκίαν τὸν Χριστὸν κηρύσσουσιν· The latter do so from love because they know that I am placed here for the defense of the gospel. (τινὲς δὲ καὶ = *but some also*; εὐδοκίαν = *good will*; Χριστὸν = *Christ*)

Matt. 11:10 This is the one about whom it is written: ἰδοὺ ἐγὼ ἀποστέλλω τὸν ἄγγελόν μου πρὸ προσώπου σου, who will prepare your way before you. (ἐγὼ = *I*; μου = *my*; προσώπου σου = *your face*) [see also Mark 2:1; Luke 7:27]

Rom. 10:5 Μωϋσῆς γὰρ γράφει τὴν δικαιοσύνην τὴν ἐκ τοῦ νόμου "The one who does these things will live by them." (Μωϋσῆς = *Moses*; γὰρ = *for*)

Digging Deeper into the New Testament Text

1) Find **Ephesians 1:3-23** in your GNT. You will find this passage to be amazingly rich in prepositions! Scan through these verses (you need not work at reading this whole passage aloud) and do the following:

   a) Find all prepositions. [Ignore for the moment any prepositions prefixed to verbs.]

   b) How many different prepositions did you find? (Which ones were they?)

   c) How many times did each of these different prepositions occur?

   d) Which preposition has been used the most? How does this relate to the frequencies supplied earlier in the first list of prepositions supplied above?

Ephesians 1:3-23? How does this relate to the frequencies supplied earlier in our lesson above?

2) Now open your Greek Interlinear to **Ephesians 1:3-23**. From our discussion above, you know that the Interlinear code for the preposition is the English letter *p* (for *p*reposition). Scan across the parsing line (the third line of the Interlinear) to check the accuracy of your work above. Did you find them all?

3) In the Interlinear, find in **Ephesians 2:5** and the English expression "made us alive with Christ." Just beneath this you will see the Greek verb συνεζωοποίησεν [Do you see that this is a combination of elements you can already recognize συν...ζωο...ποι(έω)?] On the fourth line beneath it you see its wordlist code: 5188. Go back to Appendix B, and note the "dictionary form" there provided. Then look up ***exactly this dictionary form in BDAG*** (noting the missing Greek letter!).

   a) Notice that this verb has a preposition prefixed to it.

   b) In your judgment, what is the effect of the prefixed preposition upon the simple verb meaning, according to the four options presented in our lesson above?

4) Go in Wallace's Intermediate Grammar *The Basics of NT Syntax* to pages 160-173 [*Greek Grammar Beyond the Basics*, pages 355–389]. Simply leaf through these pages for now. There is no need to understand everything you see. If you have a chance at a later point in your academic studies to venture into Advanced Greek, you will be exploring (among other things) the subtle but important insights that come when the Greek preposition is mastered.

   a) On the top of page 167 [372], note the various possible senses Wallace provides for the preposition ἐν.

   b) How would you put into your own words the warning Wallace issues regarding the "Root Fallacy" on page 165 [363]?

5) We would be remiss if we did not examine the BDAG article on the "workhorse" preposition in the GNT: ἐν.

    a) Read carefully the amazing opening paragraph. That says it all! How would you paraphrase this?

    b) Write out the 12 different general categories of sense into which BDAG organizes the usages of ἐν.

    c) Read carefully the (lengthy) category 4. What are some of your reflections on this?

Exercises

I. Short Answer

1) Of what does a <u>prepositional phrase consist</u>?

2) <u>What three classes</u> of prepositional phrases are there?

3) <u>How many</u> different (proper) <u>prepositions</u> are found in the GNT?

4) How does a preposition's "<u>handle</u>" differ from its "<u>meanings</u>?"

5) <u>What cases</u> can follow prepositions?

6) <u>What</u> does a prepositional phrase usually <u>modify</u>? (then, possibly modify?)

7) <u>Why</u> do we call these 17 prepositions "<u>proper</u>" prepositions?

8) <u>In what ways</u> could a <u>prefixed</u> preposition <u>modify</u> the meaning of a simple verb?

9) <u>What</u> is a good <u>first step</u> to take when exegeting a preposition in the GNT?

10) <u>Why</u> must one be careful (when exegeting) <u>not always to press for exact and precise differences</u> between every variation between prepositional phrases?

Solutions to Exercise 1

1) It involves a ***preposition*** and ***a noun or pronoun*** (its object).
2) There are ***temporal*** prepositional phrases. There are ***spatial*** prepositional phrases. There are ***conceptual*** prepositional phrases.
3) Only ***17***.
4) The "handle" is the simple translation value we memorize for pragmatic reasons. The "meanings" are the various possible senses a preposition may have, laid out in detail in BDAG.
5) ***Nine*** (9) prepositions can be followed by only ***one case*** (whether genitive, dative or accusative). ***Six*** (6) prepositions can be followed either by the ***genitive*** or the ***accusative*** cases. ***Two*** (2) prepositions can be followed by any of the three oblique cases (***genitive, dative,*** or ***accusative***).
6) Usually a prepositional phrase modifies a ***verb*** (and will be diagrammed under the verb). Occasionally a prepositional phrase will modify a ***noun*** (and will be diagrammed under that noun).
7) These 17 can be ***prefixed to verbs***. (Prepositions that cannot be prefixed to verbs are "improper.")
8) In direct, obvious ***addition*** of the preposition's meaning to the verb. In ***intensifying*** the meaning of the verb. In shifting the sense of the verb to what is best thought of as a completely ***new, unrelated meaning***. In bringing about ***no discernable change*** at all.
9) Consult ***BDAG*** to find the ***full range of possible senses*** for that preposition.
10) Writers may be employing ***stylistic variation*** when using: a) different prepositions in the same sense; or 2) different cases after the same preposition, but again with no shift in sense.

II. Exercise with Prepositional Phrases

Work through list of phrases below, using a card to conceal the "answer." [Remember, we're working with pragmatic "handles" here.] Work repeatedly through these until you begin to feel comfortable with working with these prepositions and their variations in meaning according to the case that follows.

<u>Prepositions (9) Allowing Only ***One Case*** to Follow:</u>

ἀντὶ τοῦ ὄχλου	instead of the crowd
ἀπὸ τοῦ ὄχλου	away from the crowd
ἐκ τοῦ ὄχλου	out of the crowd
πρὸ τοῦ ὄχλου	before the crowd
ἐν τῷ ὄχλῳ	in the crowd
σὺν τῷ ὄχλῳ	along with the crowd
ἀνὰ τὸν ὄχλον	in the midst of the crowd
εἰς τὸν ὄχλον	into the crowd
πρὸς τὸν ὄχλον	toward the crowd

Prepositions (6) Allowing **Two Cases** to Follow:

διὰ τοῦ ὄχλου	through the crowd
διὰ τὸν ὄχλον	because of the crowd
περὶ τοῦ ὄχλου	concerning the crowd
περὶ τὸν ὄχλον	around the crowd
κατὰ τοῦ ὄχλου	against the crowd
κατὰ τὸν ὄχλον	according to the crowd
ὑπὲρ τοῦ ὄχλου	in behalf of the crowd
ὑπὲρ τὸν ὄχλον	over the crowd
μετὰ τοῦ ὄχλου	with the crowd
μετὰ τὸν ὄχλον	behind the crowd
ὑπὸ τοῦ ὄχλου	by the crowd
ὑπὸ τὸν ὄχλον	underneath the crowd

Prepositions (2) Allowing **Three Cases** to Follow:

ἐπὶ τοῦ ὄχλου	on, near the crowd
ἐπὶ τῷ ὄχλῳ	on, near the crowd
ἐπὶ τὸν ὄχλον	on, near the crowd
παρὰ τοῦ ὄχλου	out from the crowd
παρὰ τῷ ὄχλῳ	beside the crowd
παρὰ τὸν ὄχλον	alongside the crowd

III. Synthetic Sentences (with Prepositional Phrases)

The sentences below gather together most of what we have learned so far, including vocabulary. For each sentence: **1)** parse each verb, including a "basic" translation of it, as if it stood alone without the rest of the sentence; **2)** identify the case, number and gender of every noun; **3)** explain the usage of the case of the noun (e.g. subject, direct object, indirect object, or genitive "of"); **4)** for each adjective, explain how it

agrees with a noun it modifies, and what position it is in; **5)** provide a smooth English translation…in normal English word order; **6)** diagram each sentence (in English, if you wish). **NOTE**: Two articles can occur together: the second article often is to be linked with the noun immediately after it, while the first article often is to be linked with a noun following the whole construction. E.g. τοὺς (τοῦ χρυσοῦ) στεφάνους

1) οἱ μετὰ τὸν ὄχλον τὰς φωνὰς τῶν πρὸ τοῦ ὄχλου οὐκ ἀκούουσι. (See p. 72, Substantive position)

2) τὸ ἅγιον εὐαγγέλιον εἰς τὰς καρδίας τῶν παιδίων ὁ διδάσκαλος σὺν τῷ ἀποστόλῳ λέγει.

3) τὸν ὄχλον ἐκ τῆς οἰκίας πρὸς τὴν ἔρημον ἀποστέλλομεν κατὰ τὸν λόγον τοῦ ἀγγέλου.

4) τὴν ἀλήθειαν τῆς μόνης βασιλείας διὰ τῆς γῆς διὰ τὴν ἀγάπην ἔτι κηρύσσω.

5) κατὰ τῶν φωνῶν τῶν ἀγγέλων τοῦ θανάτου τοῖς τέκνοις τοὺς λόγους τῆς ζωῆς δίδωσι.

6) οἱ παρὰ τῇ οἰκίᾳ τὴν δόξαν τῆς δικαιοσύνης οὐ βλέπουσι περὶ τοῦ ὄχλου τῶν καλῶν.

7) τὴν ἐν ταῖς νεκραῖς καρδίαις ἁμαρτίαν ὁ λόγος τῆς ἐξουσίας οὐκέτι λύει.

8) τοὺς τοῦ χρυσοῦ στεφάνους ἐπὶ τῶν ἁγίων τίθετε ὑπὲρ τῶν ἀποστόλων τῶν πρώτων.

9) τοὺς ὑπὸ τὴν ἐξουσίαν τῆς ἐκκλησίας ἀντὶ τῶν ἐν τῇ βασιλείᾳ τοῦ θανάτου τιμᾶτε.

10) οἱ ἐπὶ τῇ βασιλείᾳ τὰ ἔργα τῆς ζωῆς ποιοῦσι κατὰ τὸ εὐαγγέλιον πάντοτε.

7: **Pronouns**

Easing the Flow between Sentences (or clauses)

By now we've studied *seven* (of the ten) parts of speech: *verbs, nouns, articles, adverbs, interjections, adjectives and prepositions*. Now we add an *eighth*: the *pronoun*. Simply put, pronouns *stand in the place of nouns*. In Mounce's Interlinear code, a *pronoun* is signaled by an "r" (p**r**onoun).

Pronouns as Substitutes for Nouns

Consider the following pairs of sentences:

- *James* bought a *red mustang* yesterday. *James* drove the *red mustang* to church today.
- *Susan* owns *two businesses* in Fresno. The *businesses* have been performing well for *Susan*.
- *James and Susan* often walk beside the *woods*. *James and Susan* love the aroma of the *woods*.

These sentence pairs feel awkward to us because they have failed to use *pronouns* effectively. We have all learned (in our native tongues) to reduce *clutter and repetition* by substituting short, simple expressions (pronouns) the second time we mention a person or thing. Consider how these modifications work:

James bought a red mustang yesterday. James drove the red mustang to church today.   (original)

James bought a red mustang yesterday. *He* drove *it* to church today.   (modified)

Susan owns two businesses in Fresno. The businesses have been performing well for Susan.   (original)

Susan owns two businesses in Fresno. *They* have been performing well for *her*.   (modified)

James and Susan have often walked beside the woods. James and Susan love the aroma of the woods.   (original)

James and Susan have often walked beside the woods. *They* love *its* aroma.   (modified)

The Rules of Substitutes for Nouns

Somehow you and I have already learned (in our native tongues) how to make these substitutions. We know that, in these particular sentences, <u>James</u> becomes **he**, <u>mustang</u> and <u>woods</u> become **it**, <u>Susan</u> becomes **her**, and <u>James and Susan</u> become **they**. We know that **violating the rules** will create wrong and/or nonsensical expressions:

- James bought a red mustang yesterday. **His** drove **they** to church today.

- Susan owns two businesses in Fresno. **Them** have been performing well for **she**.

- James and Susan have often walked beside the woods. **Him** love **them** aroma.

In both English and Greek, certain kinds of **agreement** must hold between the **original noun** (called the **antecedent**) and the **pronoun** that replaces it. It stands to reason, for example, that:

- **James** should be replaced by a pronoun that is **masculine and singular** (he, him, his);

- **Susan** should be replaced by a pronoun that is **feminine and singular** (she, her, hers);

- An **impersonal entity** should (in English) be replaced by a pronoun that is **neuter and singular** (it, its).

But while a pronoun **must agree** with its antecedent in **gender and number**, it does **not need to agree in case**. The reason is apparent: the pronoun must be **free to function** in its own sentence (or clause) according to the grammatical needs of that clause. Notice the variation in case between a pronoun and its antecedent if these sentences were translated into Greek:

James bought a red mustang yesterday.

    [James, as <u>Subject</u>, would be <u>Nominative</u> here.]

He drove it to church today.

    [*He*, as <u>Subject</u>, would be <u>Nominative</u> here too.]

Susan owns two **businesses** in Fresno.

    [Susan, as <u>Subject</u>, would be <u>Nominative</u> here.]

    [Businesses, as <u>Direct Object</u>, would be <u>Accusative</u> here.]

They have been performing well for **her**.

    [But *her*, as <u>Indirect Object</u>, would be <u>Dative</u> here.]*

    [But *they*, as <u>Subject</u>, would be <u>Nominative</u> here.]*

James and Susan have often walked beside the **woods**.

    [Woods, as <u>Object</u> of the preposition, could be <u>Dative</u> here.]

They love *its* Aroma.

    [But *its*, as <u>Possessor</u>, would be <u>Genitive</u> here.]*

The sentences marked with asterisks (*) illustrate our point well: The pronoun will stand in the case required by its **use in its own sentence** (or clause). If a pronoun does agree in case with its antecedent in case (as in the first example), such agreement would be **purely accidental**. To restate the rule: <u>**A pronoun must agree with its antecedent in gender and number**</u> (but not necessarily in case).

An Overview of 7 Types of Greek Pronouns

Now that you understand the basic idea of pronouns, let's get a *high-altitude look* at pronouns in Greek. We will carefully study the first two types, Personal and Demonstrative pronouns, but only familiarize ourselves (for now) with the last five types.

1. Personal Pronouns

This, by far, is the most frequently used type of pronoun in the GNT, appearing over 10,000 times. It expresses all three persons, in both singular and plural. Its job is the "simple replacement" of nouns.

In Greek:	ἐγώ, ἡμεῖς	σύ, ὑμεῖς	αὐτός
In English:	I, me, my; we, us, our	you, your (singular and plural)	he, him, his, she, her, it, its, they, them, their.

English Example: **We** saw **them** at **her** party. **They** were hosting **it** at the home of **her** aunt.

2. Demonstrative Pronouns

Second in frequency in the GNT, demonstratives "point out" by drawing our attention either *towards* (here) or *away from* (there) the speaker. Given these directional options, two distinct demonstratives are needed: the *near* and the *far*.

In Greek:	οὗτος (the near demonstrative)	ἐκεῖνος (the far demonstrative)
In English:	this, these (the near demonstrative);	that, those (the far demonstrative)

English Example: Do you like the brown shoes, or the red ones? **These** are a better deal than **those**.

Only Familiarize For Now

3. Relative Pronouns

These pronouns open a new (dependent) clause linking it back to a noun in the previous clause.

In Greek:	ὅς (and all its forms)
In English:	who, whom, whose, which.

English Example: We saw them at her party, **which** was hosted at her aunt's house. I knew the sailors **who** were lost at sea. The CEO lauded the donor **whom** we met earlier.

4. Interrogative Pronouns

These pronouns allow us to ask questions (whether directly or indirectly).

In Greek:	τίς (and all its forms)
In English:	who? whom? whose? what?

English Example: **Whom** did you see at the party? **Who** was there? (Direct Question)

I was wondering **who** took my glasses from the desk. (Indirect Question)

5. Indefinite Pronouns

These pronouns allow us to speak of persons or things *not yet identified*. Indefinite pronouns share exactly the same forms with Interrogative pronouns, except that Indefinites are *enclitics* (typically lacking accent marks). Note that Interrogatives differ also by asking some kind of question.

In Greek:	τις (and all its forms)
In English:	someone, something, anyone, anything
English Example:	**Someone** was snooping around in the backyard. I don't think he took **anything**.

6. Reflexive Pronouns

These pronouns point the action of the verb *back upon the subject* of the sentence.

In Greek:	ἐμαυτοῦ, σεαυτοῦ, ἑαυτοῦ (and all their forms)
In English:	myself, ourselves, yourself, himself, herself, itself, themselves
English Example:	I really surprised **myself** by losing 10 pounds. Did <u>Jack</u> surprise **himself**?

7. Reciprocal Pronouns

These pronouns suggest a more *complex interaction* than reflexive pronouns. With the *reflexive* plural (We praised ourselves), each person could be praising him or her self *individually*. But with the *reciprocal* pronoun (We praised one another), each praised (and received praise from) *another*.

In Greek:	ἀλλήλων (and all its forms, but always plural by nature)
In English:	one another
English Example:	<u>We</u> ought to care for **one another**, while urging **one another** forward.

Demonstrative Pronouns (near οὗτος and far ἐκεῖνος)

Though Demonstratives are second in frequency, we'll deal with them first because of their simplicity. Observe the forms below, noting that they use the endings of the First and Second Declensions already familiar to you.

The Near Demonstrative

this (one), *these* (ones)		Masculine	Feminine	Neuter
Singular	nominative	οὗτος	αὕτη	τοῦτο
	genitive	τούτου	ταύτης	τούτου
	dative	τούτῳ	ταύτῃ	τούτῳ
	accusative	τοῦτον	ταύτην	τοῦτο
Plural	nominative	οὗτοι	αὗται	ταῦτα
	genitive	τούτων	τούτων	τούτων
	dative	τούτοις	ταύταις	τούτοις
	accusative	τούτους	ταύτας	ταῦτα

1) All 4 nominatives of the masculine and feminine lack the initial tau (τ), and have rough breathings.

2) The neuter nominative and accusative ending (το) follows the likeness of the article, rather than 2nd Declension nouns.

3) Every form with an ending containing alpha (α) or eta (η) will have an initial diphthong of αυ.

The Far Demonstrative

that (one), *those* (ones)		Masculine	Feminine	Neuter
Singular	nominative	ἐκεῖνος	ἐκείνη	ἐκεῖνο
	genitive	ἐκείνου	ἐκείνης	ἐκείνου
	dative	ἐκείνῳ	ἐκείνη	ἐκείνῳ
	accusative	ἐκεῖνον	ἐκείνην	ἐκεῖνο
Plural	nominative	ἐκεῖνοι	ἐκεῖναι	ἐκεῖνα
	genitive	ἐκείνων	ἐκείνων	ἐκείνων
	dative	ἐκείνοις	ἐκείναις	ἐκείνοις
	accusative	ἐκείνους	ἐκείνας	ἐκεῖνα

Uses of Demonstratives

1) As Stand-Alone Pronouns ("Substantivally", like a noun)

The near and far demonstratives can be translated rather **simply**. As we translate, we need to incorporate the various pieces of information involved: the **direction** (near or far), the **gender** (masculine, feminine, neuter), the **number** (singular or plural), and **case** (signaling the grammatical function of the pronoun in its own clause). Putting these together will come rather quickly.

οὗτος βλέπει ἐκείνην	This (man) is seeing that (woman).
αὗται βλέπουσιν ἐκείνους	These (women) are seeing those (men).
αὕτη λύει ἐκεῖνα	This (woman) is destroying those (things).
ταῦτα λύουσιν ἐκεῖνο	These (things) are destroying that (thing).

2) As Adjectives

Just as in English, the Greek demonstratives can also **modify nouns**. When they do, they will not only agree with that noun in gender, number, and case, but will always stand **in Predicate Position** with the modified noun. [Remember that the Predicate Position will be either pronoun-**article-noun** or **article-noun**-pronoun]:

οὗτος ὁ ἀπόστολος βλέπει ἐκείνην	This apostle is seeing that (woman).
αὗται βλέπουσι τοὺς ἀποστόλους ἐκείνους	These (women) are seeing those apostles.
αὕτη λύει ἐκεῖνα τὰ ἔργα	This (woman) is destroying those works.
τὰ τέκνα ταῦτα λύουσι τὸ ἔργον ἐκεῖνο	These children are destroying that work.

Personal Pronouns (1st ἐγώ, 2nd σύ, and 3rd αὐτός)

The Personal Pronouns are displayed below in all their forms (all persons, cases, numbers, and genders). The translations are stylized to represent common uses of the various cases.

		The 1st Person		The 2nd Person	
Singular	nominative	ἐγώ	(I)	σύ	(you)
	genitive	(ἐ)μοῦ	(of me, my)	σοῦ	(of you, your)
	dative	(ἐ)μοί	(to me)	σοί	(to you)
	accusative	(ἐ)μέ	(me)	σέ	(you)
Plural	nominative	ἡμεῖς	(we)	ὑμεῖς	(you)
	genitive	ἡμῶν	(of us, our)	ὑμῶν	(of you, your)
	dative	ἡμῖν	(to us)	ὑμῖν	(to you)
	accusative	ἡμᾶς	(us)	ὑμᾶς	(you)

		The 3rd Person					
		Masculine		Feminine		Neuter	
Singular	N	αὐτός	he	αὐτή	she	αὐτό	it
	G	αὐτοῦ	of him, his	αὐτῆς	of her, her	αὐτοῦ	of it, its
	D	αὐτῷ	to him	αὐτῇ	to her	αὐτῷ	to it
	A	αὐτόν	him	αὐτήν	her	αὐτό	it
Plural	N	αὐτοί	they	αὐταί	they	αὐτά	they
	G	αὐτῶν	of them, their	αὐτῶν	of them, their	αὐτῶν	of them, their
	D	αὐτοῖς	to them	αὐταῖς	to them	αὐτοῖς	to them
	A	αὐτούς	them	αὐτάς	them	αὐτά	them

1) In the 1st Person, forms with prefixed epsilon (ἐ) are **emphatic**. The unemphatic forms are enclitic (losing their accent).

2) In the 2nd Person, σοῦ, σοί, σέ are normally enclitic (losing their accent), unless they are **emphatic** (i.e., with an accent).

3) The form αὐτή should not be confused with the Demonstrative form αὕτη.

4) In the 3rd person, Masculine and Feminine pronouns can stand for any masculine or feminine noun. In that circumstance, they would not be translated as "him" (etc.) or "her" (etc.) but as "it."

The Uses of (forms of) the Personal Pronoun

1) Simple Replacement

Just as in English, the personal pronouns (I, we, you, he, she, they) can stand as **shorthand for proper names** (Bob, Ted, Jane, Billie; or Peter, James, Jesus, Thomas). This usage should be easily understood by speakers of any language.

Πέτρος τὸ εὐαγγέλιον κηρύσσει.   τὰ τέκνα τὸ εὐαγγέλιον ἀκούουσι δι᾽ <u>αὐτοῦ</u>

Peter is preaching the gospel.   The children are hearing the gospel through <u>him</u>.

Just as in English, the personal pronouns (it, they) can stand as **shorthand for nouns** that do not refer to persons (peace, house, gospel, word). This usage should be easily understood by speakers of any language.

Πέτρος <u>τὴν ἀλήθειαν</u> κηρύσσει.   τὰ τέκνα <u>αὐτὴν</u> ἀκούουσι δι᾽ αὐτοῦ

Peter is preaching the <u>truth</u>.   The children are hearing <u>it</u> through him.

In each situation above, we see that the pronoun must agree in **gender** and **number** with its antecedent (though not necessarily in case). We also see that English does not usually allow grammatical gender to be attached to nouns. Therefore all pronouns referring to **impersonal** nouns will be translated **impersonally** (it, its, they), no matter what gender they possess in Greek.

2) Emphatic

Upon reflection you will realize that there is no need for a nominative personal pronoun in a typical sentence. The nominative pronouns (I, you, he, she, it, they) are already expressed by the endings of the verb. If a **nominative personal pronoun** matching the person of the verb is used by a writer, the **unnecessary overlap** signals an **emphasis**, usually through contrast.

τὸ εὐαγγέλιον κηρύσσεις.

You are preaching the gospel. (unemphatic)

τὴν ἀλήθειαν λύει, ἀλλὰ σὺ τὸ εὐαγγέλιον κηρύσσεις.

He is destroying the truth, but **_you_** are preaching the gospel! (**emphatic**!)

(The nominative σὺ unnecessarily overlaps the 2nd person singular subject already implied by the verb form itself.)

3) Identical

When the third personal pronoun (αὐτός) stands in **Attributive Position** with any noun, the so-called **Identical** use emerges. It will be translated with the English word "**same**." The pronoun will agree with the noun in **gender**, **number** and **case**.

ὁ αὐτὸς Πέτρος	τὸ αὐτὸ εὐαγγέλιον	κηρύσσει	τοῖς αὐτοῖς τέκνοις	ἐν	τῇ οἰκίᾳ τῇ αὐτῇ
art pro noun	art pro noun		art pro noun		art noun art pro
(attributive position)	(attributive position)		(attributive position)		(attributive position)

The same Peter is preaching the same gospel to the same children in the same house.

4) **Intensive**

When the third personal pronoun (αὐτός) stands in **Predicate Position** with any noun or pronoun, the so-called **Intensive** use emerges. It will be translated by adding a form of "**-self**" to the matching (English) personal pronoun. The pronoun will agree with the noun in **gender**, **number**, and **case**. Various **nuances** of meaning can be implied by the intensive usage. "Peter himself" (see below) might mean such things as: "Peter personally and directly, not one of his aides," or "even Peter (surprise!), the very one who had earlier denied Jesus," or "Peter personally present, and not by a letter," or "Peter, the very one I just spoke of a little earlier," or "Peter, yes the famous apostle you have heard about." (BDAG supplies these and other interpretations of the intensive use of αὐτός.)

ὁ Πέτρος αὐτὸς	τὸ εὐαγγέλιον αὐτὸ	κηρύσσει	τοῖς τέκνοις αὐτοῖς	ἐν	τῇ οἰκίᾳ αὐτῇ
art noun pro	art noun pro		art noun pro		art noun pro
(predicate position)	(predicate position)		(predicate position)		(predicate position)

Peter himself is preaching the gospel itself to the children themselves in the house itself.

New Testament Exploration

John 5:43	I have come in my Father's name, καὶ οὐ λαμβάνετέ με· If someone else comes in his own name, you will receive him. (οὐ = *not*)
Luke 24:48–49	You are witnesses of these things. καὶ ἰδοὺ ἐγὼ ἀποστέλλω τὴν ἐπαγγελίαν τοῦ πατρός μου ἐφ᾽ ὑμᾶς· Now stay in the city until you have been clothed with power from on high. (ἐπαγγελίαν = *promise*; πατρός = *father*)
1 John 2:1	Τεκνία μου, ταῦτα γράφω ὑμῖν so that you might not sin. And if someone should sin, we have an advocate with the Father, Jesus Christ the righteous One.

Digging Deeper into the New Testament Text

1) Find **I John 3:3** in your GNT. See if you can spot four different types of pronouns in this one verse (Write them out and identify them.) Then scan through **I John 3:11-18**. You should be able to spot these types of pronouns: <u>demonstratives</u> (both near and far); <u>personal</u> (both emphatic and unemphatic); <u>relative</u>; <u>interrogative</u> (introducing an indirect question); and <u>reciprocal</u>.

2) Now open your Greek <u>Interlinear</u> to **I John 3:3** and **3:11-18**. You already know that the Interlinear code for pronouns is the English letter **r** (for p*r*onoun). Scan across the parsing line (the third line of the Interlinear) to <u>check the accuracy</u> of your work above. Did you find them all? You will realize that Mounce identifies all pronouns, but **not the types** of pronouns involved.

3) In the Interlinear at **I John 3:3** you see the "far" demonstrative ἐκεῖνος. On the fourth line beneath it you see its wordlist code: 1697. Go back to Appendix B, and note the "dictionary form" there provided. Then look up ***exactly this dictionary form in BDAG***. There you will see that BDAG has listed I John 3:3 under a-γ. What does this suggest for how we might understand "that one" in I John 3:3?

4) In the Interlinear find **I Thessalonians 4:13-18**. Scan though these lines. Do you recognize some vocabulary? Some propositional phrases? Some pronouns in their particular uses or positions? Do you see a particular use of the 3rd personal pronoun opening 4:16? According to our study so far, what nuance might this pronoun signify?

5) Go in Wallace's Intermediate Grammar *The Basics of NT Syntax* to pages 140-159 [*Greek Grammar Beyond the Basics*, pages 315–354]. <u>Simply leaf through these pages for now</u>. There is no need to understand everything you see. If you have a chance at a later point in your academic studies to venture into Advanced Greek, you will be exploring (among other things) the subtle but important insights that come when the Greek pronoun is mastered.

- Look at the chart on p. 142 [320] showing the statistical distribution of pronouns in the GNT. Notice the significance (for learning NT Greek) of focusing on the personal and demonstrative pronouns.

Chapter Seven Vocabulary

More Masculine Nouns of the Second Declension

This list contains more of the **22** such nouns used 100x or more in the GNT. The comments offer translation suggestions or nuances in meaning we would find listed in BDAG.

θεός	*God*	Occurring with an article which is usually **not** translated into English (ὁ θεός = "God").
κύριος	*Lord*	Often referring to God the Father or to Jesus, but occasionally simply meaning "sir."
ἄνθρωπος	*man*	Referring to male human beings, to humanity in general, or to persons of either gender.
υἱός	*son*	When coupled with ἄνθρωπος, translated "the Son of Man" (with disputed meaning).
ἀδελφός	*brother*	Referring to male siblings, or (generically) to anyone in close association.
νόμος	*law*	When with the article, often referring to the Mosaic law.
ἄρτος	*bread*	Can also refer to food in general, or to individual pieces of bread (loaf, loaves).
οὗτος	*this*	See "The Near Demonstrative" on page 86
ἐκεῖνος	*that*	See "The Far Demonstrative" on page 87

More Verbs

[It is important to memorize the roots provided in the brackets. Realize that beneath each of these present tense forms lies a deeper, more basic "root" up from which arise the various parts of a verb.]

Review of Verbs We **Already Know** (16)

λύω	[λυ]	*I destroy*
βλέπω	[βλεπ]	*I see*
τιμῶ	[τιμα]	*I honor*
κηρύσσω	[κηρυγ]	*I preach, proclaim*
ποιῶ	[ποιε]	*I make, do*
λέγω	[λεγ]	*I say*
δηλῶ	[δηλο]	*I show, explain*
ἀποστέλλω	[--στελ]	*I send (out, away)*
δίδωμι	[δο]	*I give*
λαμβάνω	[λαβ]	*I take, or receive*
τίθημι	[θε]	*I put, place, lay*
γινώσκω	[γνω]	*I know*
ἵστημι	[στα]	*I set, place, stand*
ἀκούω	[ἀκου]	*I hear, obey*
δείκνυμι	[δεικ]	*I show, explain*
γράφω	[γραφ]	*I write*

New Verbs We Are **Now Adding** (8)

βάλλω	[βαλ]	*I throw*
πίπτω	[πτ]	*I fall*
ἐγείρω	[εγερ]	*I rise*
ἀποθνῄσκω	[--θαν]	*I kill, die*
ἐσθίω	[εδ]	*I eat*
διδάσκω	[δακ]	*I teach, instruct*
πιστεύω	[πιστευ]	*I believe*
εὑρίσκω	[ευρ]	*I find, discover*

Notes about πιστεύω

This theologically important GNT verb can express a wide **variety of senses**: I believe (something to be true); I believe (someone to be reliable); I entrust (myself to something); I entrust (myself to someone); I entrust (something to someone).

Along with this variety of senses you will find a **variety of grammatical constructions** expressing these senses. You may find the various objects of faith (or entrusting) expressed by: the simple accusative, the simple dative, or by various prepositional phrases [ἐν with the dative, εἰς with the accusative, ἐπί with the dative or accusative]. Again we remind ourselves to take a deeper look at the possibilities of a Biblical passage by starting with a closer look at all the options and nuances offered by BDAG

Exercises

I. Short Answer

1) In general, <u>what do pronouns do</u>?

2) What do we call the <u>noun that is replaced</u> by a pronoun?

3) <u>How</u> must a pronoun <u>agree</u> with the noun it has replaced?

4) <u>Why</u> does a pronoun <u>not need to agree</u> with its antecedent in <u>case</u>?

5) <u>What kind</u> of pronoun opens up a <u>new subordinate clause</u>? (e.g. I know the man <u>whom</u> you saw yesterday.)

6) <u>What kind</u> of pronoun allows us to <u>ask a question</u>? (e.g. <u>Who</u> has taken his body from the tomb?)

7) <u>What kind</u> of pronoun allows us to refer to <u>what is not yet known</u>? (e.g. <u>Someone</u> must have taken him away.)

8) <u>What kind</u> of pronoun <u>refers back to the subject</u>? (e.g. He loved <u>himself</u> above all else.)

9) <u>What kind</u> of pronoun depicts <u>complex interaction</u>? (e.g. They were praising <u>one another</u> on a job well done.)

10) <u>In what position</u> are <u>demonstratives</u> found then they <u>modify nouns</u>?

11) <u>Why</u> are <u>personal</u> pronouns <u>emphatic</u> when found in the <u>nominative case</u>?

12) 12. <u>In what position</u> are <u>3rd personal</u> pronouns when they bear the <u>Identical</u> sense? (i.e. "same")

13) 13. <u>In what position</u> are <u>3rd personal</u> pronouns when they bear the <u>Intensive</u> sense? (i.e. "--self")

Solutions to Exercise I

1) They **replace nouns** to ease and simplify the flow from one sentence (or clause) to the next.
2) Replaced nouns are called **antecedents**.
3) A pronoun must agree with the noun it replaces in **gender and number** (not necessarily in case).
4) The case of the pronoun must reflect its own **usage in its own clause**, not the case (or usage) of its antecedent.
5) A **relative** pronoun.
6) An **interrogative** pronoun.
7) An **indefinite** pronoun.
8) A **reflexive** pronoun.
9) A **reciprocal** pronoun.
10) **Predicate** position. E.g. τοὺς ἀποστόλους ἐκείνους (article—noun—pronoun)
11) They **redundantly overlap** the pronoun subject already expressed by the verb ending.
12) **Attributive** position. E.g. τοῖς αὐτοῖς τέκνοις (the same children)
13) **Predicate** position. E.g. τοῖς τέκνοις αὐτοῖς (the children themselves)

II. Exercises with Pronouns

<u>Part 1: Near and Far Demonstratives:</u>

1) ἐν τῇ δόξᾳ ταύτῃ

2) κατὰ τῆς εἰρήνης ταύτης

3) δι᾽ ἐκεῖνον τὸν νόμον

4) ἐπὶ τῇ βασιλείᾳ ἐκείνῃ

5) ἐκ τοῦ εὐαγγελίου τούτου

6) παρὰ ταύτῃ τῇ οἰκίᾳ

7) σὺν τοῖς υἱοῖς ἐκείνοις

8) ὑπ᾽ ἐκείνων τῶν υἱῶν

9) ὑπὸ ταύτας τὰς ἁμαρτίας

10) ὑπὲρ τῶν ὄχλων τούτων

11) δι᾽ ἐκείνων τῶν ἐκκλησίων

12) μετὰ τοὺς ἄρτους ἐκείνους

1) ἐν τῇ δόξᾳ ταύτῃ — in this glory
2) κατὰ τῆς εἰρήνης ταύτης — against this peace
3) δι᾽ ἐκεῖνον τὸν νόμον — on account of that law
4) ἐπὶ τῇ βασιλείᾳ ἐκείνῃ — near that kingdom
5) ἐκ τοῦ εὐαγγελίου τούτου — out of this gospel
6) παρὰ ταύτῃ τῇ οἰκίᾳ — beside this house
7) σὺν τοῖς υἱοῖς ἐκείνοις — with those sons
8) ὑπ᾽ ἐκείνων τῶν υἱῶν — by those sons
9) ὑπὸ ταύτας τὰς ἁμαρτίας — under these sins
10) ὑπὲρ τῶν ὄχλων τούτων — in behalf of these crowds
11) δι᾽ ἐκείνων τῶν ἐκκλησίων — through those churches
12) μετὰ τοὺς ἄρτους ἐκείνους — behind those loaves

Part 2: Intensive and Identical Uses of αὐτός:

1) ἐν αὐτῇ τῇ δόξᾳ

2) κατὰ τῆς αὐτῆς εἰρήνης

3) διὰ τὸν αὐτὸν νόμον

4) ἐπὶ αὐτῇ τῇ βασιλείᾳ

5) ἐκ τοῦ εὐαγγελίου αὐτοῦ

6) παρὰ τῇ αὐτῇ οἰκίᾳ

7) σὺν αὐτοῖς τοῖς υἱοῖς

8) ὑπὸ τῶν υἱῶν αὐτῶν

9) ὑπὸ τὰς αὐτὰς ἁμαρτίας

10) ὑπὲρ τῶν αὐτῶν ὄχλων

11) διὰ τῶν ἐκκλησίων αὐτῶν

12) μετὰ αὐτοὺς τοὺς ἄρτους

1) ἐν αὐτῇ τῇ δόξᾳ — in the glory itself
2) κατὰ τῆς αὐτῆς εἰρήνης — against the same peace
3) διὰ τὸν αὐτὸν νόμον — on account of the same law
4) ἐπὶ αὐτῇ τῇ βασιλείᾳ — near the kingdom itself
5) ἐκ τοῦ εὐαγγελίου αὐτοῦ — out of gospel itself
6) παρὰ τῇ αὐτῇ οἰκίᾳ — beside the same house
7) σὺν αὐτοῖς τοῖς υἱοῖς — with sons themselves
8) ὑπὸ τῶν υἱῶν αὐτῶν — by the sons themselves
9) ὑπὸ τὰς αὐτὰς ἁμαρτίας — under the same sins
10) ὑπὲρ τῶν αὐτῶν ὄχλων — in behalf of the same crowds
11) διὰ τῶν ἐκκλησίων αὐτῶν — through the churches themselves
12) μετὰ αὐτοὺς τοὺς ἄρτους — behind the loaves themselves

III: Emphatics and Intensives in the Nominative

Work on recognizing the differences between the simple replacement, identical, emphatic, and intensive constructions. Remember, when the person of the pronoun **matches** the person of the verb, it is **emphatic (!)**. When the **3rd person pronoun** (αὐτός) is used in the nominative, we have the **intensive** ("-self").

1) βάλλω

2) ἀποθνήσκομεν

3) ἐγὼ βάλλω

4) ἡμεῖς ἀποθνήσκομεν

5) αὐτὸς βάλλω

6) αὐτοὶ ἀποθνήσκομεν

7) ἐγείρεις

8) διδάσκετε

9) σὺ ἐγείρεις

10) ὑμεῖς διδάσκετε

11) αὐτὸς ἐγείρεις

12) αὐτοὶ διδάσκετε

13) ἐσθίει

14) εὑρίσκουσι

15) αὐτὸς ἐσθίει

16) αὐτοὶ εὑρίσκουσι

17) αὐτὴ ἐσθίει

18) αὐταὶ εὑρίσκουσι

19) αὐτὸ ἐσθίει

20) αὐτὰ εὑρίσκουσι

Solutions to Exercise III

1) βάλλω — I am throwing
2) ἀποθνήσκομεν — we are killing
3) ἐγὼ βάλλω — *I* (emphatic) am throwing
4) ἡμεῖς ἀποθνήσκομεν — *we* (emphatic) are killing
5) αὐτὸς βάλλω — I myself am throwing
6) αὐτοὶ ἀποθνήσκομεν — we ourselves are killing
7) ἐγείρεις — you are rising
8) διδάσκετε — y'all are teaching
9) σὺ ἐγείρεις — *you* (emphatic) are rising
10) ὑμεῖς διδάσκετε — *y'all* (emphatic) are teaching
11) αὐτὸς ἐγείρεις — you yourself are rising
12) αὐτοὶ διδάσκετε — y'all yourselves are teaching
13) ἐσθίει — he/she/it is eating
14) εὑρίσκουσι — they (m, f, or n) are finding
15) αὐτὸς ἐσθίει — *he* (emphatic) is… or… he himself is eating
16) αὐτοὶ εὑρίσκουσι — *they* (emphatic) are…or…they themselves are finding
17) αὐτὴ ἐσθίει — *she* (emphatic) is… or … she herself eating
18) αὐταὶ εὑρίσκουσι — *they* (f) (emphatic) are… or…they (f) themselves are finding
19) αὐτὸ ἐσθίει — *it* (emphatic) is… or… it itself is eating
20) αὐτὰ εὑρίσκουσι — *they* (n) (emphatic) are… or…they (n) themselves are finding

IV. Synthetic Sentences (with Prepositional Phrases)

The sentences below gather together most of what we have learned so far, including vocabulary. As usual, **1)** parse verbs; **2)** identify the cases and their uses; **3)** note the position of adjectives; **4)** identify and explain pronouns; **5)** provide a smooth English translation; **6)** diagram each sentence (in English, if you wish); **7)** write out in Greek at least two sentences.

1) οἱ ἄγγελοι οὗτοι τοὺς διδασκάλους τῆς ἁμαρτίας βάλλουσιν εἰς τὴν ἔρημον ἐκείνην.

2) ἐκ τῆς γῆς αὐτῆς ὁ υἱὸς τοῦ ἀνθρώπου ἐγείρει διὰ τῆς ἐξουσίας τοῦ θεοῦ.

3) ἐκεῖνοι τὸν ἄρτον αὐτῆς τῆς ζωῆς ἐσθίουσι, καὶ ἡμεῖς τὴν δόξαν αὐτῆς βλέπομεν.

4) οἱ ἀδελφοὶ αὐτῆς ἐν τῷ αὐτῷ κυρίῳ πιστεύουσι, καὶ τὴν ἐξουσίαν αὐτοῦ καλῶς δηλοῦσι.

5) σὺν ἡμῖν τὴν βασιλείαν τοῦ θεοῦ εὑρίσκεις, ἀλλὰ ὁ ὄχλος εἰς τὰς ἁμαρτίας τῆς ἡμέρας ταύτης ἔτι πίπτει.

6) κατὰ τοῦ εὐαγγελίου τῆς ἀγάπης αὐτῆς ὑμεῖς πάλιν διδάσκετε, ἀλλὰ ἡμεῖς τοὺς λόγους ὑμῶν οὐ λαμβάνομεν.

7) 7) οἱ υἱοὶ τῆς δικαιοσύνης τοὺς υἱοὺς τῆς ἁμαρτίας οὐκ ἀποθνήσκουσιν ἐκεῖ διὰ τὸ εὐαγγέλιον τοῦτο.

8) 8) τὰ τέκνα ὑμῶν τὰς ἀγαθὰς βίβλους ταύτας ποιοῦσι, καὶ ἀποστέλλουσι νῦν αὐτὰς ὑμῖν ὑπὲρ τῶν ἀποστόλων ἐκείνων.

9) 9) αὐτοὶ τιμῶμεν τὰς ψυχὰς αὐτῶν, ἀλλὰ αὐτοὶ ὑμῖν κατὰ τῆς ἁγίας ἐκκλησίας ἡμῶν πάντοτε λέγουσι.

10) 10) αὐτοὶ τὰ ἔργα τοῦ νόμου ἐκείνου λύετε, καὶ τὴν φωνὴν τοῦ μόνου υἱοῦ ἀκούετε.

8: Conjunctions

By now we've studied *eight* (of the ten) parts of speech: *verbs, nouns, articles, adverbs, interjections, adjectives, prepositions and pronouns*. Now we add a *ninth*: the *conjunction*. Simply put, conjunctions *join things together*. In Mounce's Interlinear code, a *conjunction* is signaled by "**cj**" (**c**onjunction). [At the close of this chapter we'll round out the 10 parts of speech by dealing with *particles*, a relatively minor category.]

Co-Ordinate Conjunction (the joining of like-element together)

If we wish to join independent sentences together (and maintain the *grammatically independent* status of each clause), we must use a *Co-ordinate* conjunction. Co-ordinate conjunctions preserve the *equal power* of each clause, rather than subordinating one sentence to the other. The resulting sentence is called a *Compound Sentence*. Notice *some* of the different kinds of *logical relationships* possible between these independent clauses as illustrated by how these two clauses (below) are joined together:

Jerry will drive the squad car. Tina will drive the ambulance.	[No connection expressed = Asyndeton.]
Jerry will drive the squad car, *and* Tina will drive the ambulance.	[*and* is a Co-ordinate *additive* Conjunction]
Jerry will drive the squad car, *or* Tina will drive the ambulance.	[*or* is a Co-ordinate *alternative* Conjunction]
Jerry will drive the squad car, *but* Tina will drive the ambulance.	[*but* is a Co-ordinate *contrastive* Conjunction]

Sub-Ordinate Conjunctions (joining dependent clauses to main clauses)

While a main clause makes sense by itself without needing additional support, a *dependent clause* cannot stand alone, and must "latch onto" a main clause to survive. A dependent clause is joined to a main clause by a *Sub-ordinate* conjunction, forming a *Complex Sentence*. In the examples below, note how the dependent clause is joined via the *conjunction* to the main clause.

Jerry will drive the squad car, *if* Tom will man the radio.	[*if* is a Sub-ord. Conj. of *condition*]
Jerry will drive the squad car *though* Wilson has begged him not to.	[*though* is a Sub-ord. Conj. of *concession*]
Jerry will drive the squad car *while* Thelma is on vacation.	[*while* is a Sub-ord. Conj. of *time*]
Jerry will drive the squad car *where* John had marked the map.	[*where* is a Sub-ord. Conj. of *place*]
Jerry will drive the squad car *because* the Chief ordered him to do so.	[*because* is a Sub-ord. Conj. of *cause*]
Jerry drove the squad car *with the result that* everyone hated him.	[*with the result that* is a Sub-ord. Conj. of *result*]
Jerry will drive the squad car *in order that* Jack can drive the pumper.	[*in order that* is a Sub-ord. Conj. of *purpose*]
Jerry drove the squad car *by* holding the ignition wires together.	[*by* is a Sub-ord. Conj. of *means*]
Jerry will drive the squad car *just as* he has always driven it.	[*just as* is a Sub-ord. Conj. of *comparison*]

Diagramming Co-Ordinate and Sub-Ordinate Clauses

In the diagram below, you will notice that the co-ordinate conjunction (**but**) simply adds one main clause to the next. The second clause is not indented, or set beneath any particular part of the first sentence. Instead, the two main clauses maintain **equal status** in moving down the page from one independent clause to the next. Conversely, the two subordinate clauses (**in order that**...; **because**...) have been placed in **subservient position** up under a particular element in the main clause

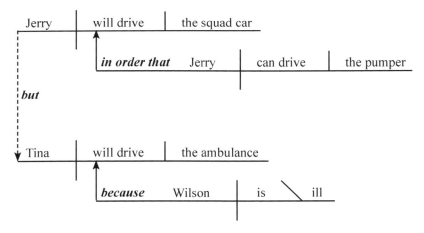

Three Types of Subordinate Clauses (Adverbial, Adjectival, Noun)

It will prove helpful to identify **three different kinds** of subordinate clauses based on which element of the main clause they specifically modify. Consider the following complex sentence:

> After they returned to Galilee, the disciples who had seen the risen Lord knew that the Gospel was true.

1) This sentence is built around **the essential kernel** of the main verb and its subject:

the disciples	knew
Subject	Verb

2) Three **subordinate clauses** have been attached to this kernel:

- An **Adverbial** Dependent Clause [After they returned from Galilee...]
- An **Adjectival** Clause [...who had seen the risen Lord...]
- A **Noun** Clause [...that the Gospel was true...]

> *After they returned to Galilee,* **the disciples** *who had seen the risen Lord* **knew** *that the Gospel was true.*

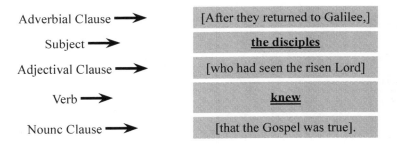

Adverbial Clause ➝	[After they returned to Galilee,]
Subject ➝	the disciples
Adjectival Clause ➝	[who had seen the risen Lord]
Verb ➝	knew
Nounc Clause ➝	[that the Gospel was true].

3) Each type of sub-ordinate clause **modifies** a **different element** in the main clause:

- **adverbial** clauses, by definition, always **modify the verb**

All of the clauses used in our illustration above [condition, concession, time, place, cause, result, purpose, means, comparison] are **adverbial**. They describe "when, where, why, or how" the action of the main verb is being accomplished.

> "After they returned to Galilee, the disciples...knew..."

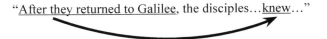

- *Adjectival* clauses, by definition, ***modify nouns or pronouns***

Clauses used to describe or identify a noun or pronoun are ***adjectival***. The most common kind of adjectival clause is introduced by a relative pronoun (not a conjunction). English relative pronouns include: <u>who</u>, <u>whose</u>, <u>whom</u>, <u>what</u>, <u>which</u>, and <u>that</u>.

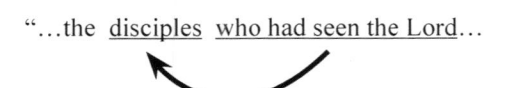

"…the <u>disciples</u> <u>who had seen the Lord</u>…

- *Noun* clauses, by definition, function as if they were ***nouns***. Such clauses, therefore, can serve as the subjects or objects of a verb.

the disciples .... knew .... <u>the Lord</u>

[Direct Object: simple noun]

[Direct Object: noun clause]

the disciples .... knew .... ***that*** <u>the Gospel was true</u>

4) When set into a diagram, each type of clause is positioned to show **which element it modifies** in the main clause:

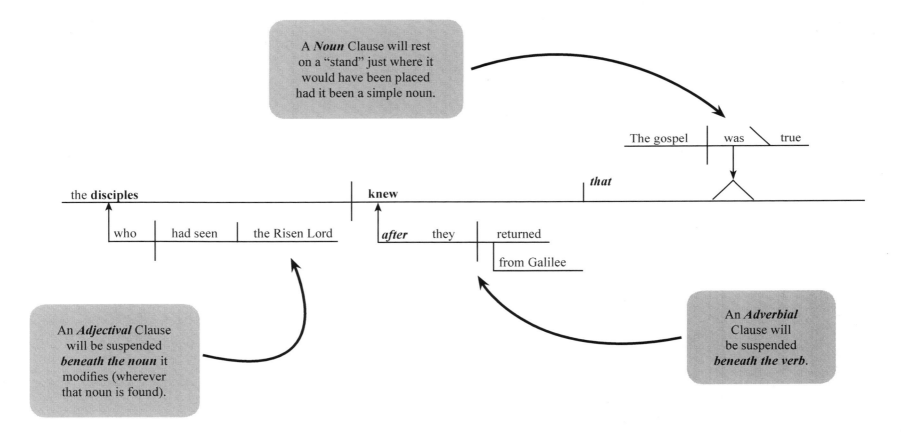

Internal Compounds

We have already described how two (or more) main clauses can be joined together by co-ordinate conjunctions to create a Compound Sentence. But the ***internal parts*** of a sentence (e.g. the subject, the verb, the object, the indirect object) can be ***compounded*** through ***co-ordinate conjunctions***. Consider the following example:

Tom ***and*** Jan   will   give ***or*** sell   their   bicycle   to   Bob, Nadine, ***and*** Willie.

    Subjects   Verbs   D. Obj.   Indirect Objects

     (2)   (s)   (1)   (3)

Notice that we have a ***compound subject*** (additive), a ***compound verb*** (alternative), and a ***compound indirect object*** (additive) created by coordinate conjunctions. As you can imagine, the possibilities are endless! We will use a diagramming strategy that creates "rocket" shapes to accommodate the expansion of parallel (co-ordinate) elements in a sentence. [There are no precise rules for how to do this. Though the basic idea is clear, many variations in diagramming such matters are possible.]

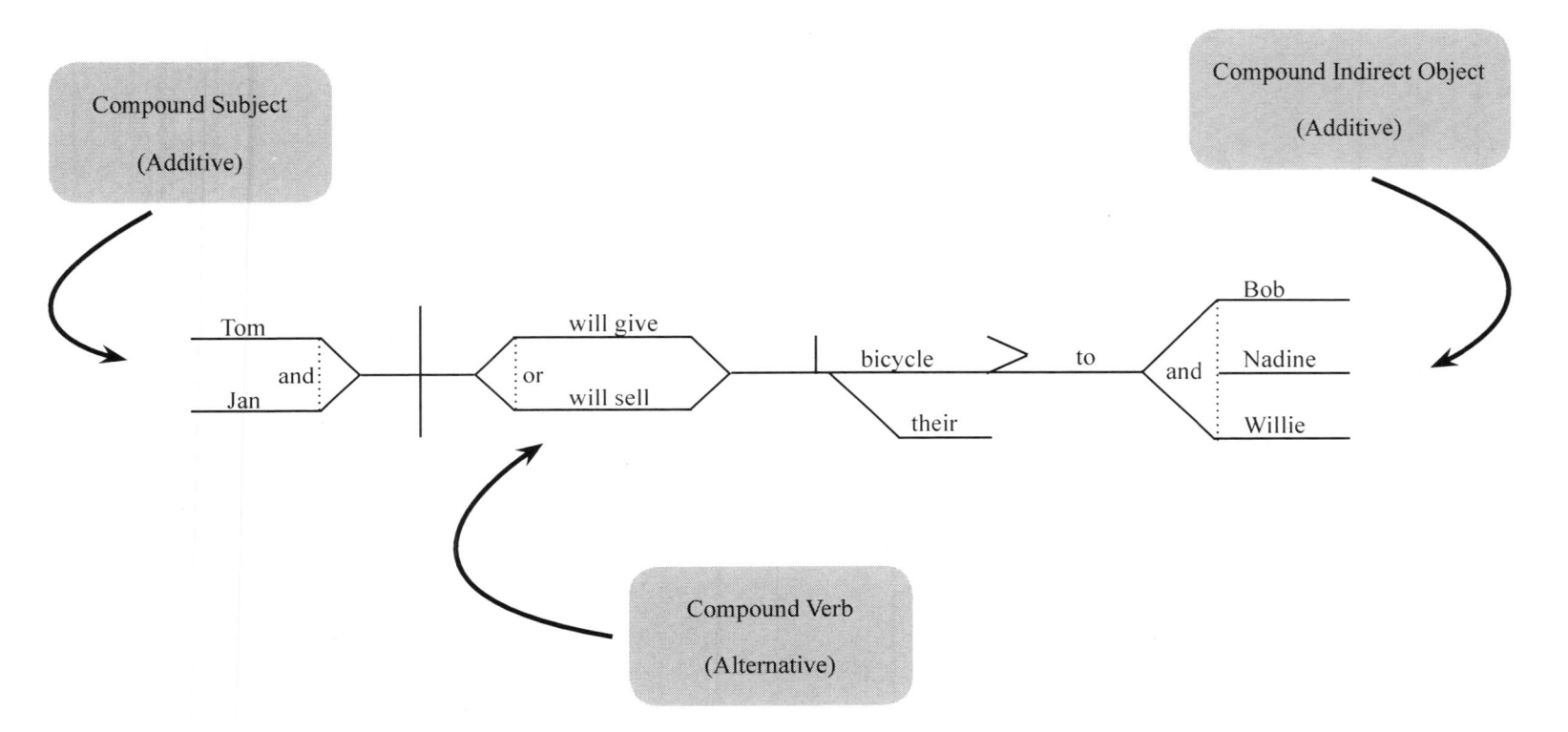

Greek Particles

One of the most interesting (and overlooked) parts of speech is the **Particle**. The name itself seems appropriate, especially if we think of those mysterious, subatomic bits of matter that can scarcely be seen or measured. Classical Greek (i.e. the version of Greek spoken in the centuries **before** Alexander the Great's conquests around 330 BC) was so rich in particles that J. D. Denniston could devote a 600-page volume to unpacking their mysteries. [J. D. Denniston. The Greek Particles. 2nd Ed. Oxford University Press, 1934.]

To illustrate that fascinating world of particles, consider how we English speakers might use the particle "***umm***" to convey a wide variety of subtle ***logical and emotional clues*** in our casual conversation:

Wow! I really like that...***umm***....green scarf you are wearing.

[Translation: Yuk! What kind of green is that? I'm trying to conceal how disgusted I am!]

So you're just going to take your summer-job income and...***umm***...buy this car?

[Translation: I'm shocked at how naïve you are. I'm trying to shame you into reality.]

Well, I want to ask you if you would...***umm***...marry me!

[Translation: I am hesitant and uncertain, but hopeful. I'm trying to avoid being too pushy.]

But by the time the NT was written, a number of the finer features of Classical Greek had almost completely eroded away. Few particles remain for us to encounter as we read the GNT. Furthermore, there isn't agreement among grammarians about just which words should be classified as particles. For some, any word that isn't neatly identifiable as one of the other nine parts of speech should be classified as a particle. According to that view, we could almost re-name particles as ***Miscellaneous***, or as the ***Trash Bin Words*** without homes elsewhere. In Mounce's Interlinear, the ***particle*** is signaled by "**pl**" (***p**article*).

New Testament Exploration

John 10:13–16

Because he is a hired hand and is not concerned about the sheep. Ἐγώ εἰμι ὁ ποιμὴν ὁ καλὸς καὶ γινώσκω τὰ ἐμὰ καὶ γινώσκουσί με τὰ ἐμά, καθὼς γινώσκει με ὁ πατὴρ κἀγὼ γινώσκω τὸν πατέρα, καὶ τὴν ψυχήν μου τίθημι ὑπὲρ τῶν προβάτων. And I have other sheep that are not from this sheepfold. I must bring them too, and they will listen to my voice, and there will be one flock and one shepherd. (ποιμὴν = *shepherd*; πατὴρ = *father*; κἀγὼ = *even I* [καί + ἐγώ]; πατέρα = *father*; ψυχήν = *soul*; προβάτων = *sheep*)

Mark 4:14–16

The sower sows the word. οὗτοι δέ εἰσιν οἱ παρὰ τὴν ὁδόν· ὅπου σπείρεται ὁ λόγος καὶ ὅταν ἀκούσωσιν, εὐθὺς ἔρχεται ὁ σατανᾶς καὶ αἴρει τὸν λόγον τὸν ἐσπαρμένον εἰς αὐτούς. And these are the ones sown on rocky ground: As soon as they hear the word, they receive it with joy. (σπείρεται = *is being sown*; ὅταν ἀκούσωσιν = *when they should hear*; σατανᾶς = *Satan*; ἐσπαρμένον = *being sown* [treat this participle as an accusative adjective]) [see also Luke 8:12]

John 10:17–18

This is why the Father loves me, because I lay down my life, so that I might take it back again. οὐδεὶς αἴρει αὐτὴν ἀπ᾽ ἐμοῦ, ἀλλ᾽ ἐγὼ τίθημι αὐτὴν ἀπ᾽ ἐμαυτοῦ. I have the authority to lay it down, and I have the authority to take it back again. This commandment I received from my Father. (ἐμαυτοῦ = *myself*)

Digging Deeper into the New Testament Text

1) Find **II Timothy 2:11-13** in your GNT. See if you can spot *four* occurrences of a *conditional* conjunction, and *two* examples of the *causal* (co-ordinate) conjunction, and *one* example of the *negative* particle.

2) Now open your Greek <u>Interlinear</u> to **II Timothy 2:11-13**. Remember that in Mounce the Interlinear code for conjunctions is *cj* (for *conjunction*), and for particles is *pl* (for *particle*). Scan across the parsing line (the third line of the Interlinear) to <u>check the accuracy</u> of your work above. Did you find them all? Now with the help of the English, you can scan through and see the NIV translation of the conjunctions and particle you have found.

3) In your GNT and Interlinear at **II Timothy 2:11 and 12** you see the word καί once in each verse. Oddly enough, you will see that Mounce does not classify this as a *conjunction*, but as an *adverb*! Though καί is used in the GNT thousands of times as a conjunction, its use in these verses is different. Look up καί *in BDAG*. Do you see that the entry is divided into two large sections, and that the NIV has apparently chosen the definition(s) provided at the opening of section 2 to guide its translation at II Timothy 2:11-12? But consider another translation possibility with a slightly different nuance: Look under 1.b, and try out letters ζ and η. How might your translation sound, if guided by these options?

4) Find **Romans 6:1-11** in your GNT. See if you can spot about *eighteen* occurrences of *conjunctions* we have looked at, *both* of the negative *particles*, and *one* example of the "μέν...δέ construction". [To keep track, write down the Greek word in question, along with the verse number in which it occurs.]

5) Now open your Greek <u>Interlinear</u> to **Romans 6:1-11**. Scan across the parsing line (the third line of the Interlinear) to <u>check the accuracy</u> of your work above. Did you find them all? Now with the help of the English, you can scan through and see the NIV translation of the conjunctions and the particle you have found. Of course you are not expected to "read the Greek" of this passage. But you can get a taste of real Greek, and can begin to see important features of the text even at this early stage in your learning.

6) In your GNT and Interlinear in *Romans 6:1-11* you see the conjunction γάρ used repeatedly. As you can imagine, this conjunction is heavily used in Paul's argumentative and explanatory passages. Look up this conjunction in BDAG, and write down the three large headings into which the senses of γάρ are arranged. How do these senses differ?

7) Go in Wallace's Intermediate Grammar *The Basics of NT Syntax* to pages 286-302 [*Greek Grammar Beyond the Basics*, pages 656–678]. <u>Simply leaf through these pages for now</u>. There is no need to understand everything you see. [If you have a chance at a later point in your academic studies to venture into Advanced Greek, you will be exploring (among other things) the subtle but important insights that come when Greek clauses are mastered.] You may notice a great deal of overlap in terminology (with what we have learned in this chapter), but that Wallace's arrangement and presentation are considerably different. In your later work in exegesis, some of Wallace's more detailed treatments may be of use to you.

Chapter Eight Vocabulary

A significant portion of our instruction regarding conjunctions and particles needs to be housed right here in our vocabulary list. Several additional pieces of information are best connected directly to the words in question.

Co-Ordinate Conjunctions

The following conjunctions can join one main (independent) clause to another, without subordinating either. [This list contains most such conjunctions occurring 100x or more in the GNT.]

καί	and	The workhorse conjunction of the GNT. Its sense is often *additive* (and). Tool Exploration (below) we will discover a far wider range of possible meanings and functions. (When repeated before two successive elements, best translated as "both....and..." καὶ οἱ ἀπόστολοι καὶ οἱ διδάσκαλοι = "Both the apostles and the teachers...")
ἀλλά	but	A strong *adversative*, often setting elements into extreme, or mutually exclusive contrast.
ἤ	or	Expresses a *disjunction* (a presentation of alternatives: x *or* y). (When repeated before two successive elements, best translated as "either....or...." ἤ οἱ ἀπόστολοι ἤ οἱ διδάσκαλοι = "Either the apostles or the teachers...")
δέ	and, but	Can signal either a simple *continuation* (*and*) or a *contrast* (*but*). Only the context can determine just which sense it will bear. This conjunction is *post-positive*. That is, *it never appears as the first word in the clause it introduces*. (It is usually the second word, and occasionally the third word.)
οὖν	therefore, then	Often used in an *inferential* sense, moving what has just been stated to introduce a logical conclusion. Also used to introduce the next event, or a new topic. This conjunction is *post-positive*.
γάρ	for	Used in a *causal* sense (which may involve a sense of *explanation* or *reason*). This conjunction is *post-positive*.

Sub-Ordinate Conjunctions

Greek is a varied and resourceful language, capable of expressing the same idea in several different ways. The following conjunctions have been organized according to the type of dependent clauses they introduce. As you will see, we are limited by our knowledge (at this point in our study of Greek) to *the Indicative Mood*. [This list contains most such conjunctions occurring 100x or more in the GNT.]

<u>Adverbial Clauses</u>

εἰ	if	Introduces a *conditional* clause:	*If* you know what should be done, then just do it!
εἰ καί	though	Introduces a *concessive* clause:	*Though* she suffers much pain, she always helps others.
ὡς	as	Introduces a *comparative* clause:	They are preaching the Gospel *as* they were taught.
καθώς	as	Introduces a *comparative* clause:	They are preaching the Gospel *as* they were taught.
ὅτε	when	Introduces a *temporal* clause:	*When* we arrived at the camp, we were warmly welcomed.
ἕως	while	Introduces a *temporal* clause:	*While* we were eating, a terrible storm arose on the lake.
οὗ	where	Introduces a *local* clause:	A fire broke out in the hotel *where* they were staying.
ὅτι	because	Introduces a *causal* clause:	They never tried to escape, *because* they feared the consequences.

In Anticipation

The following categories are currently out of our range of study, since they are typically constructed with verb forms outside the Indicative Mood. We introduce them here for exposure and information only, hoping to secure a "mental slot" for them now as we study Greek subordinate clauses.

ὥστε	with the result that	Introduces a **result** clause:	[Typically coupled with an **Infinitive**.] We overloaded the truck, **with the result that** the axle snapped.
ἵνα	in order that, so	Introduces a **purpose** clause:	[Typically coupled with a **Subjunctive**.] I stepped back, **so** you could step forward.
[no conj.]	by	**means/ manner** clauses:	[Typically expressed via a **Participle without a conjunction**.] By twisting the valve, we released a powerful stream of water.

Noun Clauses

ὅτι	that	Introduces a **noun** clause:	We believe **that** God has raised Jesus from the dead. [Note that ὅτι can introduce either a noun clause or a causal clause. Only by considering the context can we discern what sort of clause ὅτι is introducing.]

Adjectival Clauses

Since adjectival clauses are commonly introduced by **relative pronouns** (which we have not yet studied in detail), we will not be working with adjectival clauses in this chapter.

Particles

This list contains all particles used 100x or more in the GNT.

οὐ	not	The general negative used with verbs **in the Indicative Mood**
μή	not	The negative used with verbs **outside the Indicative Mood**. [Included here for exposure.]
ἀμήν	amen, truly	At the end of a prayer (e.g.), strongly affirming what has been stated: "Amen, let it be so!" When introducing a saying (as on the lips of Jesus), solemnly affirming its truthfulness: "truly…"
μέν	on one hand	Often partnering with δέ to create a pair of elements that should be seen in stronger or weaker contrast with each other. The "μέν…δέ construction" can often be translated as follows:

οἱ μὲν ἀπόστολοι κηρύσσουσιν, οἱ δὲ διδάσκαλοι διδάσκουσι.

On the one hand, the apostles are preaching, but on the other hand, the teachers are teaching.

More Masculine Nouns of the Second Declension

This list contains the **last** of the **22** such nouns used 100x or more in the GNT. The comments offer translation suggestions or nuances in meaning we would find listed in BDAG.

κόσμος	world	Referring perhaps to all that God has made, or to humanity (often in its opposition to God).
λαός	people	Often referring to a people-group or community (as in "the people of God")
δοῦλος	slave, servant	Referring to those who are (in one way or another) duty-bound to a master
οἶκος	house	A masculine word largely overlapping in meaning its feminine partner οἰκία.

ὀφθαλμός	eye	The organ of sense perception or of spiritual understanding.
τόπος	place	Referring to location in various senses: geography, status, abode, etc.
		In the singular, often referring to the sky as the abode of sun, moon and stars.
οὐρανός	heaven	In the plural, often referring to the abode of God and heavenly beings. (In this sense, it is typically translated as an English singular: ἡ βασιλεία τῶν οὐρανῶν = "the Kingdom of heaven")

Review of Verbs We _Already Know_ (24)

λύω	[λυ]	I destroy
βλέπω	[βλεπ]	I see
τιμάω*	[τιμα]	I honor
κηρύσσω	[κηρυγ]	I preach, proclaim
ποιέω*	[ποιε]	I make, do
λέγω	[λεγ]	I say
δηλόω*	[δηλο]	I show, explain
ἀποστέλλω	[--στελ]	I send (out, away)
δίδωμι	[δο]	I give
λαμβάνω	[λαβ]	I take, or receive
τίθημι	[θε]	I put, place, lay
γινώσκω	[γνω]	I know
ἵστημι	[στα]	I set, place, stand
ἀκούω	[ἀκου]	I hear, obey

δείκνυμι	[δεικ]	I show, explain
γράφω	[γραφ]	I write
βάλλω	[βαλ]	I throw
πίπτω	[πτ]	I fall
ἐγείρω	[εγερ]	I rise
ἀποθνήσκω	[--θαν]	I kill, die
ἐσθίω	[εδ]	I eat
διδάσκω	[δακ]	I teach, instruct
πιστεύω	[πιστευ]	I believe
εὑρίσκω	[ευρ]	I find, discover

*Remember that these forms will appear in "real Greek texts" only in their **contracted** forms: τιμῶ, ποιῶ, δηλῶ. They are presented in vocabulary lists (and lexicon entries) in **uncontracted** forms only to make clear which short vowel will be involved in the contractions.

New Verbs We Are _Now Adding_ (5)

μένω	[μεν]	I remain
αἴρω	[αρ]	I lift up, take away
κρίνω	[κριν]	I judge
ἔχω	[σεχ]	I have
σῴζω	[σωι]	I save

Exercises

I. Short Answer

1) In general, <u>what do conjunctions do</u>?

2) How do <u>Co-ordinate</u> conjunctions <u>differ</u> (in function) from <u>Sub-ordinate</u> conjunctions?

3) What kind of sentences do <u>Co-ordinate Conjunctions</u> create?

4) What kind of sentences do <u>Sub-ordinate Conjunctions</u> create?

5) Into what <u>three general categories</u> do <u>dependent clauses</u> fall?

6) What sorts of <u>ideas</u> do <u>Adverbial clauses</u> introduce?

7) How may a <u>Noun clause</u> <u>function</u> in a sentence?

8) <u>What is a post-positive conjunction</u>?

9) <u>What</u> is a <u>particle</u> (in the narrower sense)?

10) <u>What</u> is a <u>particle</u> (in the broader sense)?

11) How does the <u>frequency of particles</u> in the GNT compare with the same in Classical Greek?

Solutions to Exercise I

1) They ***join*** things together.
2) Co-ord. conjs join together elements of ***equal*** grammatical power [e.g. a main clause to a main clause]. Sub-ord. conjs join together elements of ***unequal*** grammatical power [i.e. a dependent clause to a main clause].
3) Co-ordinate Conjunctions create ***Compound Sentences***.
4) Co-ordinate Conjunctions create ***Complex Sentences***.
5) Adverbial clauses, Adjectival clauses, Noun clauses
6) Conditions, causes, results, purposes, concessions, comparisons, means, time, and place.
7) The entire clause can function like a noun: that is, as the subject or the object of a sentence. I believe ***the Gospel***. [The object is a simple noun]. I believe ***that Jesus is Lord***. [The object is a clause.]
8) A conjunction that will ***not appear*** as the ***first word*** in its clause.
9) A word that usually conveys a subtle emotional or rational sense.
10) Any word that can't easily be classified as one of the other nine parts of speech.
11) Except for οὐ and μή, particles are rare in the GNT, though they were frequent in Classical.

IV. Synthetic Sentences

The sentences below gather together most of what we have learned so far, including vocabulary. As usual, **1)** parse verbs; **2)** identify the cases and their uses; **3)** note the position of adjectives; **4)** identify and explain pronouns; **5)** provide a smooth English translation; **6)** diagram each sentence, with special attention to positioning clauses appropriately; **7)** and write in Greek at least two sentences.

1) νῦν μένομεν ἐν τούτῳ τῷ τόπῳ οὗ ὁ κύριος διδάσκει τὰ ἡμῶν τέκνα, καὶ γινώσκομεν ὅτι ζωὴ καὶ εἰρήνη εἰσὶν οἱ λόγοι αὐτοῦ.

2) ὁ υἱὸς τοῦ ἀνθρώπου τὸν κόσμον ἐκ τοῦ ἐσχάτου θανάτου σῴζει, εἰ πιστεύουσιν, ἀλλὰ ὁ λαός τῆς γῆς ἔτι τὴν τοῦ μόνου θεοῦ δικαιοσύνην οὐ λαμβάνει.

3) ἡμεῖς ἐν ταῖς καρδίαις ἡμῶν τὴν δόξαν τοῦ αὐτοῦ εὐαγγελίου ἔχομεν, ὑμεῖς οὖν τὰς φωνὰς τῶν ἀποστόλων ἀκούετε, εἰ καὶ νεκροί εἰσιν οὗτοι.

4) ὁ θεὸς τὴν ἁμαρτίαν τοῦ κόσμου αἴρει, ὁ γὰρ ἅγιος τῶν οὐρανῶν αὐτῷ τὴν ἰδίαν ἀγάπην δίδωσι, ὡς κηρύσσομεν.

5) σὺ μὲν μένεις πρὸ τοῦ οἴκου ἕως τὸν υἱόν μου ὁ θάνατος λύει, αὕτη δὲ τὰ τέκνα ἀποστέλλει ἀπ' ἐκείνου τοῦ οἴκου πρὸς τὴν ἔρημον ταύτην.

6) ἰδοὺ ἐκεῖνοι τοὺς διδασκάλους τῆς ἐκκλησίας
    ἀποθνήσκουσιν, ἀλλὰ ἡμεῖς κηρύσσομεν περὶ τῆς ἡμέρας
    ὅτε ὁ θεὸς τὰς τῶν ἀνθρώπων ψυχὰς κρίνει ὅτι ἐν τῇ
    ἁμαρτίᾳ μένουσι.

7) ὁ ὑπὲρ τὸν οὐρανὸν καὶ τὴν γῆν κύριος διὰ τῆς ἀληθείας
    τοὺς ἁγίους κρίνει, καὶ οἱ ἀδελφοὶ οὗτοι τοὺς ἄλλους
    διδάσκουσιν ὅτι καλὸς καὶ ἅγιός ἐστιν ὁ θεός ἡμῶν.

8) ἀμὴν ἀμὴν ὑμῖν λέγω ὅτι οἱ υἱοὶ τῆς δικαιοσύνης εἰς τὰς
    τῆς ἁμαρτίας ὁδοὺς οὐ πίπτουσι, τὸν οὖν στέφανόν μου τῆς
    ζωῆς ἔχουσιν ἐν τῇ ἡμέρᾳ τῇ ἐσχάτᾳ.

9) πάλιν ὑμῖν τὸν τῆς ζωῆς ἄρτον δίδομεν καθὼς ὁ θεὸς ἡμῖν
    αὐτὸν δίδωσιν, αὐτοὶ γὰρ οἱ ὀφθαλμοὶ ἡμῶν τὴν βασιλείαν
    τῆς δόξης βλέπουσι.

10) ὁ μὲν κόσμος τοὺς τοῦ θεοῦ δούλους κρίνει, ὁ δὲ λαὸς τοῦ
    θεοῦ τὰ δῶρα τῆς εἰρήνης καὶ ἀληθείας τῷ αὐτῷ κόσμῳ
    δίδωσι

9: Active, Middle, Passive Voices

By now we've studied **all ten** parts of speech: *verbs, nouns, articles, adverbs, interjections, adjectives, prepositions, pronouns*, *conjunctions and particles*. With these building blocks in hand we are able to understand (at least in a general and preliminary way) how **all Greek sentences are built**, however complex they may be. Of course, the roadway ahead will involve expanding our knowledge of the forms and uses of the various parts of speech.

Reviewing Verb Parsing

Throughout the preceding chapters we have kept our verbs *restricted* in tense, voice and mood to the **Present Active Indicative**. That has allowed us to focus exclusively on meeting each of the other parts of speech without unnecessary distraction. Now it's time to explore more features of Greek verbs.

As we move ahead, let's review the landscape of parsing to remind ourselves *where we've been* (marked by the bold font), and where (ultimately) we need to go:

Tenses (7):	**Present**, Imperfect, Future, Aorist, Perfect, Pluperfect, Future Perfect.
Voices (3):	**Active**, Middle, Passive.
Moods (4):	**Indicative**, Subjunctive, Imperative, Optative. (Later we will meet the <u>Participle</u> and <u>Infinitive</u> *Modes*.)
Persons (3):	**First, Second, Third**.
Numbers (2)	**Singular, Plural**.

Active and Passive Voices

We'll begin our expansion with the matter of Voice:

Active Voice

As you have experienced throughout the preceding chapters, the active voice tells us that **the persons/things involved** (I, you, he/she/it, we, y'all, they) are the ones who **perform or carry out** the action in question.

λύω	ἀποστέλλεις	διδάσκει
I am destroying	you are sending	she is teaching

εὑρίσκομεν	κρίνετε	σῴζουσι
we are finding	you are judging	they are saving

Passive Voice

By way of contrast, passive forms *reverse the polarity of action*, so that **the persons/ things involved** (I, you, he/she/it, we, y'all, they) **are acted upon by someone or something else**:

λύομαι	ἀποστέλλῃ	διδάσκεται
I am being destroyed	you are being sent	she is being taught

εὑρισκόμεθα	κρίνεσθε	σῴζονται
we are being found	you are being judged	they are being saved

1) In each of the translations of the passive above, notice how we maintained the values of the Present Tense, as well as the Indicative Mood. Remember that the **Present Tense** (in Greek) usually means "now-Time" and "on-going, continuous Aspect." Recall also that the **Indicative Mood** puts forward a factual claim, rather than a hope, command, or possibility. "I am being destroyed" declares something as a **fact**, while also expressing it as something happening **now,** and **in an ongoing way**.

2) Also, notice that "Passive" does not mean "Past." "Passive" relates to the **direction of action** (subject performing action vs. subject being acted upon), whereas "past" relates to **time** (present, past, future). Work hard to keep these two very different notions completely distinct from each other.

Passive Voice, Transitive Verbs, and Sentence Types

If you think about it very long, you will realize that no verb will function meaningfully in a passive sense unless it can take a Direct Object in its active form. Verbs which can take **Direct Objects** are called **Transitive Verbs**; verbs which cannot take **Direct Objects** are called **In-transitive Verbs**. Only Transitive verbs can be "turned around" to make sense in the passive voice:

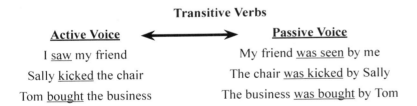

Transitive Verbs

Active Voice	**Passive Voice**
I <u>saw</u> my friend	My friend <u>was seen</u> by me
Sally <u>kicked</u> the chair	The chair <u>was kicked</u> by Sally
Tom <u>bought</u> the business	The business <u>was bought</u> by Tom

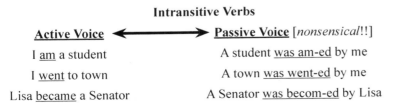

Intransitive Verbs

Active Voice	**Passive Voice** [*nonsensical*!!]
I <u>am</u> a student	A student <u>was am-ed</u> by me
I <u>went</u> to town	A town <u>was went-ed</u> by me
Lisa <u>became</u> a Senator	A Senator <u>was becom-ed</u> by Lisa

Now that we realize that only **transitive** verbs can be converted into **passive** sentences, let's take a look at four kinds of transitive sentences, and how their elements are reconfigured to make passive sentence:

Simple Transitive

God is destroying sin.

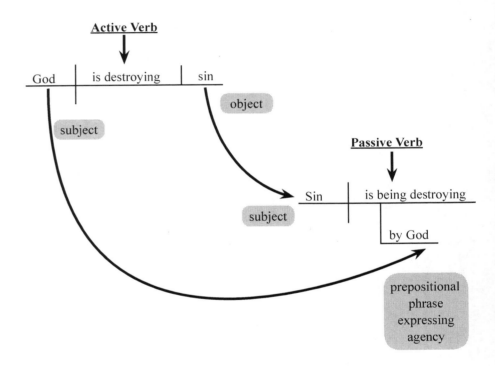

Transitive with an Indirect Object

The apostles are sending books to the children.

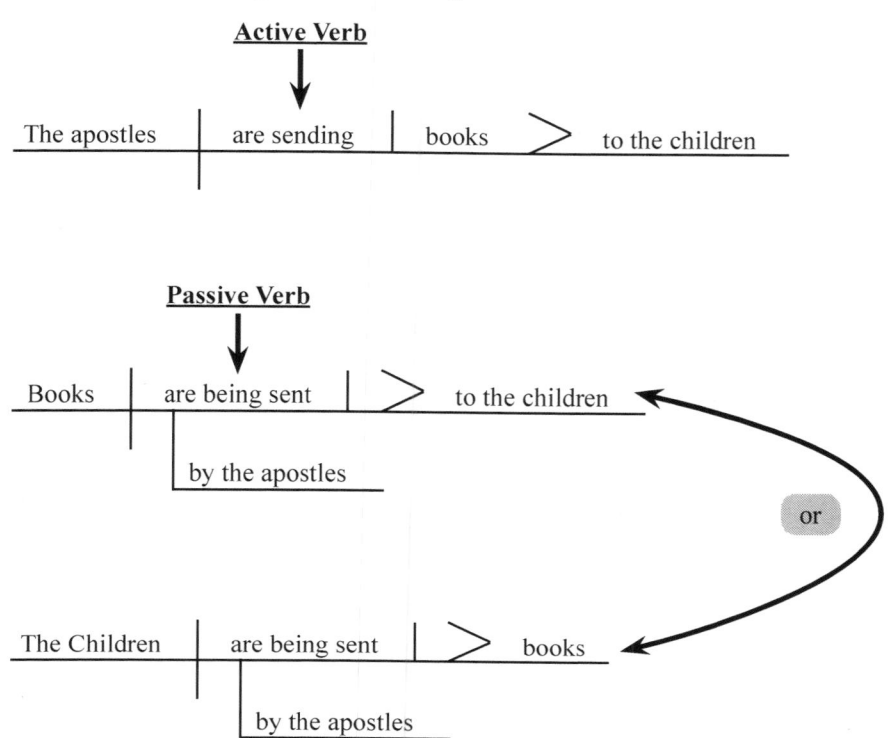

In the passive formation, either the (original) Indirect Object or the Direct Object can serve as the subject of the new passive construction. In either situation, the original subject (apostles) can be placed into a prepositional phrase in adverbial position, and is now called the "agent."

Transitive with a Predicate Accusative (noun)

God is making the Son (to be) first of all.

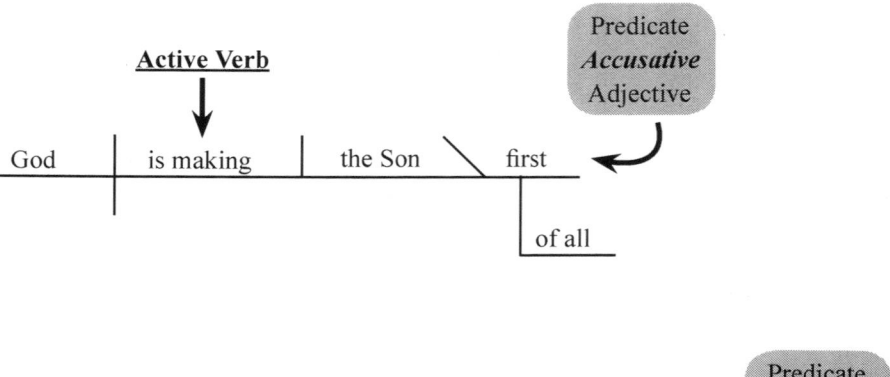

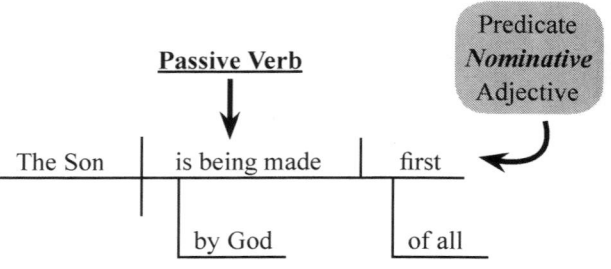

In the **ACTIVE** versions of #'s 3 and 4 above, some form of the verb "to be" is implied between the Direct Object (the Son) and the Predicate Accusatives: [… the Son (to be) Lord…; …the Son (to be) first…]. You will recall that the slanted line was our way of connecting the subject to the predicate with verbs of "being." Since such verbs essentially forge equations, it is always appropriate for the noun or adjective in the predicate to take the same case as the noun serving as the subject. In both #'s 3 and 4 above, the Direct Object (the Son) serves more or less as the subject of the implied predication, with the Predicate Noun and Adjective (Lord, first) completing the predication. If the subject of the implied predication is accusative (since "the Son" is serving primarily as the Direct Object of the main verb), it only stands to reason that the predicates (Lord, first) must also be accusative, since they are equated to "Son" via the implied linking (equation) verb (to be).

In the **PASSIVE** versions of #'s 3 and 4 above, you will notice how closely they resemble the diagram of the simple linking verb with a predicate noun or adjective: The Son is being made Lord, closely resembles The Son is Lord; The Son is being made first, closely resembles The Son is first. Verbs that can be followed by two accusatives (as in #'s 3 and 4 above) will act, when converted into passives, much like linking verbs by taking a Predicate Nominative (noun or adjective).

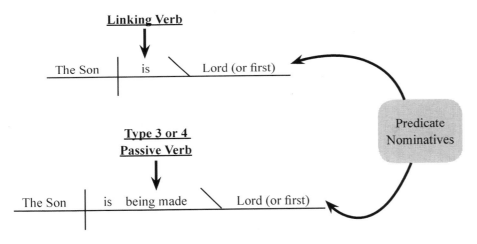

Reasons for Using the Passive

We've talked a lot about passive sentences, but haven't yet addressed **why authors would use them**…when active forms are readily available.

> Why would I say "The oak tree <u>was destroyed</u> by a bolt of lightning," rather than "A bolt of lightning <u>destroyed</u> the oak tree"?

Reasons for using the English passive largely overlap the reasons in Greek:

Stylistic Variation: Good writers have learned to vary their grammatical expression to enhance reading pleasure, interest, and ease. Biblical writers (and speakers) were often sensitive in these same ways.

Focus: Sometimes it is better to draw attention away from the actor in order to place more attention upon the action itself or its results, etc. Several different motives might be at work in such a shift:

Perhaps the actor is ***not known***

Perhaps mentioning the actor would only be ***distracting***

Perhaps the identity of the actor is ***being concealed***

Perhaps the identity of the actor is ***not important***

Obvious Agency: Often in the GNT the passive is used when, without doubt, **God** is the agent! In such a circumstance, the focus would be on the action without in any way demeaning or diminishing the role of God. [Traditionally this has been called the ***divine passive***, and explained by the Jewish hesitation to mention the divine name. But GNT writers often refer to God (θεός) without hesitation.] Most notably the ***beatitudes*** are best interpreted as divine passives:

…they shall be comforted… = …(God) will comfort them…

…they shall be satisfied… = …(God) will satisfy them…

These beatitudes leap into bold colors when we realize that "being comforted" and "being satisfied" are not the work of impersonal or generalized forces…but of God!

The Forms of the Present Passive Indicative of λύω

What do passive forms of the verb λύω look like in the <u>Present Indicative</u>?

Present *Active* Indicative		Present *Passive* Indicative	
λύω	"I am destroying…"	λύομαι	"I am being destroyed…"
λύειϛßß	"you are destroying…"	λύηßß	"you are being destroyed…"
λύει	"he/she/it is destroying"	λύεται	"he/she/it is being destroyed"
λύομεν	"we are destroying…"	λυόμεθα	"we are being destroyed…"
λύετε	"y'all are destroying"	λύεσθε	"y'all are being destroyed"
λύουσι(ν)	"they are destroying…"	λύονται	"they are being destroyed…"

An Analysis of the Endings of the Present Passive

From the forms above, you can see that the *endings* make the difference. Just switch the endings from the active ones you have already learned (ω εις ει ομεν ετε ουσι) to the passive ones (ομαι η εται ομεθα εσθε ονται), and the *polarity of action changes* in the verb from active voice to passive voice. You also remember that the active endings were composed of *two elements*: a <u>variable connecting vowel</u> and a <u>personal ending</u>. (The omicron (ο) is used before μ's and ν's; the epsilon (ε) elsewhere.) Passive endings are similar. Compare them:

Root	Connecting Vowel	Personal Ending		
λυ	ο	μι	combine to form	λύω
λυ	ο	μαι	combine to form	λύομαι
λυ	ε	σι	combine to form	λύεις
λυ	ε	σαι	combine to form	λύη (note the contraction)
λυ	ε	τι	combine to form	λύει
λυ	ε	ται	combine to form	λύεται
λυ	ο	μεν	combine to form	λύομεν
λυ	ο	μεθα	combine to form	λυόμεθα
λυ	ε	τε	combine to form	λύετε
λυ	ε	σθε	combine to form	λύεσθε
λυ	ο	ντι	combine to form	λύουσι
λυ	ο	νται	combine to form	λύονται

The Forms of the Present Passive for Contract and μι Verbs

You also recall that certain verbs (those whose roots ended in the vowels α, ε, and ο) experience a contraction of vowels between their vowel stems and the variable connecting vowels. Furthermore, you recall that another family of verbs (the so-called μι verbs) do not use a connecting vowel to join the verb stem to the personal endings. Notice how this plays out in the passive.

OMEGA CONJUGATION (using ο/ε connecting vowel)   **MI CONJUGATION** (no connecting vowel used)

	"Regular" "to destroy"	A-Contract "to honor"	E-Contract "to make"	O-Contract "to show"	"o" stem "to give"	"e" stem "to place/put"	"a" stem "to stand"	"nu" stem "to show"	Translation
1s)	λύομαι	τιμῶμαι	ποιοῦμαι	δηλοῦμαι	δίδομαι	τίθεμαι	ἵσταμαι	δείκνυμαι	**I am being -ed**
2s)	λύῃ	τιμᾷ	ποιῇ	δηλοῖ	δίδοσαι	τίθεσαι	ἵστασαι	δείκνυσαι	**You are being -ed**
3s)	λύεται	τιμᾶται	ποιεῖται	δηλοῦται	δίδοται	τίθεται	ἵσταται	δείκνυται	**He/she/it is being -ed**
1p)	λυόμεθα	τιμώμεθα	ποιούμεθα	δηλούμεθα	διδόμεθα	τιθέμεθα	ἱστάμεθα	δεικνύμεθα	**We are being -ed**
2p)	λύεσθε	τιμᾶσθε	ποιεῖσθε	δηλοῦσθε	δίδοσθε	τίθεσθε	ἵστασθε	δείκνυσθε	**Y'all are being -ed**
3p)	λύονται	τιμῶνται	ποιοῦνται	δηλοῦνται	δίδονται	τίθενται	ἵστανται	δείκνυνται	**They are being -ed**

Notes on Forms

1) You see that the 2nd singular personal ending (σαι) in the **Omega** Conjugation always contracts with previous vowels, whether with the connecting vowel alone (ο/ε), or the vowel of the verb stem itself (α, ε, or ο). In each circumstance, the sigma (σ) does not enjoy its position between vowels, drops out, and thereby instigates the contraction between vowels. But you can see in the **MI** Conjugation the unaffected personal ending, which (in these circumstances) does not contract with any preceding vowel.

2) You see in all four example verbs of the **MI** Conjugation the "pure" personal endings uncomplicated by contractions. You can also see that the verb stems are perfectly consistent and easily visible in every instance.

3) Even though you can see a fair amount of variation across these paradigms (especially with the vowel patterns connecting personal endings to verb stems), you can still discern enough of each ending to parse and translate it accurately.

The Grammatical Fate of Agents and Instruments in Passive Sentences

We have seen that the **Direct Object** of an active, transitive verb can become the **Subject** of a passive verb. We have also seen that the **Subject** (the actor/agent in an active sentence) can be expressed within a **Prepositional Phrase**:

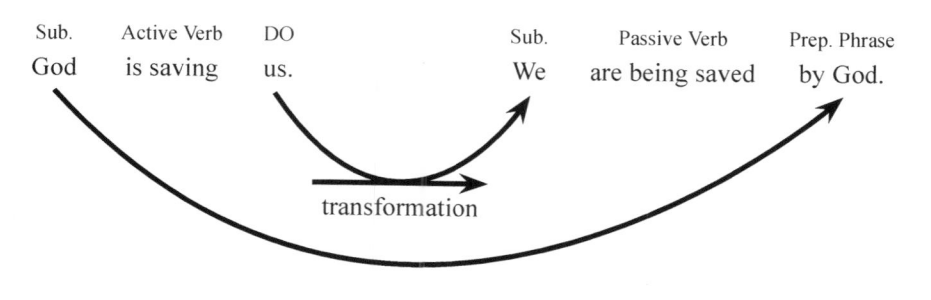

But Greek has some specific preferences about how these **Subjects** (in active sentences) **should be expressed** when the sentences are transformed into their passive counterparts:

- If the **Subject** (the "do-er") in an active sentence is a **person** (e.g. **God** is saving us), then in the passive transformation that person will be set in the **Genitive** Case with the preposition ὑπό. The "doer" is now called the **Personal Agent.** "We are being saved <u>by God</u> (ὑπὸ τοῦ θεοῦ)

- If the **Subject** (the "do-er") in an active sentence is a **thing** (e.g. **The word** is saving us), then in the passive transformation that thing will usually be set in the **Dative** Case without a preposition. The "doer" is now called the **Impersonal Means.** "We are being saved <u>by the word</u> (τῷ λογῷ)

The Middle Voice

Verbs in the Middle Voice imply that **the persons involved** (I, you, he/she/it, we, y'all, they) **are performing** the action, but **are somehow more intimately involved in the action** than usual. This **foggy notion** must be teased out circumstance by circumstance, with a fair amount of interpretive wiggle room remaining. To illustrate some of these interpretive possibilities, imagine finding our verb λύω as an indisputable **Middle**. How might we translate it to convey a **middle sense**?

We <u>are destroying</u> (ourselves).	[A middle verb could imply that the action is reflexive: **directly self-inflicted**.]
We <u>are destroying</u> our health.	[A middle verb could emphasize our actions are **ultimately affecting our own bodies**.]
We (ourselves) <u>are destroying</u> the counterfeit money.	[A middle verb could imply that we are acting **personally and directly**, not through an intermediary.]

Middle Voice Forms

Oddly enough, the forms of the Middle Voice (in the Present Indicative) **share the forms** of the **Passive Voice**! Only by examining other factors can we tell whether we are dealing with a Middle or a Passive.

But because true (and undisputed) Middles are relatively **rare** in the GNT, we will not spend <u>much</u> time at this point working with them. When you encounter **Middle/Passive** forms in our exercises, you should <u>typically</u> treat them as **Passives**…or as Deponents (see below).

Deponent Verbs

A significant number of Greek verbs share an important characteristic: though they are **Middle/Passive in form**, they should be translated **actively**. They have traditionally been called Deponent verbs because they seem to have "*laid aside*" their active forms (the Latin verb *deponere* means "to lay aside").

New Testament Exploration

John 9:12–14	They said to him, "Where is that man?" He said, "I do not know." Ἄγουσιν αὐτὸν πρὸς τοὺς Φαρισαίους τόν ποτε τυφλόν. Now, the day on which Jesus made the mud and opened his eyes was a Sabbath. (Φαρισαίους = *Pharisees*; ποτε τυφλόν = *formerly blind*)
Gal 5:17–18	For the flesh has desires that are opposed to the Spirit, and the Spirit opposed to the flesh, for these are opposed to each other, so that you all cannot do what you want. εἰ δὲ πνεύματι ἄγεσθε, οὐκ ἐστὲ ὑπὸ νόμον. (πνεύματι = *by the Spirit*)
Matt 21:25–26	From where was John's baptism? From heaven or from people? They discussed among themselves, saying, "If we should say from heaven, he will say to us all, 'Therefore, why did you not believe him?' But if we should say from people, φοβούμεθα τὸν ὄχλον, for they all consider John to be a prophet."

Digging Deeper into the New Testament Text

1) Find **Mark 1:9** and **13** in your GNT. See if you can spot *two* occurrences of *Personal Agency* employing ὑπό with the Genitive.

2) Now open your Greek Interlinear to **Mark 1:9** and **13**. You should easily find these two Agent Phrase in English and Greek. But what about the passive verbs? In Mounce, the sign of the passive (*p*) can be seen in the parsing line under the respective verbs:

In the case of the first verb, the code would run as follows:

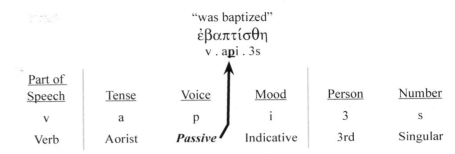

"was baptized"
ἐβαπτίσθη
v . api . 3s

Part of Speech	Tense	Voice	Mood	Person	Number
v	a	p	i	3	s
Verb	Aorist	*Passive*	Indicative	3rd	Singular

In the case of the second verb, the code would run as follows:

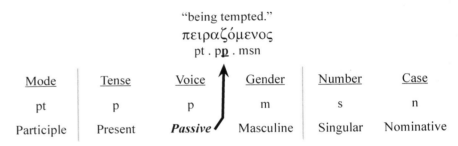

"being tempted."
πειραζόμενος
pt . pp . msn

Mode	Tense	Voice	Gender	Number	Case
pt	p	p	m	s	n
Participle	Present	*Passive*	Masculine	Singular	Nominative

It's *not necessary* to know the vocabulary words in these verses, or understand yet what a *Participle* is, or know what the *Aorist* Tense signifies. It is enough to see what we know, and begin to get accustomed to picking through real GNT sentences to recognize what we have learned.

In English, convert these two passive verbs into active ones. How would they sound?

3) In your Interlinear at **II Corinthians 4:8-9** you will find a flurry of passives (though they are in participial form). Look for the code: pt.pp. xxx. You should find 5 of them. Write down the English translations of these participles. Do you hear the passive sense in the translations that are supplied by the NIV?

Note that *no agents* are supplied! What motivation (might you conjecture) could be at work for using the passive? (Review the three reasons offered in the lesson above.)

4) In your Interlinear at **II Corinthians 4:8-9,** you will find the English word "forsaken," with the Greek participle ἐγκαταλειπόμενοι beneath it.

By using its vocabulary code (1593), you can find it in Appendix B, and then find its entry in **BDAG**. As you examine this entry, notice that this same verb is used in Mark 15:34 and Matthew 27:46. How interesting that forsakenness was not Paul's experience, but was Jesus' experience. But note the subtle "wiggle-room" allowed by the **BDAG** definition at that point: "...of *feeling* or being forsaken by God..." With BDAG's support, might we say that Jesus may **not actually** have been forsaken by God (though he may have felt it so)?

5) Go in Wallace's Intermediate Grammar *The Basics of NT Syntax* to pages 187-191 [*Greek Grammar Beyond the Basics*, pages 431–441]. Simply leaf through these pages for now. There is no need to understand everything you see. In later studies as needed, you may find it helpful to work more carefully with these pages and the distinctions they offer.

Chapter Nine Vocabulary

ἄγω	[αγ]	*I draw, lead.* Also found with 18 different prefixes [e.g. συνάγω (I draw together, gather)]	
–βαίνω	[βα]	*I go* Always with a prefix [e.g. ἀναβαίνω (I am going up); καταβαίνω (I am going down)].	
φέρω	[φερ]	*I carry, bring, lead.* Also found with 14 different prefixes [e.g. προσφέρω (I bring to, offer)]	

Deponent Verbs

(passive in form, active in translation)

γίνομαι	[γεν]	*I become.*	Like εἰμί, can serve as an equative verb (followed by a predicate nominative).
ἀποκρίνομαι	[κριν]	*I answer.*	Clearly a prefixed form of κρίνω, but deponent. Takes a Dative Object.
φοβέομαι	[φοβε]	*I fear, dread*	An Epsilon-Contract verb. See the Middle/Passive forms of ποιέω above.
πορεύομαι	[πορευ]	*I go.*	Found with 10 different prefixes.
ἔρχομαι	[ερχ]	*I come, go.*	Found with 18 different prefixes. Used over 600x without a prefix.
ἐξέρχομαι		*I go out.*	A prefixed form of ἔρχομαι.
εἰσέρχομαι		*I go into, enter.*	A prefixed form of ἔρχομαι.
ἀπέρχομαι		*I go away.*	A prefixed form of ἔρχομαι.

Exercises

I. Short Answer

1) In <u>what three different voices</u> may Greek verbs be found? What does each generally suggest?

2) What kind of verbs can be converted into passives?

3) When a sentence is converted from active to passive form, what happens to the (original) Direct Object?

4) What four different kinds of transitive sentences are there? Identify them with English examples.

5) When verbs in <u>Sentence-types 3 and 4</u> (see question 4 above) are made <u>passive</u>, how do they <u>resemble copulative verbs</u>?

6) What <u>three reasons</u> did we consider for using the <u>passive voice</u> (when the active is available)?

7) In the GNT, <u>who</u> is likely the <u>agent</u> of many passive verbs though the agent remains <u>unexpressed</u>?

8) In passive constructions, <u>how are agents expressed</u>?

9) In the Present Indicative, <u>what forms</u> does the <u>Middle Voice</u> take?

10) <u>How common</u> is it to encounter a "true" Middle in the GNT?

11) <u>What</u> is a <u>Deponent</u> Verb?

Solutions to Exercise I

1) The **Active**: subject is performing the action. The **Middle**: subject is somehow portrayed as more intimately involved in the action. The **Passive**: subject is being acted upon.
2) Only transitive verbs: verbs taking direct objects.
3) It usually becomes the Subject of the passive verb.
4) (1) Simple Direct Object: John is building a house. (2) Direct Object with Indirect Object: John is sending the letter to Wilma. (3) Direct Object with (Noun) Predicate Accusative: John made James the president. (4) Direct Object with (Adjective) Predicate Accusative: John made James uncomfortable.
5) They resemble copulative verbs (equation verbs) in that they are completed by a **Predicate Nominative**.
6) Stylistic variation. Focus on something other than the agent (with various motives possible). The Agent is obvious.
7) **God** [frequently called the "divine passive"].
8) **Personal Agents** are expressed as the **Genitive Objects** of ὑπό. **Impersonal Means** are found in the **Dative**, usually without a preposition.
9) They share the forms of the passive. One must appeal to other factors to tell how to distinguish the two.
10) Not common at all. Most Middle/Passive forms will be Passives or Deponents.
11) A verb with Middle/Passive endings that must be translated actively.

II. Drills with Passives

Increase your skill with passive verbs (along with Personal Agents and Impersonal Means) with these pairs of mirrored sentences. Personal pronouns are <u>overly used</u> in order to be as helpful as possible.

1) ὁ θεὸς σῴζει ἐμέ. ἐγὼ σῴζομαι ὑπὸ τοῦ θεοῦ.

2) οἱ ἀπόστολοι διδάσκουσί σε. σὺ διδάσκῃ ὑπὸ τῶν ἀποστόλων.

3) τὸ τέκνον γράφει τὴν βίβλον. ἡ βίβλος γράφεται ὑπὸ τοῦ τέκνου.

4) τὸ εὐαγγέλιον ἀποστέλλει ἡμᾶς. ἡμεῖς ἀποστελλόμεθα τῷ εὐαγγελίῳ.

5) ἡ ἀλήθεια κρίνει ὑμᾶς. ὑμεῖς κρίνεσθε τῇ ἀληθείᾳ.

6) ἡ ἁμαρτία ἀποθνήσκει τοὺς διδασκάλους. οἱ διδάσκαλοι ἀποθνήσκονται τῇ ἁμαρτίᾳ

<u>Solutions to Exercise II</u>

1) ὁ θεὸς σῴζει ἐμέ. God is saving me. ἐγὼ σῴζομαι ὑπὸ τοῦ θεοῦ. I am being saved by God.

2) οἱ ἀπόστολοι διδάσκουσί σε. The apostles are teaching you. σὺ διδάσκῃ ὑπὸ τῶν ἀποστόλων. You are being taught by the apostles.

3) τὸ τέκνον γράφει τὴν βίβλον. The child is writing the book. ἡ βίβλος γράφεται ὑπὸ τοῦ τέκνου. The book is being written by the child.

4) τὸ εὐαγγέλιον ἀποστέλλει ἡμᾶς. The gospel is sending us. ἡμεῖς ἀποστελλόμεθα τῷ εὐαγγελίῳ. We are being sent by the gospel.

5) ἡ ἀλήθεια κρίνει ὑμᾶς. The truth is judging you. ὑμεῖς κρίνεσθε τῇ ἀληθείᾳ. You are being judged by the truth.

6) ἡ ἁμαρτία ἀποθνῄσκει τοὺς διδασκάλους. Sin is killing the teachers. οἱ διδάσκαλοι ἀποθνῄσκονται τῇ ἁμαρτίᾳ. The teachers are being killed by sin.

III. *Synthetic Sentences*

The sentences below gather together most of what we have learned so far, including vocabulary. As usual, **1)** parse verbs; **2)** identify the cases and their uses; **3)** note the position of adjectives; **4)** identify and explain pronouns; **5)** provide a smooth English translation; **6)** diagram each sentence, with special attention to positioning clauses appropriately; **7)** and write out in Greek at least two sentences.

1) εἰς τὴν βασιλείαν τῶν οὐρανῶν ἡ ἐκκλησία ἄγεται ὑπὸ τοῦ ἡμῶν κυρίου, οὗ τοῖς υἱοῖς τῆς δικαιοσύνης καὶ ἡ ζωὴ καὶ εἰρήνη δίδονται.

2) τὰ δῶρα ταῦτα πάλιν δίδονται τοῖς τέκνοις τοῖς κάλοις ὑπὸ τῶν διδασκάλων αὐτῶν, εἰ καὶ οὐκ ἔχουσι χρυσόν.

3) ὁ θεὸς τὸν ἴδιον υἱὸν κύριον τοῦ κόσμου ποιεῖ, ἀλλὰ οἱ ἄγγελοι δοῦλοι τῆς ἐκκλησίας ποιοῦνται ὑπὸ τοῦ αὐτοῦ θεοῦ. (See earlier discussion of Predicate Accusatives page 111)

4) σὺν τοῖς ἡμῶν ἀδελφοῖς πρὸς τὴν οἰκίαν ταύτην πορεύῃ, ἕως κατὰ τὸν λόγον τοῦ κυρίου οἱ ἀπόστολοι εἰς ἐκείνην τὴν ἔρημον ἀπέρχονται.

5) καὶ τὸν θεὸν καὶ τοὺς λόγους αὐτοῦ τιμῶμεν, ὅτι ἀκούει καὶ τοῖς ἰδίοις τέκνοις ἀποκρίνεται ἐν τῇ ὥρᾳ τοῦ θανάτου.

6) αἱ ὑμῶν καρδίαι διὰ τοῦ λόγου τοῦ θεοῦ ποιοῦνται οἶκοι τῆς δικαιοσύνης. οὐκέτι οὖν τὸν ἔσχατον θάνατον ἢ τὰς φωνὰς τοῦ ὄχλου φοβεῖσθε.

7) ἰδοὺ ἐγώ εἰμι ἡ ὁδὸς καὶ ἡ ἀλήθεια καὶ ἡ ζωή, καθὼς πάντοτε οἱ ἀδελφοὶ οἱ ἀγαθοὶ ὑμῶν ἐν τῷ κόσμῳ τούτῳ κηρύσσουσι καὶ διδάσκουσι.

8) νῦν καὶ πιστεύομεν καὶ γινώσκομεν ὅτι ἡ δόξα τοῦ εὐαγγελίου τῷ κόσμῳ ὑπὸ τῆς ἐκκλησίας δηλοῦται.

9) ἐκεῖ οἱ ἄγγελοι τοῦ θεοῦ καταβαίνουσιν ἀπὸ τῶν οὐρανῶν καὶ εἰς τοὺς οὐρανοὺς ἀναβαίνουσι, ἕως ὧδε τὰ ἔργα τοῦ νόμου τοῖς λόγοις τῆς ἀληθείας λύονται.

10) ἀμὴν ἀμὴν ἅγιος ὁ θεὸς ἡμῶν, καὶ διὰ τῆς ἀγάπης τοῦ αὐτοῦ θεοῦ γινόμεθα ἅγιοι ἐν ταῖς ἡμῶν καρδίαις.

10: Imperfect Tense

Throughout the preceding chapters we have kept our verbs **restricted** in tense and mood to the **Present Indicative**. In the last chapter we expanded our understanding of **Voice** to include the Middle (rare) and Passive (fairly common), along with Deponent Verbs. Now we will explore three more Indicative **Tenses** [**Imperfect, Future and Aorist**] in chapters 10, 11 and 12 respectively.

Reviewing Verb Parsing

Again let's review the landscape of parsing to remind ourselves **where we've been** (marked by the bold font):

Tenses (7):	<u>**Present**</u>, Imperfect, Future, Aorist, Perfect, Pluperfect, Future Perfect.
Voices (3):	<u>**Active**</u>, <u>**Middle**</u>, <u>**Passive**</u>. [**Just expanded in Chapter Nine.**]
Moods (4):	<u>**Indicative**</u>, Subjunctive, Imperative, Optative. (Later we will meet the <u>Participle</u> and <u>Infinitive</u> Modes.)
Persons (3):	<u>**First, Second, Third**</u>.
Numbers (2)	<u>**Singular, Plural**</u>.

The Imperfect Tense (logic and basic sense)

As you remember from Chapter Two, the Tenses of the Indicative Mood express a combination of **Time** and **Aspect**. At each intersection (except for two) stands a set of forms we call a **Tense**. As you can easily see from the chart below, the Greek **Imperfect** Tense combines the **Past Time** with **Internal Aspect**.

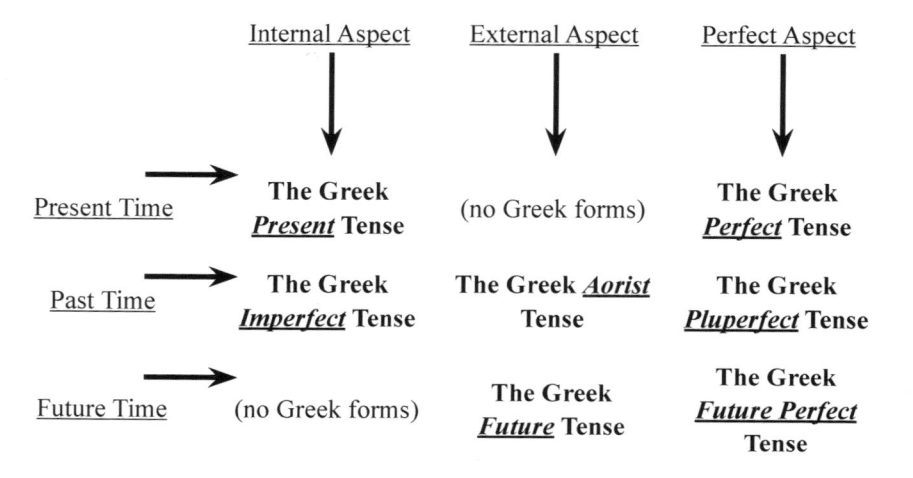

	Internal Aspect	External Aspect	Perfect Aspect
Present Time	**The Greek** *Present* **Tense**	(no Greek forms)	**The Greek** *Perfect* **Tense**
Past Time	**The Greek** *Imperfect* **Tense**	**The Greek** *Aorist* **Tense**	**The Greek** *Pluperfect* **Tense**
Future Time	(no Greek forms)	**The Greek** *Future* **Tense**	**The Greek** *Future Perfect* **Tense**

You can discern how the combination of Past Time with Internal Aspect sounds **in English** in the following expressions:

I <u>was teaching</u>	You <u>were being found</u>	They <u>were destroying</u>
We <u>were being taught</u>	She <u>was leading</u>	He <u>was being led</u>
You <u>were going</u>	They <u>were being sent</u>	It <u>was being spoken</u>
I <u>was throwing</u>		

Reexamine each of the examples until you can see clearly just how Past Time and Internal (continuous) Aspect are combined, whether the Voice of these sentences is Active or Passive.

The Forms of the Imperfect (Active and Middle/Passive) of λύω

Study the forms of λύω as given below, along with the translations provided:

Imperfect Active Indicative

ἔλυον	"I was destroying…"
ἔλυεςßß	"you were destroying…"
ἔλυε(ν)	"he/she/it was destroying"
ἐλύομεν	"we were destroying…"
ἐλύετε	"y'all were destroying"
ἔλυον	"they were destroying…"

Imperfect Passive Indicative

ἐλυόμην	"I was being destroyed…"
ἐλύουßß	"you were being destroyed…"
ἐλύετο	"he/she/it was being destroyed"
ἐλυόμεθα	"we were being destroyed…"
ἐλύεσθε	"y'all were being destroyed"
ἐλύοντο	"they were being destroyed…"

The Augment

Perhaps the most immediate feature of the Imperfect you notice is a smooth-breathing epsilon (ἐ) prefixed to every form. This is called a **syllabic augment** (because it adds a whole syllable to the verb), and will be found on all verbs (beginning with a consonant) in **past-time Tenses** of the **Indicative Mood**. [Remember from your earlier work that there are three past-time tenses in the Indicative Mood: the Imperfect, the Aorist, and the Pluperfect.]

The augment is simple enough in verbs beginning with a **consonant**: it is simply a prefixed epsilon (ἐ). But if a verb begins with a **vowel or diphthong**, this initial vowel or diphthong is **lengthened**, and is called a **temporal augment**. [In the pronunciation of Ancient Greek, it seems that long vowels were held for a *longer time* than short vowels. To lengthen a vowel would involve lengthening the *time or duration* of its pronunciation. Such an augment, therefore, could naturally be called a *temporal augment*.]

With the temporal augments, the pattern of lengthening follows (almost exactly) the pattern of relationships between short and long vowels you learned in Chapter One. We have supplied an arrow to show the pathway followed (for temporal augments in verbs) when short vowels are lengthened into long vowels:

	Short			Long	
"a" type	alpha	[α]	→	alpha	[α]
"e" type	epsilon	[ε]	→	eta	[η]
"o" type	omicron	[o]	→	omega	[ω]
"i" type	iota	[ι]	→	iota	[ι]
"u" type	upsilon	[υ]	→	upsilon	[υ]

You should notice two features about the pathways of vowel lengthening in this chart:

1) The short alpha (α) does not lengthen into long alpha (α) as one might expect, but rather into eta (η).

2) There is no visual difference between short and long iotas (ι), or between short and long upsilons (υ). [Though not visible, the distinction is important in Classical Greek poetry (e.g.), where the lengths of the vowels must fit into precise patterns as each line of poetry is constructed.]

If a verb begins with a **diphthong**, the temporal augment can follow **one of two pathways**:

1) The initial vowel of the diphthong can be <u>temporally</u> lengthened (with perhaps the iota dropping into subscript form);

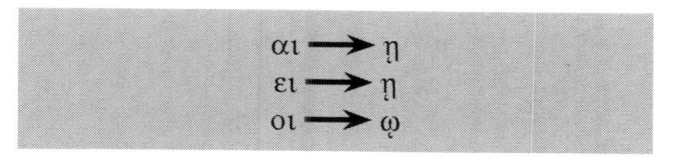

2) or, the diphthong will <u>not be lengthened at all</u>.

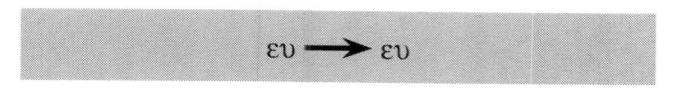

If a verb is **prefixed with a preposition**, the augmentation (of either kind) will be found **between** the preposition and the simple verb, <u>not out at the very beginning of the whole compound verb</u>.

> E.g., the verb ἐκλύω [a compound formed with the preposition ἐκ and the verb λύω] would appear in the (first singular, active) Imperfect as
> ἐκέλυον.

If the **prefixed preposition** ends in a vowel, the vowel is dropped as the augmentation is added.

> ἀποστέλλω
> ἀπ_στελλον
> ἀπέστελλον

The Endings of the Imperfect

You've also noticed that the endings are a bit different. Because we've shifted into **past time**, the personal endings must shift to a set called **Secondary Personal Endings**. The good news is that Greek has only two sets of personal endings: **Primary** and **Secondary**. By learning the personal endings of the Present and Imperfect Tenses, you will have learned both sets. All other finite verb forms (in all other tenses and moods) will use either Primary or Secondary Personal Endings.

Just as the endings of the Present Tense were composed of **two elements** (a <u>variable vowel</u> and a <u>personal ending</u>) so it is with the Imperfect:

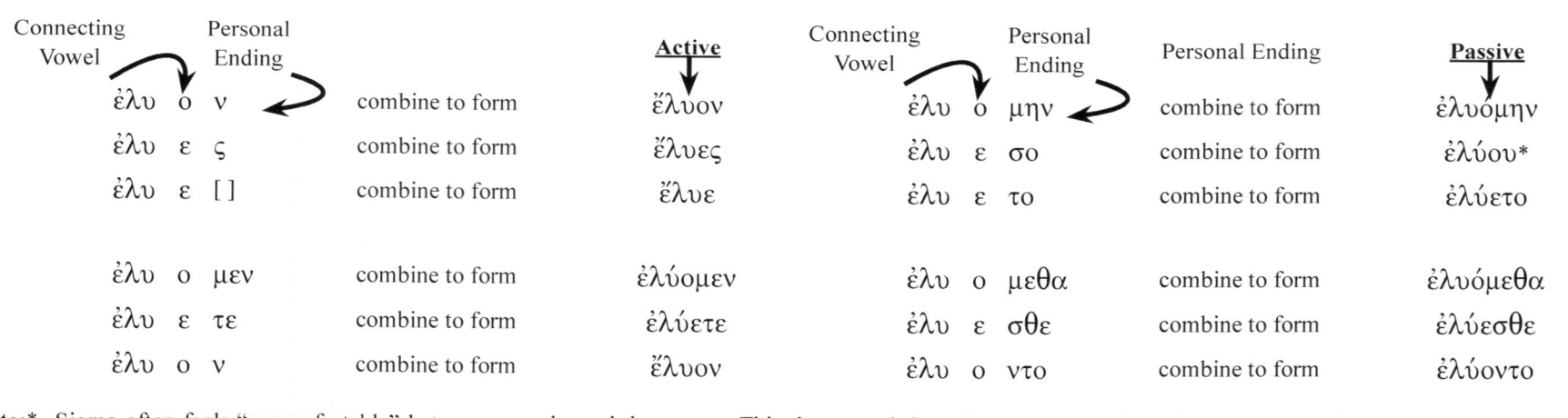

Note:* Sigma often feels "uncomfortable" between vowels, and drops out. This departure brings the two vowels into direct contact with each other, precipitating contraction (compare with the dynamics of contract verbs).

The Forms of the Imperfect for all Verb Types

Omega Conjugation (using o/ε connecting vowel)				**Mi Conjugation** (no connecting vowel used)				**Translation**
"Regular"	A-Contract	E-Contract	O-Contract	"o" stem	"e" stem	"a" stem	"nu" stem	
"to destroy"	"to honor"	"to make"	"to show"	"to give"	"to place/put"	"to stand"	"to show"	

Imperfect Active

ἔλυον	ἐτίμων	ἐποίουν	ἐδήλουν	ἐδίδουν	ἐτίθην	ἵστην	ἐδείκνυν	**I was -ing**
ἔλυες	ἐτίμας	ἐποίεις	ἐδήλους	ἐδίδους	ἐτίθεις	ἵστης	ἐδείκνυς	you were -ing
ἔλυε	ἐτίμα	ἐποίει	ἐδήλου	ἐδίδου	ἐτίθει	ἵστη	ἐδείκνυ	he/she/it was -ing
ἐλύομεν	ἐτιμῶμεν	ἐποιοῦμεν	ἐδηλοῦμεν	ἐδίδομεν	ἐτίθεμεν	ἵσταμεν	ἐδείκνυμεν	we were -ing
ἐλύετε	ἐτιμᾶτε	ἐποιεῖτε	ἐδηλοῦτε	ἐδίδοτε	ἐτίθετε	ἵστατε	ἐδείκνυτε	you were -ing
ἔλυον	ἐτίμων	ἐποίουν	ἐδήλουν	ἐδίδοσαν	ἐτίθεσαν (or ἐδίδουν)	ἵστασαν	ἐδείκνυσαν	they were –ing

Imperfect Middle/Passive

ἐλύομην	ἐτιμώμην	ἐποιούμην	ἐδηλούμην	ἐδιδόμην	ἐτιθέμην	ἱστάμην	ἐδεικνύμην	**I was being -ed**
ἐλύου	ἐτιμῶ	ἐποίου	ἐδηλοῦ	ἐδίδοσο	ἐτίθεσο	ἵστασο	ἐδείκνυσο	you were being -ed
ἐλύετο	ἐτιμᾶτο	ἐποιεῖτο	ἐδηλοῦτο	ἐδίδοτο	ἐτίθετο	ἵστατο	ἐδείκνυτο	he/she/it was being -ed
ἐλυόμεθα	ἐτιμώμεθα	ἐποιούμεθα	ἐδηλούμεθα	ἐδιδόμεθα	ἐτιθέμεθα	ἱστάμεθα	ἐδεικνύμεθα	we were being -ed
ἐλύεσθε	ἐτιμᾶσθε	ἐποιεῖσθε	ἐδηλοῦσθε	ἐδίδοσθε	ἐτίθεσθε	ἵστασθε	ἐδείκνυσθε	you were being -ed
ἐλύοντο	ἐτιμῶντο	ἐποιοῦντο	ἐδηλοῦντο	ἐδίδοντο	ἐτίθεντο	ἵσταντο	ἐδείκνυντο	they were being -ed

Notes on Forms

1) You see that the 2nd singular personal ending (σο) in the **Omega** Conjugation always contracts with previous vowels, whether with the connecting vowel alone (o/ε), or the vowel of the verb stem itself (α, ε, or o). In each circumstance, the sigma (σ) does not enjoy its position between vowels, drops out, and thereby instigates the

contraction between vowels. But you can see in the **MI** Conjugation the unaffected personal ending, which (in these circumstances) does not contract with any preceding vowel.

2) You see in all four example verbs of the **MI** Conjugation the "pure" personal endings uncomplicated by contractions. You can also see that the verb stems are perfectly consistent and easily visible in every instance.

3) Even though you can see a fair amount of variation across these paradigms (especially with the vowel patterns connecting personal endings to verb stems), you can still discern enough of each ending to parse and translate it accurately.

The Uses of the Imperfect

The Greek Imperfect has several of the same "senses" as does the English Imperfect. One way to improve the depth of your reading (whether in English or in the GNT) is to ask which "sense" of the Imperfect might be at work in a given passage.

<table>
<tr>
<td>Descriptive/
Dramatic:</td>
<td>Oftentimes we will use the "was x'ing" expression in English simply to tell a story more *vividly*, to help listeners get into the feel of the event. Instead of "the mummy stood up," we could say, "The mummy was standing up…!"</td>
</tr>
<tr>
<td>Customary:</td>
<td>Sometimes Greek writers employed an Imperfect to describe behaviors that regularly or *habitually* took place. A good translation of a Customary Imperfect might be: "John *would regularly* pray far into the night," or "John *usually* prayed far into the night," or "John *used to* pray far into the night." [Note, there would be no separate words for *usually*, *would regularly*, or *used to* in the Greek. The Imperfect tense (along with the context) could convey these notions.]</td>
</tr>
<tr>
<td>Iterative:</td>
<td>Sometimes Greek writers wanted to highlight the *repetitive* nature of an action which was not necessarily a matter of custom or habit. A good translation of such an Iterative Imperfect might be: "Jane was *repeatedly* wiping the brow of the crash victim," or "Jane *kept on* wiping the brow of the crash victim." [Again, no separate words for *repeatedly*, or *kept on* would be required Greek. The Imperfect tense (along with the context) could convey these notions.]</td>
</tr>
</table>

The Formation of the 1st Principal Part from Various Verb Roots

In our vocabulary lists up to this point, we have been placing the *root* of each verb in *brackets* without explanation. Now we need to draw back the curtain to reveal the connections between the verb root and the many various forms that Greek verbs can take. The key to it all is to understand that a *verb root* must be transformed into (one of) *six different principal parts* so that *all the various forms of a verb* can then be constructed from those principal parts. When you can clearly see this movement from (one) *root*, through (six) *principal parts*, to (dozens of) *verb forms*, you will "get it"! In other words, you can think of the six principal parts as the *middle men*, or as *traffic hubs*. You can't travel from a verb root to any particular form of a Greek verb without traveling through one of the six principal parts.

This means, of course, that we have *already* been "traveling through" the First Principal Part *without knowing it!* That's right! All forms of the Present and Imperfect Tenses of the Indicative mood are built from the **FIRST** Principal Part. But how is the First Principal Part itself built?

To understand how this works, imagine that a *verb root* must be sent into **The First Principal Part Factory**, which will convert the root into a *finished product* (the First Principal Part) through one of several *manufacturing processes*. The *engineer* who accepts the verb root into the factory makes a (somewhat mysterious) *choice* as to which *assembly line* (A–F) the root should travel. Since those assembly lines differ from one another in their machinery, *the appearance of the finished product* (the First Principal Part) *will depend entirely upon the assembly line chosen by the engineer!*

To visualize the process, study the diagram below. Notice the different "machinery" used in the various assembly lines.

Now we can examine how the verbs we have learned so far travel down different assembly lines to form the First Principal Part.

[In what follows, we will stay at a general level of analysis, and will not be supplying in-depth explanations of how each assembly line works. As you will see, numbers of adjustments are required when various consonants and vowels come into contact with each other. At a later point in your study of Greek, you will find a more precise accounting for these changes intriguing and enlightening.]

Assembly Line A

As you can see in the diagram, there are no machines or workers on Assembly Line A! Nothing happens! The verb root enters the Line and exits the line without any changes* being made, except that (conceptually speaking!) the product is "stamped" with its new identification tag: "First Principal Part." [*Well, O.K.! Sometimes the length of the root vowel is lengthened, or extended into a diphthong…but other than *that* (!), nothing happens.]

Many verbs we have studied have traveled down Assembly Line A. In the following forms (Present Active Indicative, 1st person, singular) notice the underlined portion. It is the unmodified verb root, clearly visible, now functioning as the First Principal Part (from which the Present Tense must be formed):

$$\underline{λύω} \qquad \underline{λέγω} \qquad \underline{βλέπω} \qquad \underline{ἄγω} \qquad \underline{φέρω}$$

$$\underline{κρίνω} \qquad \underline{γραφω} \qquad \underline{ἀκούω} \qquad \underline{πιστεύω} \qquad \underline{ν}ω$$

$$\underline{τιμάω} \qquad \underline{δηλόω} \qquad \underline{ποιέω} \qquad \underline{φοβέομαι}$$

[We show these contract verbs in uncontracted form to show the root]

$$\underline{πορεύομαι} \qquad \underline{ἔρχομαι}$$

[Including all of the many compound forms of these verbs.]

$$\underline{ἔχω}$$

[The root is actually σεχ, but the sigma (σ) has dropped off.]

Assembly Line B

The process of (iota) reduplication [is this word itself redundant?] takes the ***initial consonant*** of the root, ***repeats*** it, and connects it to the root by means of an ***iota*** (ι). Sometimes the results are clearly visible and immediately understandable. At other times, a secondary procedure partly masks the original reduplication process.

Root	First Principal Part	Explanation
δο	δίδωμι	The delta (δ) is reduplicated. [Don't worry about the lengthening of the omicron.]
θε	τίθημι	The theta (θ) is reduplicated. [Two thetas in succession must be changed to τ… θ.]
στα	ἵστημι	The sigma (σ) is reduplicated. [The initial sigma reduces to a rough breathing.]
πτ	πίπτω	The pi (π) is reduplicated.
γνω	γινώσκω	The gamma (γ) is reduplicated. [The second gamma then drops out.]
δακ	διδάσκω	The delta (δ) is reduplicated. [Note the second process of adding σκω.]
γεν	γίνομαι	The gamma (γ) is reduplicated. [The second gamma drops out, etc.]

Assembly Line C

We have not yet learned any verbs using this Assembly Line. [Of the 16 or so verbs in the NT in this category, none is used frequently enough to detain us in this first semester of our work.]

Assembly Line D

In the most puzzling of all Assembly Lines, a "consonantal iota" (actually an English "y" sound) is added to the end of the verb root. This "consonantal iota" is never visible in Greek spelling, but has left evidence of its presence by changing other letters in the verb root.

Root	First Principal Part	Explanation
βαλ	βάλλω	The suffixed iota causes the lambda (λ) to be doubled.
στελ	ἀποστέλλω	The suffixed iota causes the lambda (λ) to be doubled.
σωιδ	σῴζω	The suffixed iota converts the delta (δ) into a ζ. The iota is then subscripted.
κηρυγ	κηρύσσω	The suffixed iota converts the gamma (γ) into a σσ.
εγερ	ἐγείρω	The suffixed iota ultimately lengthens the root vowel (ε) into a diphthong (ει).
αρ	αἴρω	The suffixed iota ultimately lengthens the root vowel (α) into a diphthong (αι).

Assembly Line E

Along this Line a liquid consonant (λ μ ν ρ) in *some* form will be attached to the root. Sometimes it will be attached to the end of the root; otherwise positioned internally. Sometimes the liquid letter will bring along its own vowel (thereby creating an additional syllable).

Root	First Principal Part	Explanation
λαβ	λαμβάνω	A mu (μ) is inserted, and an alpha-nu syllable (αν) is attached to the end.
δεικ	δείκνυμι	A nu-upsilon syllable (νυ) suffix is attached.
βα	βαίνω	A nu (ν) is added, which results (because of other "complications" we won't mention) in the alpha (α) being transformed into a diphthong (αι).

Assembly Line F

Here the suffix (ι)σκω is added to the stem.

Root	First Principal Part	Explanation
γνω	γινώσκω	Notice that this word has also traveled Line B for reduplication. (See p. 143)
αποθαν	ἀποθνῄσκω	The alpha (α) of the root is "zeroed out," and an eta (η) is added to compensate for the loss. Then the iota (ι) of the suffix ισκω is subscripted beneath the eta (η).
δακ	διδάσκω	Notice that this word has also traveled Line C for reduplication
ευρ	εὑρίσκω	Here the suffix is ισκω

Assembly Line "G"

Some evidence exists that a very old Assembly Line, which added the suffix θι to form the First Principle Part, had for a time been operational. Only a few traces of its work remain.

Root	First Principal Part	Explanation
εδ	ἐσθίω	The delta (δ), when followed by a theta (θ), was converted into a sigma (σ).

Root, the 1st Principal Part, and the Lexical Entry

The value of knowing the verb root will emerge more clearly in the next chapter when we study the Future tense. You will discover that the Future, along with many other Greek verb tenses, is built from *one of the other five Principal Parts*, not built from the First!

And yet, unfortunately, it is the First Principal Part (rather than the root) which has been chosen by tradition to stand as a verb's "name tag," or Lexical Entry, in most Greek dictionaries. So you will be told, for example, that the Greek verb meaning "take/receive" is λαμβάνω, and you will imagine (unwisely) that from *this* form all other forms of this verb will be built. By now you know that λαβ (and *not* λαμβάνω) is the root of this verb from which all the various forms of this verb will ultimately be derived. You must learn, therefore, to recognize the Dictionary Entry (e.g. λαμβάνω) merely as one "branch office" of a verb, and must remember that the "corporate office" which runs all the "branch offices" may not look much like the Dictionary Entry.

Neuter Plural Subjects with 3rd Singular Verbs

In the GNT it is common to find a neuter plural subject taking a 3rd singular verb (instead of a 3rd plural verb).

The "Normal:"	τὰ τέκνα βλέπουσι τὸν κύριον	The children are seeing the Lord.
A common "Abnormality:"	τὰ τέκνα βλέπει τὸν κύριον	The children are seeing the Lord.

The Imperfect Indicative of εἰμί

Because the verb "to be" is stative (i.e. not expressing action, but state), it is not really appropriate to parse it with "voice" (Active, Middle, or Passive), even though Mounce treats these forms (in his Interlinear Code) as Active. We will simply *omit* reference to *voice*, so that we will parse ἤμην as "Imperfect, —, Indicative, First Person, Singular."

	Singular	Plural
1st	ἤμην	ἦμεν
2nd	ἦς	ἦτε
3rd	ἦν	ἦσαν

New Testament Exploration

Matt 26:57–58   Now the ones who had arrested Jesus led him to Caiaphas, the high priest, where the scribes and the elders had gathered. ὁ δὲ Πέτρος ἠκολούθει αὐτῷ ἀπὸ μακρόθεν all the way to the high priest's courtyard, and after going in, he sat with the guards to see the outcome.

John 3:34–36   For the one whom God sent is speaking the words of God, for not by measure does he give the Spirit. ὁ πατὴρ ἀγαπᾷ τὸν υἱὸν καὶ πάντα δέδωκεν ἐν τῇ χειρὶ αὐτοῦ. The one who believes in the Son has eternal life. The one who rejects the Son will not see life, but God's wrath remains on him. (πατὴρ = *father*; πάντα δέδωκεν = *he has given all things*; χειρὶ = *hand*)

John 10:16–17   And I have other sheep that are not from this sheepfold. I must bring them too, and they will hear my voice, and there will be one flock and one shepherd. Διὰ τοῦτό με ὁ πατὴρ ἀγαπᾷ ὅτι ἐγὼ τίθημι τὴν ψυχήν μου, so that I might take it back again. (πατὴρ = *father*; ψυχήν = *soul*)

Matt 1:25   When Joseph awoke from sleep he did what teh angel of the Lord told him. He took his wife, καὶ οὐκ ἐγίνωσκεν αὐτὴν until she gave birth to a son, and he called his name Jesus.

Digging Deeper into the New Testament

1) Find **Mark 5:21-43** in your GNT, and in the Greek Interlinear. Read the ***entire episode*** (the raising of Jairus' daughter, and the healing of the bleeding woman) ***in English(!)***. For practice in pronouncing ***Greek***, read *5:24* aloud repeatedly.

2) Now we want to do a "treasure hunt" in the Greek Interlinear, searching for Imperfects throughout **Mark 5:21-43**. In order to do this, you need to know that the code Mounce has devised signals ***Imperfects*** with an "i" ***immediately following*** the initial part-of-speech designation [the part-

of-speech code for a verb is "v"]. Therefore, anytime you see a code beginning with "v.i…." you know you have an Imperfect verb on you hands. [And since the Imperfect Tense is found only in the Indicative Mood, the "mood slot" in the code of Imperfect verbs will be an "i" as well. The pattern for the Imperfect, then, would be **v.i?i.??**. (We've put question marks for voice, person, and number.)] You can see this code at work in the first verb of ***Mark 5:28***:

In this circumstance, the code should be interpreted as follows:

"thought"
ἔλεγεν
v.**i**ai.3s

Part of Speech	Tense	Voice	Mood	Person	Number
v	i	a	i	3	s
Verb	*Imperfect*	active	Indicative	3rd	Singular

Now scan through this entire passage (5:21-43) to <u>find all Imperfect verbs</u>. [You should find eleven (11) of them.] <u>Write each one out (in Greek), along with the English Translation (New International Version) supplied in the Interlinear at that point</u>.

Three (3) of the Imperfects you found are forms of εἰμί. Their Imperfect sense ("was") is fairly routine, and won't delay us further. But the seven (7) other Imperfects you found deserve closer inspection. For only one of them (5:32) does the NIV attempt in any way to convey the sense of the Imperfect. There the translators have chosen the expression "kept looking around" to convey the persistent, on-going effort of Jesus to detect who had touched him. Such a touch adds drama to the story, allowing us as readers to sense (perhaps) the woman's growing fear as Jesus keeps looking, and looking and looking…

But for each of the other six (6) Imperfects, the NIV has chosen to "flattened" the translation, giving English readers no clue that a Greek Imperfect lies beneath. Work with each of these verbs, and test out different ways of conveying the Imperfect [e.g., "kept x-ing", "x-ed and x-ed", "continually x-ed", "repeatedly x-ed", "went on x-ing", "habitually x-ed"]. Notice how much richer the story becomes, as these interpretive possibilities come into play. <u>This is why we're learning Greek!</u>

3) In your Interlinear at **5:24** you will find the English word "followed," with the Greek Imperfect verb ἠκολούθει beneath it. By using its vocabulary code (199), you can find it in Appendix B of the Interlinear, and then find its entry in **BDAG**. Examine this entry, noticing the five (5) different senses this verb may have from passage to passage. Which sense best applies here in Mark? How might you know that option 3 [to be a committed follower] probably does not work here? Do you see how a Greek word might have a "theologically insignificant" sense, while in other contexts might bear a "highly theologically significant" sense?

4) In Wallace's Intermediate Grammar *The Basics of NT Syntax* find pages 232-238 [*Greek Grammar Beyond the Basics*, pages 540–553]. Read these pages carefully, and follow closely the various nuances (subtle senses) of the Imperfect described here. Which uses of the Imperfect can be translated into English with a simple "was/were x'ing" formula, and which cannot? You might want to highlight Wallace's translation proposals (which he also calls 'keys to identification') to help you identify more clearly each nuance.

Chapter Ten Vocabulary

We will now add our last installment of vocabulary for this semester, bringing our total to around 160 words. [Chapters 11 and 12 will have no new vocabulary.] With the words below added into your memory bank, you will have learned most words that occur 100 times or more in the GNT. [The major exception is the set of third declension nouns and adjectives used 100 times or more, about 20 in number.]

The following words, all contract verbs, follow the same pattern as the alpha or epsilon contract verbs you have already learned. Notice that they all form their First Principal Part by moving down **Assembly Line A** (i.e. no change is made to the verb root). The verb root is easily visible in the Dictionary Entry (the First Principal Part).

Alpha Contract Verbs [Shown uncontracted to reveal the root]

ὁράω	[ορα]	*I see, perceive, experience*	Found with 7 different prefixes.
ἀγαπάω	[αγαπα]	*I love.*	Found with 0 different prefixes!
ζάω	[ζα]	*I live, I am alive.*	Found with 2 different prefixes.
γεννάω	[γεννα]	*I beget, I sire, I give birth to.*	Found with 1 prefix.

Epsilon Contract Verbs [Shown uncontracted to reveal the root]

λαλέω	[λαλε]	*I speak.*	Found with 6 different prefixes.
καλέω	[καλε]	*I call.*	Found with 10 different prefixes.
ζητέω	[ζητε]	*I seek.*	Found with 4 different prefixes.
ἀκολουθέω	[ακολουθε]	*I follow.*	Found with 5 different prefixes. [… "I follow someone" (in the dative)]

The Imperfect of the Verb "To Be"

	Singular		Plural	
1st	ἤμην	I was	ἦμεν	we were
2nd	ἦς	you were	ἦτε	you were
3rd	ἦν	he/she/it was	ἦσαν	they were

Exercises

I. Short Answer

1) <u>What time</u> (past, present or future) does the Greek <u>Imperfect</u> Tense signify?

2) <u>What aspect</u> (internal/continuous, external/undefined, or perfect) does the Greek <u>Imperfect</u> Tense signify?

3) How would you express (in English) these notions of time and aspect (of the Imperfect Tense) with the verb "run" in the first person singular, active voice?

4) From <u>which Principal Part</u> is the Greek <u>Imperfect</u> Tense built?

5) With what <u>set of personal endings</u> is the Greek <u>Imperfect</u> Tense built?

6) What <u>two kinds of augment</u> appear with Greek verbs in past-time tenses?

7) <u>How many</u> different <u>Principal Parts</u> would a "regular" Greek verb have?

8) From what <u>basic element</u> are <u>all Principal Parts</u> formed?

9) Even though we may find the word λαμβάνω in a Greek Lexicon, why is it that the other Principal Parts (and therefore many other forms of this word) will **not** be formed from this **Entry form**?

<u>Solutions to Exercise I</u>

1) past
2) internal/continuous
3) I was running (notice: past time; internal/continuous aspect)
4) the First Principal Part
5) secondary personal endings
6) syllabic [prefixed as an epsilon to a verb beginning with a consonant]; temporal [lengthening initial vowel of a verb so beginning]
7) six [We have only encountered the First Principal Part to this point.]
8) the Verb Root
9) Because the Entry Form is not the Root; it is only the First Principal Part. Tradition has dictated that we identify verbs by their First Principal Parts, not by their Roots. Perhaps in some ideal world we might all use dictionaries organized by Roots!

II. Drills with Present and Imperfect Verb Tenses

Increase your skill in recognizing, parsing and translating the Imperfect Tense with the following drills. Notice that the left-hand column contains Present Tense verbs, and that we move into the new territory of the Imperfect as we shift to the right-hand column. <u>Go over this exercise repeatedly until it begins to "flow" easily.</u>

It should also be helpful to forge a clear link between the "information" that the parsing gives us (e.g. Present Active Indicative, 2nd person Plural) and the English translation we supply (e.g. ya'll are sending…). Work through this drill repeatedly, until you understand exactly how the parsing information results in an accurate English translation.

1) Working with the verb: ἐγὼ

    a) ἐγὼ σῴζω τὰς βίβλους.

    b) ἐγὼ ἔσῳζον τὰς βίβλους.

    c) ἐγὼ σῴζομαι ὑπὸ τοῦ θεοῦ.

    d) ἐγὼ ἐσῳζόμην ὑπὸ τοῦ θεοῦ.

2) Working with the verb: διδάσκω

    a) σὺ διδάσκεις τοὺς ἀποστόλους.

    b) σὺ ἐδίδασκες τοὺς ἀποστόλους.

    c) σὺ διδάσκῃ ὑπὸ τῶν ἀποστόλων.

    d) σὺ ἐδιδάσκου ὑπὸ τῶν ἀποστόλων.

3) Working with the verb: τέκνον

    a) τὸ τέκνον γράφει τὴν βίβλον.

    b) τὸ τέκνον ἔγραφε τὴν βίβλον.

    c) ἡ βίβλος γράφεται ὑπὸ τοῦ τέκνου.

    d) ἡ βίβλος ἐγράφετο ὑπὸ τοῦ τέκνου.

4) Working with the verb: εὐαγγέλιον

    a) ἡμεῖς κηρύσσομεν τὸ εὐαγγέλιον.

    b) ἡμεῖς ἐκηρύσσομεν τὸ εὐαγγέλιον.

    c) ἡμεῖς ἀποστελλόμεθα τῷ εὐαγγελίῳ.

    d) ἡμεῖς ἀπεστελλόμεθα τῷ εὐαγγελίῳ.

5) Working with the verb: κόσμος

    a) ὑμεῖς κρίνετε τὸν κόσμον.

    b) ὑμεῖς ἐκρίνετε τὸν κόσμον.

    c) ὑμεῖς κρίνεσθε ὑπὸ τῶν ἀποστόλων.

    d) ὑμεῖς ἐκρίνεσθε ὑπὸ τῶν ἀποστόλων.

6) Working with the verb: διδάσκαλος

    a) οἱ διδάσκαλοι λύουσι τὴν ἁμαρτίαν.

    b) οἱ διδάσκαλοι ἔλυον τὴν ἁμαρτίαν.

    c) οἱ διδάσκαλοι ἀποθνήσκονται τῇ ἁμαρτίᾳ.

    d) οἱ διδάσκαλοι ἀπεθνήσκοντο τῇ ἁμαρτίᾳ

Solutions to Exercise II

1) a) ἐγὼ σῴζω τὰς βίβλους. I am saving the books. (Present Active Indicative, 1st Sing)
b) ἐγὼ ἔσῳζον τὰς βίβλους. I was saving the books. (Imperfect Active Indicative, 1st Sing)*
c) ἐγὼ σῴζομαι ὑπὸ τοῦ θεοῦ. I am being saved by God. (Present Mid/Pass Indicative, 1st Sing)
d) ἐγὼ ἐσῳζόμην ὑπὸ τοῦ θεοῦ. I was being saved by God. (Imperfect Mid/Pass Indicative, 1st Sing)

2) a) σὺ διδάσκεις τοὺς ἀποστόλους. You are teaching the apostles. (Present Active Indicative, 2nd Sing)
b) σὺ ἐδίδασκες τοὺς ἀποστόλους. You were teaching the apostles. (Imperfect Active Indicative, 2nd Sing)
c) σὺ διδάσκῃ ὑπὸ τῶν ἀποστόλων. You are being taught by the apostles. (Present Mid/Pass Indicative, 2nd Sing)

d) σὺ ἐδιδάσκου ὑπὸ τῶν ἀποστόλων. You were being taught by the apostles. (Imperfect Mid/Pass Indicative, 2nd Sing)

3) a) τὸ τέκνον γράφει τὴν βίβλον. The child is writing the book. (Present Active Indicative, 3rd Sing)
b) τὸ τέκνον ἔγραφε τὴν βίβλον. The child was writing the book. (Imperfect Active Indicative, 3rd Sing)
c) ἡ βίβλος γράφεται ὑπὸ τοῦ τέκνου. The book is being written by the child. (Present Mid/Pass Indicative, 3rd Sing)
d) ἡ βίβλος ἐγράφετο ὑπὸ τοῦ τέκνου. The book was being written by the child. (Imperfect Mid/Pass Indicative, 3rd Sing)

4) a) ἡμεῖς κηρύσσομεν τὸ εὐαγγέλιον. We are preaching the gospel. (Present Active Indicative, 1st Plural)
b) ἡμεῖς ἐκηρύσσομεν τὸ εὐαγγέλιον. We were preaching the gospel. (Imperfect Active Indicative, 1st Plural)
c) ἡμεῖς ἀποστελλόμεθα τῷ εὐαγγελίῳ. We are being sent by the gospel. (Present Mid/Pass Indicative, 1st Plural)
d) ἡμεῖς ἀπεστελλόμεθα τῷ εὐαγγελίῳ. We were being sent by the gospel. (Imperfect Mid/Pass Indicative, 1st Plural)

5) a) ὑμεῖς κρίνετε τὸν κόσμον. You are judging the world. (Present Active Indicative, 2nd Plural)
b) ὑμεῖς ἐκρίνετε τὸν κόσμον. You were judging the world. (Imperfect Active Indicative, 2nd Plural)
c) ὑμεῖς κρίνεσθε ὑπὸ τῶν ἀποστόλων. You are being judged by the apostles. (Present Mid/Pass Indicative, 2nd Plural)
d) ὑμεῖς ἐκρίνεσθε ὑπὸ τῶν ἀποστόλων. You were being judged by the apostles. (Imperfect Mid/Pass Indicative, 2nd Plural)

6) a) οἱ διδάσκαλοι λύουσι τὴν ἁμαρτίαν. The teachers are destroying sin. (Present Active Indicative, 3rd Plural)
b) οἱ διδάσκαλοι ἔλυον τὴν ἁμαρτίαν The teachers were destroying sin. (Imperfect Active Indicative, 3rd Plural)*
c) οἱ διδάσκαλοι ἀποθνήσκονται τῇ ἁμαρτίᾳ. The teachers are being killed by sin. (Present Mid/Pass Indicative, 3rd Plural)
d) οἱ διδάσκαλοι ἀπεθνήσκοντο τῇ ἁμαρτίᾳ The teachers were being killed by sin. (Imperfect Mid/Pass Indicative, 3rd Plural)
*Note: Remember that the forms (blue family) of the First Person Singular and Third Person Plural are identical (ον) in the Imperfect Active Indicative. Only the context of the Greek sentence can guide you in deciding how to parse the form. There may be occasions when the context itself could be ambiguous, and interpretations of the passage would then differ.

III. Synthetic Sentences

The sentences below gather together most of what we have learned so far, including vocabulary. As usual, **1)** parse verbs; **2)** identify the cases and their uses; **3)** note the position of adjectives; **4)** identify and explain pronouns; **5)** provide a smooth English translation; **6)** diagram each sentence, with special attention to positioning clauses appropriately; **7)** and write out at least two sentences in Greek.

1) ἡ δόξα τοῦ θεοῦ διὰ τῆς ἐκκλησίας ἐδηλοῦτο, καὶ τὰ ἔργα τῆς δικαιοσύνης ὑπὸ τῶν ἁγίων ἀποστόλων ἐποιοῦντο.

2) αἱ ἀλήθειαι τῆς βασιλείας τῷ ὄχλῳ ἐλαλοῦντο καλῶς, καθὼς οἱ διδάσκαλοι ἐκεῖνοι αὐτὰς ἐκ τῶν πρώτων ἀποστόλων ἤκουον.

3) εἰ τὸν ἡμῶν κύριον ἐν ταῖς καρδίαις ὑμῶν ἀγαπᾶτε, γινώσκετε ὅτι αὐτὸς τὰ τέκνα τῆς ἀγάπης καὶ εἰρήνης πάντοτε γεννᾷ.

4) εἰ καὶ ἐκ τῶν ὅδων τοῦ θανάτου τὰ ὑμῶν τέκνα ἐκαλοῦντο, οὐκέτι τῷ κυρίῳ τῆς ζωῆς ἠκολούθουν ἢ ἐλάμβανον τὸ δῶρον τῆς βασιλείας αὐτοῦ.

5) ἐν ταύτῃ τῇ ἡμέρᾳ ἐν οὐρανοῖς κατὰ τὸν νόμον τῆς ἀγάπης ζῆτε, ἐπι γὰρ τῆς γῆς ἐν ἐκείνῃ τῇ ἡμέρῃ τὸν ἄρτον τῆς ζωῆς ἠσθίετε.

6) οἱ υἱοὶ τῆς εἰρήνης ἀπεθνήσκοντο ὑπὸ τοῦ διδασκάλου ἐκείνου, νῦν δὲ αὐτὸς κηρύσσει ὅτι ὁ κύριος ἡμῶν ὁ υἱὸς τοῦ θεοῦ ἦν καί ἐστίν.

7) διὰ τὸ εὐαγγέλιον εἰς τὸν κόσμον εἰσηρχόμην, ἐκ δὲ τοῦ αὐτοῦ κόσμου ἐξήρχοντο διὰ τὴν ἁμαρτίαν καὶ τὸν θάνατον.

8) ὑπὸ τὴν ἐξουσίαν τῆς ἁμαρτίας ἡ ψυχή μου νεκρὰ ἦν, ἀλλὰ νῦν ἐν τῇ τοῦ μόνου υἱοῦ τοῦ θεοῦ δόξῃ ζῶ, καὶ ἐν ταῖς ὅδοις τῆς δικαιοσύνης πορεύομαι.

9) εἰ καὶ ὁ θεὸς ὁ ἅγιος αὐτοὺς ἐκάλει, οἱ υἱοὶ τῶν ἀνθρώπων οὐκ ἀπεκρίνοντο ὅτι οἱ αὐτῶν ὀφθαλμοὶ τὰς τῆς ἀληθείας ὅδους ἐφοβοῦντο.

10) τὰ ἕτερα εὐαγγέλια ὑπὸ τῶν ἑτέρων ἀποστόλων ἐκηρύσσετο, ἡμεῖς δὲ τὸ εὐαγγέλιον τοῦτο ὅτι ὁ ἡμῶν θεὸς τοὺς νεκροὺς ἐγείρει.

11 : The Future Tense

Pulling it all together: The Conception and the Construction of Verbs

You might say that we've been riding on two separate rails as we've been studying verbs. One rail is the ***conceptual framework***, or the world of ideas involved with verbs. As you know, verbs have certain characteristics (tense, voice, mood, person, number) that convey various ideas that are combined in any given verbal form. If we hope to interpret accurately any particular verb we meet in the GNT, we must provide a "meaning" for each of the "ideas" embedded in that particular verb form appropriate to that literary context.

The other rail we have been traveling is that of verb formation, or ***verb construction***. How are the various verb forms assembled? Out of what parts and pieces is a particular verb form built? In previous lessons we have learned that the verb ***Root*** is the bedrock element which is transformed into (usually) six ***Principal Parts***, to which may be added a variety of ***Accessories*** (augments, connecting vowels, personal endings) to make the individual verb forms we actually meet in Greek texts.

Now we want to bring these two rails closer together. When you see how verb *form* and verb *function* interconnect, the Greek verb system will "click together" in your mind. But before snapping these rails together, we need to finish building an overview of 1) verb ***construction*** and of 2) verb ***conception***.

Overview of the Construction of the Greek Verb

We have already learned that a ***Verb Root*** lies at the very bottom of every Greek verb. We also now know that the verb root must go through various "factories" or "manufacturing processes" to be converted into each of the six ***Principal Parts*** from which the many (different) actual Greek verb forms are built. We could map the overall process as follows:

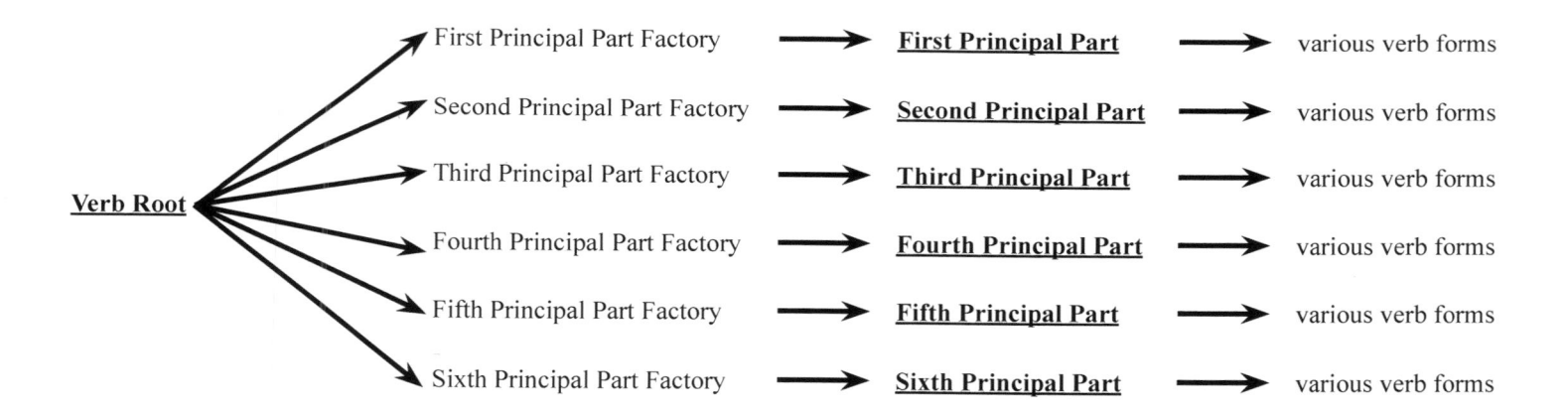

Let's see what this looks like with a real Greek verb. Standard Greek reference resources (e.g. lexicons, grammars) will tell us that the *six Principal Parts* of λύω are as follows:

First Pr. Prt.	Second Pr. Prt.	Third Pr. Prt.	Fourth Pr. Prt.	Fifth Pr. Prt.	Sixth Pr. Prt.
λύω	λύσω	ἔλυσα	λέλυκα	λέλυμαι	ἐλύθην

[An Extremely Important Note: If I could stand on my head and scream, or create a flashing neon sign right at this point…I would! Ponder what follows until it sinks in completely: When we look up a Greek verb in the dictionary (e.g. in BDAG the form λύω), we are seeing that verb's FIRST PRINCIPAL PART, not its ROOT!! In other words, the dictionary entry is NOT the basic form from which all other forms of that verb are built. The dictionary entry (the First Principal Part) is simply one of several offshoots the root will generate.

This realization must be followed by a second, equally important, realization: that the dictionary entry (i.e. the First Principal Part) must NOT be imagined to be the BASIC form of the verb from which the other Principal Parts are formed. It is necessary that we tell ourselves over and over that the First Principle Part is not necessarily "first" or "foremost" or "more important" in any meaningful way. All the Principal Parts are "brothers and sisters" of equal standing, each descending directly from their single parent (the root) and not from another Principal Part.**]**

It wouldn't hurt for us to be redundant here to make our point as clearly as possible. We have simply rearranged the diagram on the previous page to show in yet another way how the verb root and the dictionary entry are two completely different entities.

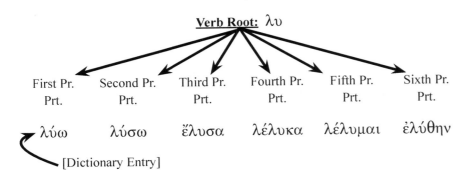

Note again that there is NO genetic movement from the First to the Second Principal Part (and so on). Each Principal Part is a direct offspring from the Root, and is NOT a child of any other Principal Part. So when you look up a verb in BDAG, you must insist (in your own mind) on identifying that dictionary entry simply as one child among other children (the other Principal Parts). [Unfortunately, most dictionaries never identify a verb's root (the parent form).]

Another **un**helpful habit of tradition is that we are usually given (in various verb lists) a verb's Principal Parts in their "dressed up" forms. Take a look again at the list of Principal Parts for the verb λύω below. This time, we'll strip augments, connecting vowels, and personal endings from the Principal Part to reveal the "naked Principal Part" hidden inside.

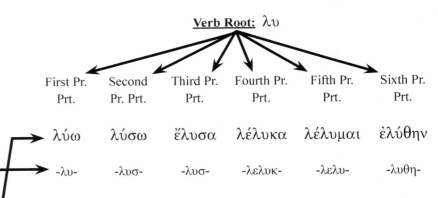

Dressed-up Forms: An *actually-occurring* 1st person singular form (in a specific tense/voice/mood) used to *represent* all other forms within the lineage of that Principal Part.

"Naked" Forms: The *theoretical* "stem" from which all forms found within this lineage are actually formed.

In other words, the Verb Root is transformed into "naked" Principal Parts, to which then are added various <u>augments</u>, <u>connecting vowels</u>, <u>suffixes</u>, and <u>personal endings</u> to construct all "real" verb forms. Below we have placed the *clothed* Principal Parts in *parentheses*, in order to draw attention to the "*naked*" forms, which are the real points of genesis for their respective families.

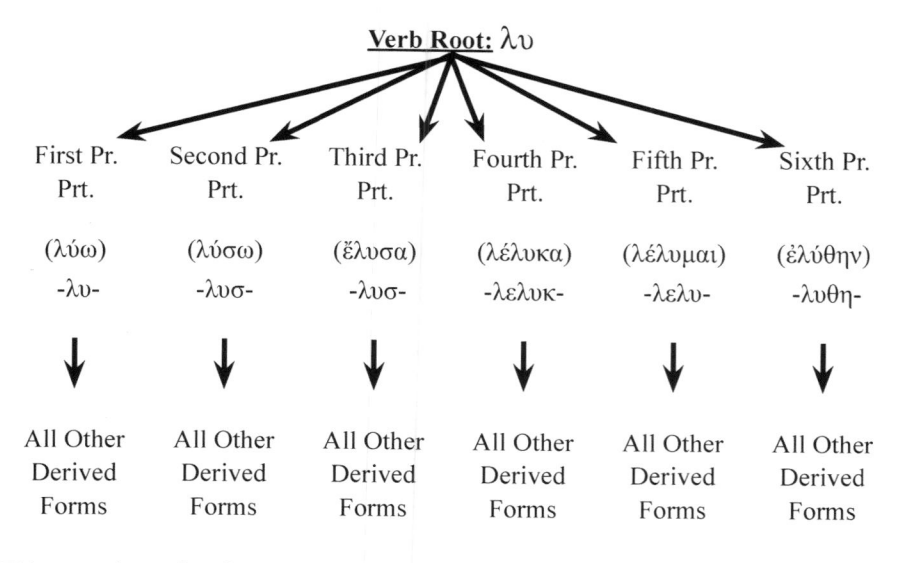

Verb Root: λυ

First Pr. Prt.	Second Pr. Prt.	Third Pr. Prt.	Fourth Pr. Prt.	Fifth Pr. Prt.	Sixth Pr. Prt.
(λύω)	(λύσω)	(ἔλυσα)	(λέλυκα)	(λέλυμαι)	(ἐλύθην)
-λυ-	-λυσ-	-λυσ-	-λελυκ-	-λελυ-	-λυθη-
All Other Derived Forms	All Other Derived Forms	All Other Derived Forms	All Other Derived Forms	All Other Derived Forms	All Other Derived Forms

This overview of verb construction will carry us far. As we continue learning new verb Tenses and Moods, we will see that they are formed by *attaching* a variety of *accessories* (augments, suffixes, connecting vowels, personal endings, declensional endings) onto the *naked Principal Parts*.

Conceptual Overview of the Greek Verb

We have already done significant work (in Chapter Two) establishing and explaining the categories of *Mood*, *Tense*, *Voice*, *Person* and *Number*. [You might want to review that material if it is foggy.] The *following chart* synthesizes these matters into a visual arrangement, while extending and adding a few elements. Study the following features of the chart:

1) From the top, the largest division relates to *Aspect*. The chart shows that all Greek verbs must fall within one of three Aspects: <u>Internal</u> (ongoing, repeated action viewed as "in process"); <u>External</u> (action viewed as a whole, without interest in its duration or internal stages); <u>Perfect</u> (action viewed as finished with an extended effect of some sort).

2) The vertical columns of Aspect are further divided into *Voice*. You can see that the Internal and Perfect Aspects do not have separate forms for Middle and Passive voices, while the External Aspect makes distinction between Middle and Passive forms.

3) You see that the vertical columns of Aspect and Voice extend downward, fully intersecting the four *Moods*, and beneath them two *Modes*. You are familiar with Moods [Indicative, Subjunctive, Imperative, Optative], which register different ways of presenting reality. The Modes work a completely different angle: an *Infinitive* is a verb functioning like a *noun*; while a *Participle* is a verb functioning like an *adjective*. [We will touch more on this in Chapter Twelve.]

4) You can see that each *intersection* between the vertical columns [Aspect, Voice] and horizontal rows [Moods (with time) and Moods and Modes (without time)] have a three-element "*name,*" e.g. the "Aorist Active Indicative" or the "Perfect Mid/Passive Participle". [We have omitted the Mood/Mode portion of the name from each intersection to save space. You should attach it yourself.] If you listen to the (whole!) name of the intersection, you can immediately locate that intersection on the chart, and (more importantly) know its *characteristics* [in terms of mood, tense, voice, and aspect].

5) You can also see that *Time* (the fixing of an action into real past, real present, or real future) is a creature *only of the Indicative Mood*! No Mood or Mode (other than the Indicative) should be spoken of as expressing past, present, or future time. When non-Indicative Moods or Modes do imply some "time value" within a sentence, that "time value" is derived from and relative to other elements in the sentence. **Note this well**: Given the fact that "time" is an independent characteristic operating only in the Indicative Mood, we must realize that "tradition" has again created confusion by naming the Internal-Aspect Tenses of the Subjunctive, Imperative, Optative, Infinitive, and Participle as "Present" Tenses. There is nothing necessarily "Present" about them! Yes, they

belong to the same family of verb forms that form the Present Indicative (hence their name), but their Tense significance has nothing to do with "present time." In these moods and modes, "Present Tense" means only *Internal Aspect*!

	Internal Aspect		External Aspect			Perfect Aspect	
	Active	Mid/Pass	Active	Middle	Passive	Active	Mid/Pass
Indicative [Mood] Present Time	**Present** Active	**Present** Mid/Pass	(no forms)	(no forms)	(no forms)	**Perfect** Present	**Perfect** Mid/Pass
Past Time	**Imperfect** Active	**Imperfect** Mid/Pass	**Aorist** Active	**Aorist** Middle	**Aorist** Passive	**PluPerfect** Active	**PluPerfect** Mid/Pass
Future Time	(no forms)	(no forms)	**Future** Active	**Future** Middle	**Future** Passive	**Fut. Perfect** Active	**Fut. Perfect** Mid/Pass
Subjunctive [Mood]	**Present** Active	**Present** Mid/Pass	**Aorist** Active	**Aorist** Middle	**Aorist** Passive	(rare or n/a)	(rare or n/a)
Imperative [Mood]	**Present** Active	**Present** Mid/Pass	**Aorist** Active	**Aorist** Middle	**Aorist** Passive	(rare or n/a)	(rare or n/a)
Optative [Mood]	**Present** Active	**Present** Mid/Pass	**Aorist** Active	**Aorist** Middle	**Aorist** Passive	(rare or n/a)	(rare or n/a)
Infinitive [Mood]	**Present** Active	**Present** Mid/Pass	**Aorist** Active	**Aorist** Middle	**Aorist** Passive	**Perfect** Active	**Perfect** Mid/Pass
Participle [Mood]	**Present** Active	**Present** Mid/Pass	**Aorist** Active	**Aorist** Middle	**Aorist** Passive	**Perfect** Active	**Perfect** Mid/Pass

1) In order to absorb the chart well, you will find it necessary to "mull it over." A great way to do this is to read aloud, block-by-block, each "name" in each intersection. (Be sure to add the name of the Mood/Mode to create the necessary 3-part identification for each intersection.) Go through the chart row-by-row (horizontally), then column-by-column (vertically). For example, if you were reading the first column (from top to bottom) you would say: "Present-Active-Indicative; Imperfect-Active-Indicative; Present-Active-Subjunctive; Present-Active-Imperative; Present-Active-Optative; Present-Active-Infinitive; Present-Active-Participle." If you were reading the Infinitive row you would say: "Present-Active-Infinitive; Present-Middle/Passive-Infinitive; Aorist-Active-Infinitive; Aorist-Middle-Infinitive; Aorist-Passive-infinitive; Perfect-Active-Infinitive; Perfect-Middle/Passive-Infinitive.

2) You will notice that certain blocks either have no forms or are very rare, especially in the columns of the Perfect Aspect. One likely cause for lower usage was the complexity and length of the Greek verb forms in these locations. Actual Greek speakers found simpler ways to express their ideas than using the "full blown" forms that would have stood in these blocks.

Integrating Principal Parts with the Conceptual Overview of the Verb

The time has come to pull it all together. In the chart on the next page we will see that the mechanisms for generating the forms of Greek verbs [root, principal part] *correlate nicely* with the conceptual overview displayed on the previous page. As you study the integrated chart you will notice the following patterns of interaction:

First Principal Part:	From this building block are built all forms in both columns of the Internal Aspect.
Third Principal Part:	From this building block are built all* forms in the Active and Middle columns of External Aspect [*except for the Active and Middle Future Indicative].
Sixth Principal Part:	From this building block are built all forms in the Passive column of External Aspect.
Fourth Principal Part:	From this building block are built all forms in the Active column of Perfect Aspect.
Fifth Principal Part:	From this building block are built all forms in the Middle/ Passive column of Perfect Aspect.
Second Principal Part:	From this building block are built *only* the Future Active and Middle of the Indicative Mood.

As you pour over the integrated chart on the following page and grasp its interlocking features (both in terms of verb formation and in terms of parsing information), you will find yourself extremely well positioned for absorbing all future instruction (from Intermediate to Advanced levels) regarding the Greek verb. Every minute spent mastering this unified vision will yield a harvest far exceeding the initial cost of seed!

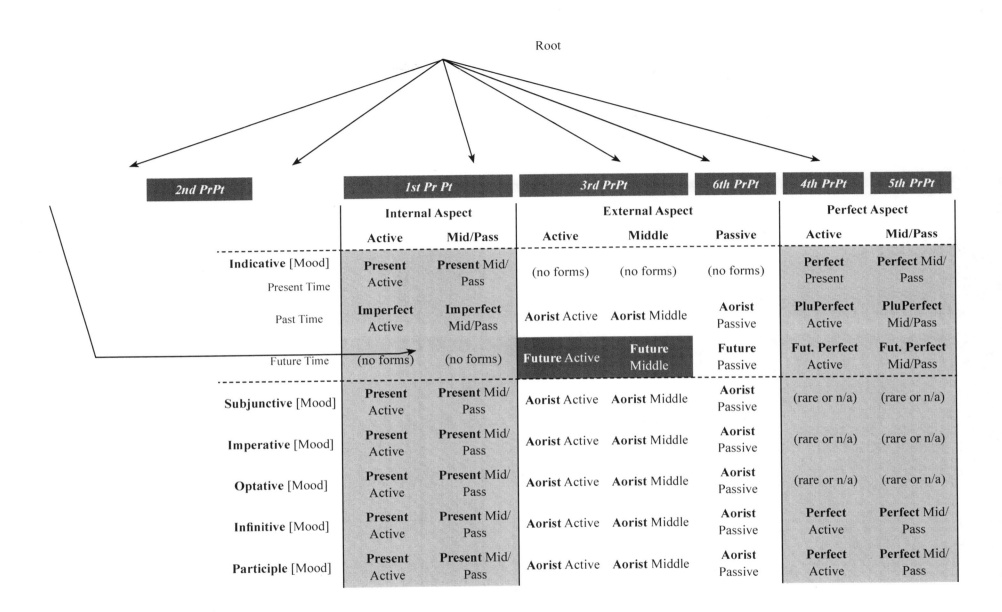

The Future Tense (its basic idea)

Now that we have taken the time to project the entire landscape of the Greek verb, it should be much easier to learn the Future Tense. From the unified chart above you can see several features of the Greek Future without much trouble:

1)   The Future is found *only in the Indicative Mood*. [With few exceptions in the GNT, time is "fixed" or "determined" only in the Indicative Mood.]

2)   You can see that the Future Tense has *External Aspect*. [By and large, the Future Tense views an action as a whole, not as a progressive or staged series. This does not mean that the action itself is not progressive or staged "in the real world," only that the writer's perspective, presentation, and interests are External, "outside the event," viewing it as a whole.]

3)   You can see that the Future Tense will have three (3) sets of forms which express *Active, Middle* and *Passive Voices* distinctly. [In other words, there is no sharing of forms by the Middle and Passive as in Present and Imperfect Tenses.]

4)   You can see that the *Future Active* and *Future Middle* will be formed from the Second Principal Part, while the *Future Passive* will be formed from the Sixth Principal Part.

The Forms of the Future (Active, Middle, and Passive) Indicative of λύω

Future Active Indicative		*Future* Middle Indicative		*Future* Passive Indicative	
λύσω	"I will destroy"	λύσομαι	"I myself will destroy"	λυθήσομαι	"I will be destroyed"
λύσειςßß	"you will destroy"	λύσηßß	"you yourself will destroy"	λυθήσῃ	"you will be destroyed"
λύσει	"he/she/it will destroy"	λύσεται	"he/she/it himself will destroy"	λυθήσεται	"he/she/it will be destroyed"
λύσομεν	"we will destroy"	λυσόμεθα	"we ourselves will destroy"	λυθησόμεθα	"we will be destroyed"
λύσετε	"y'all will destroy"	λύσεσθε	"y'all yourselves will destroy"	λυθήσεσθε	"y'all will be destroyed"
λύσουσι(ν)	"they will destroy"	λύσονται	"they themselves will destroy"	λυθήσονται	"they will be destroyed"

The Formation of the Future

As you read through these forms, you probably noticed that you've met all of these *endings before*! That's really good news! All of the personal endings (and their connecting vowels) in the Future come straight over from the forms of the Present Active and Middle/Passive [Indicative] we have already learned. [These endings are called Primary Endings.]

What this means, of course, is that what *distinguishes* these Future forms from the Present forms is that the Future is built from the *Second* Principal Part (in the Active and Middle Voices) and the *Sixth* Principal Part (in the Passive Voice), *not from the*

First. We now need to understand how these two Principal Parts (second and sixth) are manufactured from the verb root.

The Formation of the Second Principal Part

The Second Principal Part is formed from the verb Root, as you certainly should know by now! But the optional Assembly Lines are fewer than those found in the First Principal Part Factory.

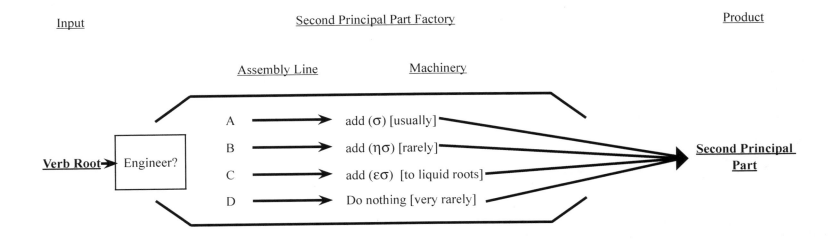

The "no-problem" Verbs *(add σ or ησ to the Verb Root)*

For **most** of the verbs we have learned, **Assembly Line A** is the pathway chosen by our mysterious engineer. As with λύσω, the **sigma is added** to the root, and personal endings [connecting vowels and endings] are added without difficulty.

1st PrinPart (Dictionary Entry)	Translation	Verb Root	2nd PrinPart (Fut/Act/Ind/1s)	Translation	Comments
λύω	*I am destroying*	[λυ]	λύσω	*I will destroy*	Perfectly regular and obvious
ἀκούω	*I am hearing*	[ακου]	ἀκούσω	*I will hear*	Perfectly regular and obvious
πιστεύω	*I am believing*	[πιστευ]	πιστεύσω	*I will believe*	Perfectly regular and obvious
πορεύομαι	*I am going*	[πορευ]	πορεύσομαι	*I will go*	Deponent (mid) in the Future as well

The "mi" verbs turn out to be very predictable, once it is realized (as now we should!) that we build the 2nd Principal Part from the verb Root, not the Dictionary Entry (1st PrinPrt). In these verbs the vowel which ends the root is lengthened before the sigma.

1st PrinPart (Dictionary Entry)	Translation	Verb Root	2nd PrinPart (Fut/Act/Ind/1s)	Translation	Comments
ίδωμι	*I am giving*	[δο]	δώσω	*I will give*	Perfectly regular and obvious
ἵστημι	*I am setting*	[στα]	στήσω	*I will set*	Perfectly regular and obvious
τίθημι	*I am placing*	[θε]	θήσω	*I will place*	Perfectly regular and obvious

Short vowels at the end of a verb root are lengthened as the sigma is added: α to η; ε to η; and ο to ω.

1st PrinPart (Dictionary Entry)	Translation	Verb Root	2nd PrinPart (Fut/Act/Ind/1s)	Translation	Comments
ἀγαπάω	*I am loving*	[ἀγαπα]	ἀγαπήσω	*I will love*	Perfectly regular and obvious
ζάω	*I am living*	[ζα]	ζήσω	*I will live*	Perfectly regular and obvious
τιμάω	*I am honoring*	[τιμα]	τιμήσω	*I will honor*	Perfectly regular and obvious
ἀκολουθέω	*I am following*	[ἀκολουθε]	ἀκολουθήσω	*I will follow*	Perfectly regular and obvious
ζητέω	*I am seeking*	[ζητε]	ζητήσω	*I will seek*	Perfectly regular and obvious
καλέω	*I am calling*	[καλε]	καλέσω	*I will call*	Epsilon does not lengthen!
ποιέω	*I am making*	[ποιε]	ποιήσω	*I will make*	Perfectly regular and obvious
δηλόω	*I am showing*	[δηλο]	δηλώσω	*I will show*	Perfectly regular and obvious

1st PrinPart (Dictionary Entry)	Translation	Verb Root	2nd PrinPart (Fut/Act/Ind/1s)	Translation	Comments
βαίνω	*I am going*	[βα]	βήσομαι	*I will go*	Deponent in the Future
γινώσκω	*I know*	[γνο]	γνώσομαι	*I will know*	Deponent in the Future

A few verbs travel down Assembly Line B, forming the 2nd Principal Part by adding ησ to the Verb Root.

1st PrinPart (Dictionary Entry)	Translation	Verb Root	2nd PrinPart (Fut/Act/Ind/1s)	Translation	Comments
γίνομαι	*I am becoming*	[γεν]	γενήσομαι	*I will become*	Deponent in the Future as well.
εὑρίσκω	*I am finding*	[ευρ]	εὑρήσω	*I will find*	Perfectly regular and obvious.

The "some-problem" Verbs (adding σ to Verb Roots ending in mutes [π, β, φ, κ, γ, χ, τ, δ, θ])

If a verb root ends in a "mute" consonant, that consonant will contract with the sigma to form the 2nd Principal Part. Yet even after the contraction (amalgamation) has take place, the "s" sound can easily be heard, signaling the Future. The contraction pattern is:

	Mute Final Consonant of Verb Root				**2nd PrinPrt Suffix**		**Result**	
	Voiceless	Voiced	Asperate					
Labial (lips)	π	β	φ	+	σ	=	ψ	(labial + σ = ψ)
Velar (throat)	κ	γ	χ	+	σ	=	ξ	(velar + σ = ξ)
Dental (teeth)	τ	δ	θ	+	σ	=	σ	(dental + σ = σ)

1st PrinPart (Dictionary Entry)	Translation	Verb Root	2nd PrinPart (Fut/Act/Ind/1s)	Translation	Comments
ἄγω	*I am leading*	[αγ]	ἄξω	*I will lead*	Regular contraction, see above.
βλέπω	*I am seeing*	[βλεπ]	βλέψω	*I will see*	Regular contraction, see above.
γράφω	*I am writing*	[γραφ]	γράψω	*I will write*	Regular contraction, see above.
δείκνυμι	*I am showing*	[δεικ]	δείξω	*I will show*	Regular contraction, see above.
διδάσκω	*I am teaching*	[δακ]	διδάξω	*I will teach*	(See #1 below)
ἔχω	*I am having*	[σεχ]	ἕξω	*I will have*	(See #2 below)
κηρύσσω	*I am preaching*	[κηρυγ]	κηρύξω	*I will preach*	Regular contraction, see above.
λαμβάνω	*I am receiving*	[λαβ]	λήμψομαι	*I will receive*	(See #3 below)
σῴζω	*I am saving*	[σωδ]	σώσω	*I will save*	Regular contraction, see above.

Additional Notes:

1) Though the root technically is δακ, the reduplication continues in all Principal Parts as if the verb root were διδακ.

2) The loss of the initial sigma leaves its mark in the form of a rough breathing.

3) The root vowel has lengthened, and a mu (μ) has been retained, perhaps on analogy with the 1st Principal Part.

The "big-problem" Verbs (adding εσ to liquid roots)

One aggravating feature of the Greek verb relates to the Future (Active and Middle) of verbs whose roots end in a Liquid Consonant (λ, μ, ν, or ρ). It appears that an εσ is added to the verb root, but that the resulting combination of liquid-epsilon-sigma-connecting vowel (ε, ο) regularly ejects the sigma and contracts the remaining vowels. Observe the transformation:

(For Comparison) Present Tense	Root	Original Future Form	Loss of Sigma	Contracted Form	Translation
κρίνω	[κριν]	κρινέσω	κρινέ-ω	κρινῶ	*I will judge*
κρίνεις	[κριν]	κρινέσεις	κρινέ-εις	κρινεῖς	*you will judge*
κρίνει	[κριν]	κρινέσει	κρινέ-ει	κρινεῖ	*he/she/it will judge*
κρίνομεν	[κριν]	κρινέσομεν	κρινέ-ομεν	κρινοῦμεν	*we will judge*
κρίνετε	[κριν]	κρινέσετε	κρινέ-ετε	κρινεῖτε	*you will judge*
κρίνουσι	[κριν]	κρινέσουσι	κρινέ-ουσι	κρινοῦσι	*they will judge*

As you observe these liquid futures, two unpleasant facts will dawn upon you:

1) **Four** (4) of these Liquid Future forms **are similar to** their Liquid Present Tense counterparts, <u>with the exception of the accent</u>! Instead of the comfort of seeing a sigma (σ) to mark the 2nd Principal Part, we see only a shift in the placement and type of accent:

κρίνω	*I am judging*	κρινῶ	*I will judge*
κρίνεις	*you are judging*	κρινεῖς	*you will judge*
κρίνει	*he/she/it is judging*	κρινεῖ	*he/she/it will judge*
κρίνουσι	*they are judging*	κρινοῦσι	*they will judge*

2) The endings of ***all*** of these Liquid Future forms ***are exactly the same as*** the <u>Present Tense</u> forms of <u>Epsilon (ε) Contract Verbs</u> (like ποιέω). By adding the εσ, then losing the sigma, the remaining epsilon now stands ready to contract with the "endings" just as happens in all Epsilon (ε) Contract Verbs in the Present.

Epsilon (ε) Contract <u>Present</u>	<u>Translation</u>	Liquid <u>Future</u>	<u>Translation</u>
ποιῶ	*I am making*	κρινῶ	*I will judge*
ποιεῖς	*you are making*	κρινεῖς	*you will judge*
ποιεῖ	*he/she/it is making*	κρινεῖ	*he/she/it will judge*
ποιοῦμεν	*we are making*	κρινοῦμεν	*we will judge*
ποιεῖτε	*you are making*	κρινεῖτε	*you will judge*
ποιοῦσι	*they are making*	κρινοῦσι	*they will judge*

When we see *circumflexes* over these endings but see *no preceding liquid consonant* (λ, μ, ν, or ρ), we should conclude that it is a Contract verb in the <u>Present</u>. When a *liquid consonant* precedes these endings, it is likely a Liquid verb in the <u>Future</u>.

1st PrinPart (Dictionary Entry)	Translation	Verb Root	2nd PrinPart (Fut/Act/Ind/1s)	Translation	Comments
αἴρω	*I am lifting up*	[αρ]	ἀρῶ	*I will lift up*	Regular Liquid formation.
βάλλω	*I am throwing*	[βαλ]	βαλῶ	*I will throw*	Regular Liquid formation.
ἐγείρω	*I am raising*	[εγερ]	ἐγερῶ	*I will raise*	Regular Liquid formation.
κρίνω	*I am judging*	[κριν]	κρινῶ	*I will judge*	Regular Liquid formation.
μένω	*I am staying*	[μεν]	μενῶ	*I will stay*	Regular Liquid formation.
ἀποστέλλω	*I am sending*	[-στελ]	ἀποστελῶ	*I will send*	Regular Liquid formation.
ἀποθνήσκω	*I am dying*	[-θαν]	ἀποθανοῦμαι	*I will die*	<u>Deponent Liquid</u>
ἀποκρίνομαι	*I am answering*	[-κριν]	ἀποκρινοῦμαι	*I will answer*	<u>Deponent Liquid</u>

Suppletive ("Salvage Yard") Verbs

Imagine that you're 16 years old, desperately want a car, but have no money. Imagine that your Uncle Ned, who owns a Salvage Yard (we used to call them "junk yards") graciously allows you to take any of his wrecked cars you want. But as you examine them, you discover that not one of them is complete: this one has no engine, that one has no front end, the other one has no rear half, and so on. So, with your Uncle Ned's permission (!) and acetylene torch, you cut a good front end from a Chevy Malibu, a good cabin area from a Dodge Charger, and a good rear end from a Ford Pinto. Then with Uncle Ned's welder you connect them together and…presto…(via some mechanical magic)…you've got your "car." You call it the "Chev-odg-ord." Whether you realize it or not, you have yourself a "Suppletive" car: a single vehicle made from completely diverse genetic stock.

How does this work with verbs? You know that a "normal" verb has one Root which flows genetically into the formation of six Principal Parts. But imagine that a given verb Root was **Defective**, only sprouting into two or three Principal Parts, and therefore not able to "express itself" in the full range of verb Tenses (etc.). Imagine that a different Root (but one with a similar meaning!) likewise has failed to sprout into all of its Principal Parts. Now imagine that you could "marry" these two roots to create a "whole" verb with a fuller range of Principal Parts! Now you have "one" verb made out of several Defective Roots.

Though there are fewer than 10 "Chev-odg-ord" verbs in the GNT, several of them have common meanings and are frequently encountered. We've already met five (5) of them (in their Present and Imperfect Tenses) without knowing it. Now when we move to the Future, we discover that a "marriage" must have taken place with a completely different root to create a "hybrid verb," a Suppletive. Examine below:

1st PrinPart (Dictionary Entry)	Translation	Verb Root 1	2nd PrinPart (Fut/Act/Ind/1s)	Translation	Verb Root 2
λέγω	*I am saying*	[λεγ]	ἐρῶ	*I will say*	[ερ]
ὁράω	*I am seeing*	[ορα]	ὄψομαι	*I will see*	[οπ]
ἐσθίω	*I am eating*	[εσθ]	φάγομαι	*I will eat*	[φαγ]
ἔρχομαι	*I am coming*	[ερχ]	ἐλεύσομαι	*I will come*	[ελευθ]
φέρω	*I am carrying*	[φερ]	οἴσω	*I will carry*	[οι]

As you might realize, these Futures need to be learned as if they were new vocabulary words. From now on, you will need to fuse together in your mind these forms: λέγω and ἐρῶ; ὁράω and ὄψομαι; ἐσθίω and φάγομαι; ἔρχομαι and ἐλεύσομαι; φέρω and οἴσω. *We* may not appreciate these marriages, but **they're** doing just fine! [By the way, you might notice that nothing is done to the root φαγ to generate the 2nd Prinicipal part. It has traveled down Assembly Line D.]

Comments on Future Middle Form

As you know from all of our work above, the Future Tense has forms that distinctively stand in the Middle. In the examples we presented with λύω in the Future Middle [λύσομαι etc.], we offered a translation that *drew attention to the active subject*: "I *myself* will destroy." As we suggested in Chapter Two, a true Middle (i.e. not a Deponent form to be translated like an Active) requires a great deal of exegetical awareness and skill to translate properly. Even so, there will be considerable disagreement among scholars over how best to interpret a true Middle in any given circumstance. Therefore, the Future Middle forms we will work with (in our exercises below) will be ***Deponents only*** [to be translated simply Actively]. When you see these Middle endings, translate them Actively, and call them Deponents. For your convenience, we have collected the ten (10) verbs we have learned to this point whose Futures are Deponent.

1st PrinPart (Dictionary Entry)	Translation	Verb Root	2nd PrinPart (Fut/Act/Ind/1s)	Translation	
πορεύομαι	*I am going*	[πορευ]	πορεύσομαι	*I will go*	
ὁράω	*I am seeing*	[ορα]	ὄψομαι	*I will see*	(Suppletive)
ἐσθίω	*I am eating*	[εσθ]	φάγομαι	*I will eat*	(Suppletive)
ἔρχομαι	*I am coming*	[ερχ]	ἐλεύσομαι	*I will come*	(Suppletive)
γίνομαι	*I am becoming*	[γεν]	γενήσομαι	*I will become*	
γινώσκω	*I am knowing*	[γνο]	γνώσομαι	*I will know*	
βαίνω	*I am going*	[βα]	βήσομαι	*I will go*	
λαμβάνω	*I am receiving*	[λαβ]	λήμψομαι	*I will receive*	
ἀποκρίνομαι	*I am answering*	[-κριν]	ἀποκρινοῦμαι	*I will answer*	
ἀποθνήσκω	*I am dying*	[-θαν]	ἀποθανοῦμαι	*I will die*	

The Future Passive and The 6th Principal Part

From the unified chart it is clear that the Future Passive is formed from the sixth Principal Part, to which are joined the same endings as are found in the Middle. Look again at the whole Paradigm below:

***Future* Active Indicative**		***Future* Middle Indicative**		***Future* Passive Indicative**	
λύσω	"I will destroy"	λύσομαι	"I myself will destroy"	λυθήσομαι	"I will be destroyed"
λύσειςββ	"you will destroy"	λύσηββ	"you yourself will destroy"	λυθήση	"you will be destroyed"
λύσει	"he/she/it will destroy"	λύσεται	"he/she/it himself will destroy"	λυθήσεται	"he/she/it will be destroyed"
λύσομεν	"we will destroy"	λυσόμεθα	"we ourselves will destroy"	λυθησόμεθα	"we will be destroyed"
λύσετε	"y'all will destroy"	λύσεσθε	"y'all yourselves will destroy"	λυθήσεσθε	"y'all will be destroyed"
λύσουσι(ν)	"they will destroy"	λύσονται	"they themselves will destroy"	λυθήσονται	"they will be destroyed"

The obvious job that remains is grasping the formation of the *sixth Principal Part*. Only two Assembly Lines exist:

Input   Sixth Principal Part Factory   Product

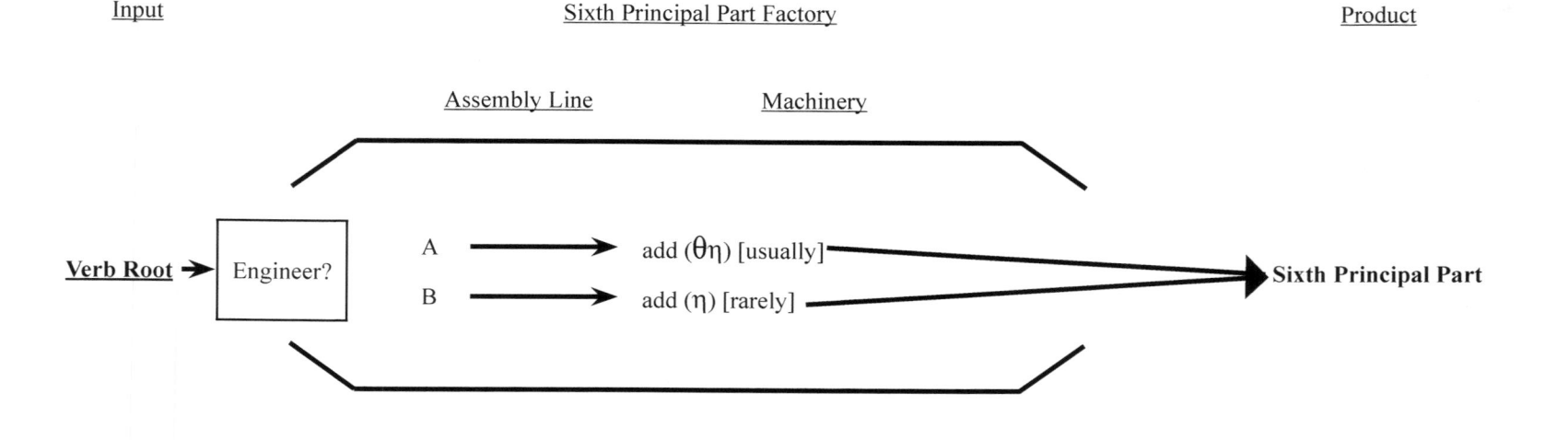

Assembly Line   Machinery

Verb Root → Engineer?

A → add (θη) [usually]

B → add (η) [rarely]

→ **Sixth Principal Part**

Almost all the verbs we know will travel down Assembly Line A. More good news is that the **theta** (θ) added by Assembly Line A is **never effaced**, **never eliminated**, **never contracted** to change its own appearance! This means that we should spot the sixth Principal Part fairly easily.

As presented in grammars, lexicons and vocabulary lists, the sixth Principal Part is "dressed up" in the representative form of the <u>Aorist Passive Indicative, 1st singular</u>. See the example given with λύω below:

First Pr. Prt.	Second Pr. Prt.	Third Pr. Prt.	Fourth Pr. Prt.	Fifth Pr. Prt.	Sixth Pr. Prt.
λύω	λύσω	ἔλυσα	λέλυκα	λέλυμαι	ἐλύθην

In order to find the "naked" form, we need to strip off the augment (ε) [remembering that the Aorist Indicative is a past-time verb] as well as the secondary active personal ending (ν). We are left with λυθη as the <u>basic Principal Part</u>, to which we must add a <u>sigma</u> (σ) to mark the Future dimension. Then come the <u>Primary Middle/Passive personal endings</u> attached via the appropriate <u>connecting vowels</u> (ο or ε).

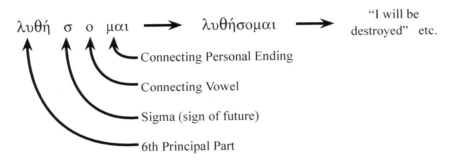

As we move through the various forms of the Future Passive, you will notice that not all verbs we have learned actually have a sixth Principal Part, giving us less work to do. If a verb is not transitive (i.e. does not take a Direct Object when in the Active Voice), it will not have passive forms (excepting certain Deponent verbs).

Most of the following verbs need little comment. The theta-eta-sigma (θησ) sequence is clear, and the basic root you have learned is quite visible. Only the occasional lengthening of final root vowels will slightly modify appearances:

1st PrinPart (Dictionary Entry)	Translation	Verb Root	6th PrinPart (naked)	<u>Future Passive Ind.</u> 1st person singular	Translation
λύω	*I am destroying*	[λυ]	λυθη-	λυθήσομαι	*I will be destroyed*
ἀκούω	*I am hearing*	[ακου]	ἀκουθη-	ἀκουθήσομαι	*I will be heard*
πιστεύω	*I am believing*	[πιστευ]	πιστευθη-	πιστευθήσομαι	*I will be believed*

1st PrinPart (Dictionary Entry)	Translation	Verb Root	6th PrinPart (naked)	Future Passive Ind. 1st person singular	Translation
δίδωμι	*I am giving*	[δο]	δοθη-	δοθήσομαι	*I will be given*
τίθημι	*I am placing*	[θε]	τεθη-	τεθήσομαι	*I will be placed*
ἀγαπάω	*I am loving*	[ἀγαπα]	ἀγαπηθη-	ἀγαπηθήσομαι	*I will be loved*
τιμάω	I am honoring	[τιμα]	τιμηθη-	τιμηθήσομαι	I will be honored
ποιέω	*I am making*	[ποιε]	ποιηθη-	ποιηθήσομαι	*I will be made*
δηλόω	*I am showing*	[δηλο]	δηλωθη-	δηλωθήσομαι	*I will be shown*
αἴρω	*I am lifting up*	[αρ]	ἀρθη-	ἀρθήσομαι	*I will be lifted up*
ἐγείρω	*I am raising*	[εγερ]	ἐγερθη-	ἐγερθήσομαι	*I will be raised*

In the verbs below, the final gamma (γ) or kappa (κ) has been aspirated [becoming a chi (χ)] under the influence of the theta (θ). Otherwise these forms are very recognizable. [You can experience the change by pronouncing these letters, unchanged, before the theta. Just the presence of the aspiration in the theta causes the speaker to aspirate the previous consonant.]

1st PrinPart (Dictionary Entry)	Translation	Verb Root	6th PrinPart (naked)	Future Passive Ind. 1st person singular	Translation
ἄγω	*I am leading*	[ἀγ]	ἀχθη-	ἀχθήσομαι	*I will be led*
δείκνυμι	*I am showing*	[δεικ]	δειχθη-	δειχθήσομαι	*I will be shown*
διδάσκω	*I am teaching*	[δακ]	διδαχθη-	διδαχθήσομαι	*I will be taught*
κηρύσσω	*I am preaching*	[κηρυγ]	κηρυχθη-	κηρυχθήσομαι	*I will be preached*

As you might have expected, **Suppletive** verbs keep up their tricky ways. While λέγω and ὁράω will use the same root as you met in the 2nd Principal Part, φέρω has now employed a third distinct root to form the 6th Principal Part. The good news continues to be that the theta-eta-sigma (θησ) sequence remains clearly visible, making these verbs easy to parse.

1st PrinPart (Dictionary Entry)	Translation	Verb Root	6th PrinPart (naked)	Future Passive Ind. 1st person singular	Translation
λέγω	*I am saying*	[ερ]	ἐρρεθη-	ἐρρεθήσομαι	*I will be spoken*
ὁράω	*I am seeing*	[οπ]	ὀφθη-	ὀφθήσομαι	*I will be seen*
φέρω	*I am carrying*	[ενεγ]	ἐνεχθη-	ἐνεχθήσομαι	*I will be carried*

A few remaining verbs manifest oddities that we will not attempt to explain at this point. The first (γνωσθη-) has an unexpected internal sigma; the next two (κληθη-, βληθη-) transpose the order of letters in their root; the next pair (σωθη-, κριθη-) seem to have lost the last letter of their roots; and the final pair (-σταλη-, γραθη-) are the only ones (of the verbs we've learned) that go down Assembly Line B (using no theta). But note again, **these forms are still quite recognizable**.

1st PrinPart (Dictionary Entry)	Translation	Verb Root	6th PrinPart (naked)	Future Passive Ind. 1st person singular	Translation
γινώσκω	*I know*	[γνο]	γνωσθη-	γνωσθήσομαι	*I will be known*
καλέω	*I am calling*	[καλε]	κληθη-	κληθήσομαι	*I will be called*
βάλλω	*I am throwing*	[βαλ]	βληθη-	βληθήσομαι	*I will be thrown*
σῳζω	*I am saving*	[σωδ]	σωθη-	σωθήσομαι	*I will be saved*
κρίνω	*I am judging*	[κριν]	κριθη-	κριθήσομαι	*I will be judged*
ἀποστέλλω	*I am sending*	[-στελ]	-σταλη-	ἀποσταλήσομαι	*I will be sent*
γράφω	*I am writing*	[γραφ]	γραφη-	γραφήσομαι	*I will be written*

Interpretive Meaning of the Future Indicative

The Greek Future Tense works quite like the English Future Tense. Basically there are three (3) distinct uses of future forms, with the examples below illustrating these uses in either language:

1) <u>Simple Predictive Future</u>: "Tomorrow I **will drive** out to the beach to take a walk." [Projecting what **will** happen.]

2) <u>Imperatival Future</u>: "Amy, tomorrow you **will clean** your room up! Any questions?" [Requiring what **must** happen.]

3) <u>Deliberative Future</u>: "**Should** we **sell** our stock and **invest** in real estate?" [Considering what **should** happen.]

The Future Indicative of εἰμί

	Singular	Plural
1st	ἔσομαι	ἐσόμεθα
2nd	ἔσῃ	ἔσεσθε
3rd	ἔσται	ἔσονται

New Testament Exploration

Matt 25:45–46   Then he will answer them, saying, Truly, I say to you all, just as you did not do it for the least of these, you did not do it for me. καὶ ἀπελεύσονται οὗτοι εἰς κόλασιν αἰώνιον, οἱ δὲ δίκαιοι εἰς ζωὴν αἰώνιον. (κόλασιν αἰώνιον = *eternal punishment*; δίκαιοι = *righteous*; αἰώνιον = *eternal*)

Matt 13:40–41   Therefore, just as the weeds are collected and burned with fire, so it will be at the end of the age. ἀποστελεῖ ὁ υἱὸς τοῦ ἀνθρώπου τοὺς ἀγγέλους αὐτοῦ, and they will gather from his kingdom everything that causes sin and the ones who practice lawlessness.

Matt 13:49–50   It will be this way at the end of the age. Angels will come and separate the evil from the righteous καὶ βαλοῦσιν αὐτοὺς εἰς τὴν κάμινον τοῦ πυρός· where there will be weeping and gnashing of teeth. (κάμινον = *furnace*; πυρός = *fire*)

Luke 1:13–14   But the angel said to him, "Do not be afraid, Zechariah, for your prayer has been heard, καὶ ἡ γυνή σου Ἐλισάβετ γεννήσει υἱόν σοι καὶ καλέσεις τὸ ὄνομα αὐτοῦ Ἰωάννην. And this will be joy and gladness, and many will rejoice at his birth.

Rev 3:12   The one who conquers I will make him a pillar in the temple of my God, and he will never depart from it καὶ γράψω ἐπ᾽ αὐτὸν τὸ ὄνομα τοῦ θεοῦ μου καὶ τὸ ὄνομα τῆς πόλεως τοῦ θεοῦ μου, the new Jerusalem that comes down out of heaven from my God, and my new name as well. (ὄνομα = *name*; πόλεως = *city*)

Digging Deeper into the New Testament Text

1) Find **I Corinthians 15:51-2** and **I Thessalonians 4:16-17** in your GNT, and read these verses aloud repeatedly. As you read, you should recognize several vocabulary words and much of the grammar. See if you can pick out the Futures…before you turn to the Interlinear. How many Futures are there? What features of the forms allowed you to recognize them as Futures even if you have not yet learned these particular vocabulary words?

2) Now check the same verses in the Greek <u>Interlinear,</u> searching for Futures. In order to do this, you need to know that the code Mounce has devised signals **Futures** with an "f" **_immediately following_** the initial part-of-speech designation [the part-of-speech code for a verb is "v"]. Therefore, anytime you see a code beginning with "v.f…." you know you have a Future verb on you hands. You can see this code at work in the first verb of **I Cor. 15:51**:

In this circumstance, the code should be interpreted as follows:

"will sleep"
κοιμηθησόμεθα
v . fpi . 1pl

Part of Speech	Tense	Voice	Mood	Person	Number
v	f	p	i	1	pl
Verb	**_Future_**	passive	Indicative	1st	plural

[Though Mounce parses this verb as a Passive in form, it likely functions as a Deponent to be translated Actively: "We shall…sleep…" See below in our work with **BDAG**.]

3) In your Interlinear at **I Cor. 15:51** you will find the English word "sleep," with the Greek Future verb κοιμηθησόμεθα beneath it. By using its vocabulary code (3121), you can find it in Appendix B of the Interlinear, and then find its entry in **BDAG**. Examine this entry in **BDAG**, noticing the different senses this verb may have from passage to passage. Which

sense best applies here in I Corinthians? [**BDAG** helps us out by citing this very passage.] One of the great values of **BDAG** is its citation of extra-biblical passages for their contrastive value. What pagan literary passage does **BDAG** offer in contrast to its citation of I Cor. 15:18 which would have set Paul's gospel apart from its cultural backdrop?

Note also that **BDAG** has a clarifying note just before sense #1: "…in our lit. only in pass. and w. act. sense…" This may seem at first too cryptic to decode, but isn't too difficult after all. It means: "[This verb κοιμάω] is [found] in our lit[erature] (i.e. the GNT) only in pass[ive forms] and [is to be translated] w[ith an] active sense." In other words, the GNT writers treat this verb as a Deponent verb.

4) In Wallace's Intermediate Grammar *The Basics of NT Syntax* find pages 244-245 [*Greek Grammar Beyond the Basics*, pages 566–571]. Read these pages carefully, and follow closely the various nuances (subtle senses) of the Future described here. [No need to make this overly complicated. We've covered these uses in our treatment above.] Which use of the Future likely dominates the passages we have been working with? [**I Corinthians 15:51-2** and **I Thessalonians 4:16-17**].

Chapter Eleven Vocabulary

We are adding no truly new vocabulary. But because the Suppletive verbs are showing roots we have not seen before, it might be helpful to list them here:

Root	1st PrinPrt.	Root	2nd PrinPart	Root	6th PrinPrt
λεγ	λέγω	ἐρ	ἐρῶ	ἐρ	ῥηθη- (or ῥεθη-)
ὁρα	ὁράω	ὀπ	ὄψομαι	ὀπ	ὀφθη-
ἐσθ	ἐσθίω	φαγ	φάγομαι		
ἐρχ	ἔρχομαι	ἐλευθ	ἐλεύσομαι		
φερ	φέρω	οἰ	οἴσω	ἐνεγ	ἐνεχθη-

The Future forms of εἰμί are best added here, and should appear very "familiar" to you:

	Singular		Plural	
1st	ἔσομαι	I will be	ἐσόμεθα	we will be
2nd	ἔσῃ	you will be	ἔσεσθε	you will be
3rd	ἔσται	he/she/it will be	ἔσονται	they will be

Note that the 2nd singular undergoes the same contraction you find in the regular Primary Middle/Passive forms, and that the 3rd singular appears to drop the expected epsilon (ε) connecting vowel.

Exercises

I. Short Answer

1) <u>What time</u> (past, present or future) does the Greek <u>Future</u> Tense signify?

2) <u>What aspect</u> (internal/continuous, external/undefined, or perfect) of does the Greek <u>Future</u> Tense signify?

3) How would you express (in English) these notions of time and aspect (of the Future Tense) with the verb "run" in the first person singular, active voice?

4) From <u>which Principal Part</u> is the Greek <u>Future</u> Tense (active and middle voices) built?

5) From <u>which Principal Part</u> is the Greek <u>Future</u> Tense (passive voice) built?

6) With what <u>set of personal endings</u> is the Greek <u>Future</u> Tense built?

7) Does an <u>augment</u> appear with Greek verbs in the Future Tense?

8) <u>How many</u> different <u>Principal Parts</u> would a "regular" Greek verb have?

9) From what <u>basic element</u> are <u>all Principal Parts</u> individually formed (in "regular" transitive verb)?

10) What are ***Suppletive verbs***?

11) <u>How</u> is the 2nd <u>Principal Part</u> most commonly formed?

12) <u>How</u> is the 6th <u>Principal Part</u> most commonly formed?

13) <u>Very generally</u>, how are the six Principal Parts distributed across the unified chart?

14) <u>What</u> are the <u>three uses</u> of the Future Tense? Explain each.

Solutions to Exercise I

1) future (Whew!)
2) external, viewed as a simple whole
3) I will run (notice: future time; external/simple aspect)
4) the 2nd Principal Part
5) the 6th Principal Part
6) primary personal endings
7) no [augments appear only in the past time tenses of the Indicative (Imperfect, Aorist, Pluperfect)]
8) six
9) the Verb Root
10) The joining together of several (two or more) Defective verbs (that are similar in meaning) to create a single set of Principal Parts that now function as a single "verb." As you look across the Principal Parts of a Suppletive verb, you will realize that its Principal Parts are derived from (two or more) different Roots.
11) by adding sigma (σ) to the Verb Root
12) by adding theta-eta (θη) to the Verb Root
13) All Principal Parts (except the 2nd) control vertical columns of the chart, with all verb forms in a given column formed from the Principal Part positioned over it. The 2nd Principal Part interrupts this pattern, forming the Future Active and Middle forms in the Indicative.
14) Predictive: [Projecting what will happen.]. Imperatival: [Requiring what must happen.].

   Deliberative: [Considering what should happen.]

II. Drills with Present, Imperfect, and Future Verb Tenses

Increase your skill in recognizing, parsing and translating all three Tenses we have learned [Present, Imperfect, Future]. Notice that the left-hand column contains Present Tense verbs in a full sentence, while the center column and the right column offer replacement verbs in the Imperfect and Future respectively. <u>Go over this exercise repeatedly until it begins to "flow" easily.</u>

1) Working with the verb: σῴζω

   a) ἐγὼ σῴζω τὰς βίβλους. - ἔσῳζον - σώσω

   b) ἐγὼ σῴζομαι ὑπὸ τοῦ θεοῦ. - ἐσῳζόμην - σωθήσομαι

2) Working with the verb: διδάσκω

   a) σὺ διδάσκεις τοὺς ἀποστόλους. - ἐδίδασκες - διδάξεις

   b) σὺ διδάσκῃ ὑπὸ τῶν ἀποστόλων. - ἐδιδάσκου - διδαχθήσῃ

3) Working with the verb: τέκνον

    a) τὸ τέκνον γράφει τὴν βίβλον. - ἔγραφε - γράψει

    b) ἡ βίβλος γράφεται ὑπὸ τοῦ τέκνου. - ἐγράφετο - γραφήσεται

4) Working with the verb: ἀγαπάω

    a) ἡμεῖς ἀγαπῶμεν τὸν θεόν. - ἠγαπῶμεν - ἀγαπήσομεν

    b) ἡμεῖς ἀγαπώμεθα ὑπὸ τοῦ θεοῦ. - ἠγαπώμεθα - ἀγαπηθησόμεθα

5) Working with the verb: κρίνω

    a) ὑμεῖς κρίνετε τὸν κόσμον. - ἐκρίνετε - κρινεῖτε

    b) ὑμεῖς κρίνεσθε ὑπὸ τῶν ἀποστόλων - ἐκρίνεσθε - κριθήσεσθε

6) Working with the verb: διδάσκαλος

    a) οἱ διδάσκαλοι λύουσι τὴν ἁμαρτίαν. - ἔλυον - λύσουσι

    b) οἱ διδάσκαλοι λύονται τῇ ἁμαρτίᾳ. - ἐλύοντο - λυθήσονται

Solutions to Exercise II

1) a) ἐγὼ σῴζω τὰς βίβλους. I am saving the books. (**Present** Active Indicative, 1st Sing) ἔσῳζον was saving (**Imperf.Act.Ind.1stSg**) σώσω will save (**Fut.Act.Ind.1stSg**)
b) ἐγὼ σῴζομαι ὑπὸ τοῦ θεοῦ. I am being saved by God. (**Present** Mid/Pass Indicative, 1st Sing) ἐσῳζόμην was being saved (**Imperf.M/P.Ind.1stSg**) σωθήσομαι will be saved (**Fut.P.Ind.1stSg**)

2) a) σὺ διδάσκεις τοὺς ἀποστόλους. You are teaching the apostles. (**Present** Active Indicative, 2nd Sing) ἐδίδασκες were teaching (**Imperf.Act.Ind.2ndSg**) διδάξεις will teach (**Fut.Act.Ind.2ndSg**)
b) σὺ διδάσκῃ ὑπὸ τῶν ἀποστόλων. You are being taught by the apostles. (**Present** Mid/Pass Indicative, 2nd Sing) ἐδιδάσκου were being taught (**Imperf.M/P.Ind.2ndSg**) διδαχθήσῃ will be taught (**Fut.P.Ind.2ndSg**)

3) a) τὸ τέκνον γράφει τὴν βίβλον. The child is writing the book. (**Present** Active Indicative, 3rd Sing) ἔγραφε was writing (**Imperf.Act.Ind.3rdSg**) γράψει will write (**Fut.Act.Ind.3rdSg**)

b) ἡ βίβλος γράφεται ὑπὸ τοῦ τέκνου. The book is being written by the child. (**Present** Mid/Pass Indicative, 3rd Sing) ἐγράφετο was being written (**Imperf.M/P.Ind.3rdSg**) γραφήσεται will be written (**Fut.P.Ind.3rdSg**)

4) a) ἡμεῖς ἀγαπῶμεν τὸν θεόν. We are loving God. (**Present** Active Indicative, 1st Plural) ἠγαπῶμεν were loving (**Imperf.Act.Ind.1st Pl**) ἀγαπήσομεν will love (**Fut.Act.Ind.1st Pl**)
b) ἡμεῖς ἀγαπώμεθα ὑπὸ τοῦ θεοῦ. We are being loved by God. (**Present** Mid/Pass Indicative, 1st Plural) ἠγαπώμεθα were being loved (**Imperf. M/P.Ind.1st Pl**) ἀγαπηθησόμεθα will be loved (**Fut.P.Ind.1st Pl**)

5) a) ὑμεῖς κρίνετε τὸν κόσμον. You are judging the world. (**Present** Active Indicative, 2nd Plural) ἐκρίνετε were judging (**Imperf.Act.Ind.2nd Pl**) κρινεῖτε will judge (**Fut.Act.Ind.2nd Pl**)
b) ὑμεῖς κρίνεσθε ὑπὸ τῶν ἀποστόλων You are being judged by the apostles. (**Present** Mid/Pass Indicative, 2nd Plural) ἐκρίνεσθε were being judged (**Imperf.M/P.Ind.2nd Pl**) κριθήσεσθε will be judged (**Fut.P.Ind.2nd Pl**)

6) a) οἱ διδάσκαλοι λύουσι τὴν ἁμαρτίαν. The teachers are destroying sin. (**Present** Active Indicative, 3rd Plural) ἔλυον were destroying (**Imperf.Act.Ind.3rd Pl**) λύσουσι will destroy (**Fut.Act.Ind.3rd Pl**)
b) οἱ διδάσκαλοι λύονται τῇ ἁμαρτίᾳ. The teachers are being destroyed by sin. (**Present** Mid/Pass Indicative, 3rd Plural) ἐλύοντο were being destroyed (**Imperf.M/P.Ind.3rd Pl**) λυθήσονται will be destroyed (**Fut.P.Ind.3rd Pl**)

III. Synthetic Sentences

The sentences below gather together most of what we have learned so far, including vocabulary. As usual, **1)** parse verbs; **2)** identify the cases and their uses; **3)** note the position of adjectives; **4)** identify and explain pronouns; **5)** provide a smooth English translation; **6)** diagram each sentence, with special attention to positioning clauses appropriately; **7)** and write out in Greek at least two sentences.

1) ἡ ἐκκλησία τὴν δόξαν τοῦ θεοῦ διὰ τοῦ λόγου διδαχθήσεται, καὶ τὰ ἔργα τῆς δικαιοσύνης οἱ ἅγιοι ἀπόστολοι ποιήσουσι.

2) οἱ λόγοι τῆς βασιλείας τῷ λαῷ ἐρρηθήσονται, καθὼς οἱ ἄγγελοι ἐκεῖνοι αὐτοὺς ἐκ τῶν οὐρανῶν κηρύσσουσι.

3) εἰ ἐν ταῖς καρδίαις ὑμῶν τὴν ἀλήθειαν τοῦ εὐαγγελίου ἀγαπήσετε, γνώσεσθε ὅτι ἡ ἀλήθεια οὐχ ὑπὸ τῶν τέκνων τῆς ἁμαρτίας λυθήσεται.

4) εἰ καὶ ἐκ τῶν ὁδῶν τοῦ θανάτου τὰ ἡμῶν τέκνα οἱ ἀπόστολοι οὗτοι καλέσουσι, τὸν λόγον τῆς ζωῆς οὐκ ἀκούσουσι, τὴν δὲ βασιλείαν τοῦ θεοῦ οὐ λήμψονται.

5) ἐν ἐκείνῃ τῇ ἡμέρᾳ εἰς τοὺς οὐρανοὺς διὰ τῆς ἐξουσίας τοῦ
   υἱοῦ εἰσελεύσεσθε, τὸ γὰρ δῶρον τῆς ζωῆς ὑπὸ τοῦ θεοῦ
   ὑμῖν δοθήσεται.

6) οἱ διδάσκαλοι τῆς εἰρήνης οὐκ ἐλύοντο ὑπὸ τοῦ
   διδασκάλου τοῦ θανάτου, ἀλλὰ ὑπὸ τοῦ θεοῦ
   γνωσθήσονται εἰς δὲ τοὺς οὐρανοὺς αὐτοῦ ἀχθήσονται.

7) εἰς τὸν κόσμον εἰσελεύσομαι διὰ τὸ εὐαγγέλιον, ἐκ δὲ
   τοῦ αὐτοῦ κόσμου διὰ τὴν ἁμαρτίαν καὶ τὸν θάνατον
   ἐξελεύσῃ; [Note punctuation, and third use of the Future.]

8) νῦν διὰ τὴν ἐξουσίαν τῆς ἁμαρτίας ἡ ψυχή μου νεκρά,
   ἀλλὰ ἐν ἐκείνῃ τῇ ἡμέρᾳ τῇ δόξῃ τοῦ θεοῦ ἐγερθήσομαι, ἡ
   δὲ ψυχή μου ἁγία ἔσται καὶ ὑπὸ τοῦ θεοῦ ὀφθήσεται.

9) οἱ υἱοὶ τῶν ἀνθρώπων κατὰ τὴν ἀλήθειαν κριθήσονται,
   ὁ γὰρ ἅγιος αὐτοὺς ἐκάλει, ἀλλὰ οὐκ ἐπίστευον τοὺς
   δούλους τοῦ εὐαγγελίου.

10) εἰ καὶ τὸ εὐαγγέλιον κηρύσσομεν ὅτι οἱ νεκροὶ
    ἐγερθήσονται ὑπὸ τοῦ θεοῦ, ὁ κόσμος ἐν ταῖς ἁμαρτίαις
    αὐτοῦ νεκρός ἐστίν, καὶ οὐ λήμψεται τὴν φωνὴν τῶν ἁγίων.

12: Aorist Tense

The Aorist Indicative (logic and ideas)

To this point we have learned three (3) verb Tenses in the **Indicative** Mood: the **Present** (Active and Middle/Passive), the **Imperfect** (Active and Middle/Passive), and the **Future** (Active, Middle, and Passive). Just as importantly, we have learned not only **how they are formed** (on the basis of the First, Second and Sixth Principal Parts) but also **where they are located** on a unified verb chart. We can discern many important features of a Tense by examining its position on the chart as it intersects such columns and rows as Aspect, Voice, Mood, and Time.

Now as we turn to the **Aorist Indicative**, we will discover that we have already done most of the heavy lifting back in chapters Ten and Eleven. With an understanding of the **Principal Parts** (as formed from the verb Root) along with an overall **conceptual map** of the Greek verb, we can engage the **Aorist Indicative** fairly directly. From the unified chart re-presented on the next page you can see key features of the **Aorist Indicative** without much trouble:

1) The Aorist Tense **_in the Indicative Mood_** is as **past-time Tense**. The three (3) past-time Tenses of the Indicative (Imperfect, Aorist, and Pluperfect) will signal past-time by their **augments**, and can be found in a horizontal row within the Indicative.

<u>Important Note</u>: As you look down the column of External Aspect, you will notice that all of the boxes (except for the Future Tense] are named "Aorist." But only in the Indicative Mood does "past-time" horizontally intersect the column of Aorist Tenses. This means that the Aorist Tenses, **outside the Indicative Mood**, have **no necessary reference to the past.** Therefore in the Subjunctive, Imperative, Optative, Infinitive, and Participle the Aorist Tense essentially indicates External Aspect: **an action viewed and presented as a whole**. This is why it is absolutely necessary always to distinguish the Aorist Indicative from Non-Indicative Aorists! Put another way, **only in the Indicative Mood** does the **Aorist Tense** signify External Aspect **and** past-time!

2) You can see that the Aorist Indicative expresses **External Aspect**. [By and large, the entire External-Aspect column contains verb forms that view an action as a whole, not as a progressive or staged series. This does not mean that the action itself is not progressive or staged "in the real world,"

only that the writer's perspective, presentation, and interests are External, "outside the event," viewing it as a whole.]

3) You can see that the Aorist Tense will have three (3) sets of forms which express **Active, Middle** and **Passive Voices** distinctly. [In other words, there is no sharing of forms by the Middle and Passive as in Present and Imperfect Tenses.]

4) You can see that the **Aorist Active** and **Aorist Middle** will be formed from the <u>Third</u> Principal Part, while the **Aorist Passive** will be formed from the <u>Sixth</u> Principal Part.

Unified Overview

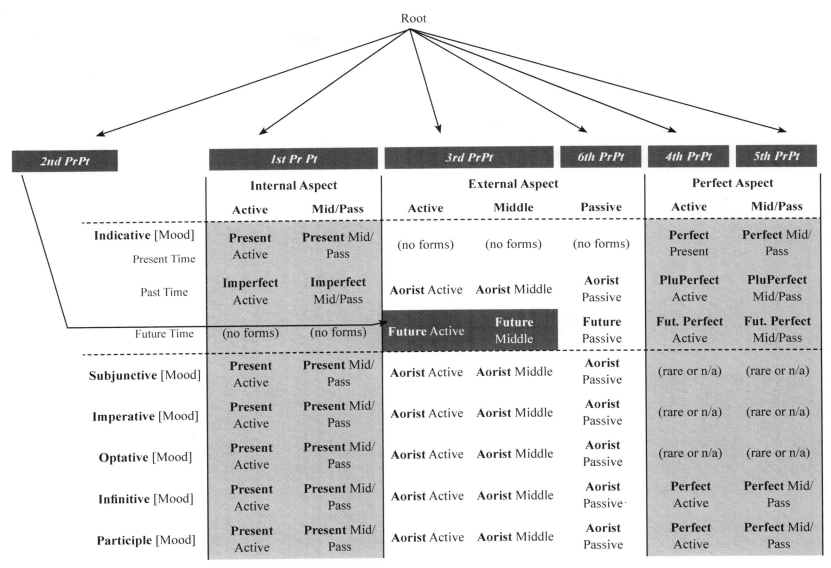

The Formation of the 3rd Principal Part

Since it is clear from the chart that the *Aorist Active and Middle Tenses* (down the entire External-Aspect column) are formed from the *Third Principal Part*, we must learn how this particular Principal Part is formed. From the diagram below you can see that a verb Root may travel down any of five (5) Assembly Lines:

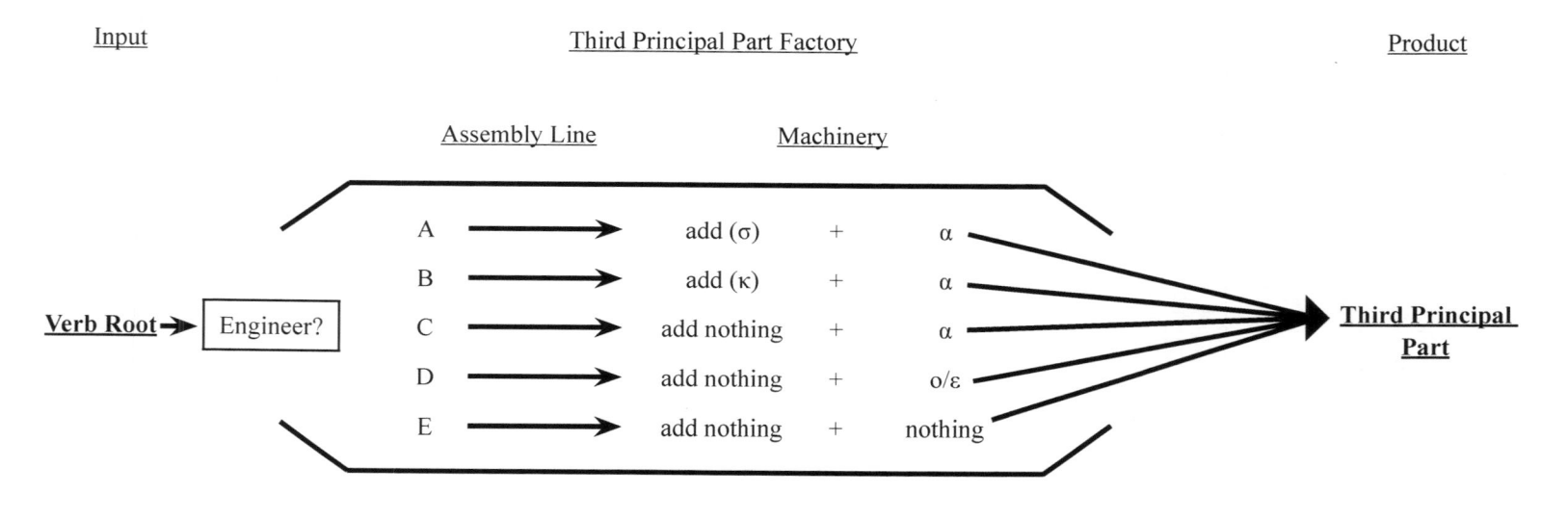

Input	Third Principal Part Factory	Product

Some Traditional Labels

We've been using the images of *Assembly Lines* to describe the different ways verb Roots undergo transformation into Principal Parts. But in the standard Greek tools that you will be using (lexicons, grammars), a traditional nomenclature is used. (Notice that any form using an alpha connecting vowel (α) is known as a "First" Aorist.)

A $\longrightarrow$ add (σ) + α = "*First* Aorist" (type 1?)

B $\longrightarrow$ add (κ) + α = "*First* Aorist" (type 2?)

C $\longrightarrow$ add nothing + α = "*First* Aorist" (type 3?)

D $\longrightarrow$ add nothing + ο/ε = "*Second* Aorist"

E $\longrightarrow$ add nothing + nothing = "*Root* Aorist"

Some Historical Comments

A beginning grammar is not the place to engage in complex explanations about the evolution of a language. But an occasional comment can prove helpful. You might be interested to know that the so-called "Second" Aorists and "Root" Aorists are the earliest (i.e. oldest) strategies the Greek language employed to express an Aorist Tense. In the evolution of the Greek language, the so-called "First" Aorists gained only a toehold before growing in frequency in usage over time. When we reach the GNT, the "First" Aorists had gained the upper hand. Keep these two things in mind: 1) The names "First" and "Second" are poorly chosen, obscuring the chronological priority of the so-called "Second" aorists; 2) Many verbs will have both "First" and "Second" Aorist forms, with one foot in the "old" world and one in the "new." On occasion there may be a shade of difference in meaning between the two. Consult BDAG for help here. [You might look up ἵστημι to see how complex this can become.]

Assembly Line "A"

Many Greek verbs travel down Assembly Line "A," adding **sigma (σ)** to the **Root**. An important feature of this pathway is the use of **alpha (α)** as a <u>connecting vowel</u> joining the "naked" <u>Principal Part</u> to the <u>Personal Endings</u> in the **Indicative**. Observe how these elements, along with the <u>augment</u>, unite to form the ***Aorist Active and Middle Indicative***. (We'll demonstrate this four-fold combination of elements with the 1st Person Plural of the Active.)

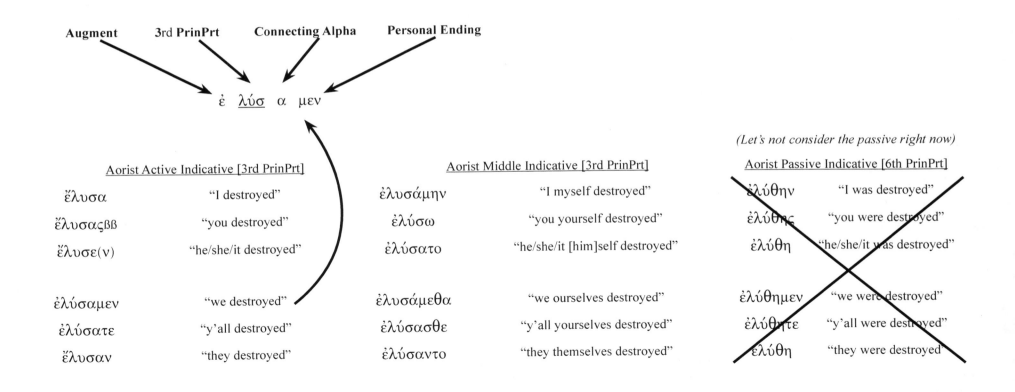

The Personal Endings of Assembly Line "A"

You may have noticed that the Personal Endings used above are the same as those used by the **Imperfect**. Since both the **Imperfect Indicative** and **Aorist Indicative** are **past-time Tenses**, it is only natural that they both would use **Secondary Personal Endings**.

Don't be too distracted by the wrinkles (!!!) that have emerged at three (3) points. (The "expected" components are set in brackets, while the actual "outcomes" lie beyond the arrows.)

- In the 1st Singular Active: The Personal Ending (ν) is not actually used, exposing the alpha (α) to be the last letter of the word.

- In the 3rd Singular Active: The alpha (α) is exchanged for an epsilon (ε), perhaps under influence from another Tense. The nu (ν) shown in parentheses is not a personal ending, but the moveable nu easing pronunciation if the following word (in a given sentence) begins with a vowel.

- In the 2nd Singular Middle: The regular contraction to omega (ω) occurs between alpha (α) and omicron (ο) when the sigma (σ) of the personal ending drops out. You may recall that intervocalic sigmas often drop out.

Aorist Active Indicative		**Aorist Middle Indicative**	
[ἔλυσ-α-ν] ➤	ἔλυσα !!!	[ἐλυσ-ά-μην] ➤	ἐλυσάμην
[ἔλυσ-α-ς] ➤	ἔλυσας	[ἐλύσ-α-σο] ➤	ἐλύσω !!!
[ἔλυσ-α-(ν)] ➤	ἔλυσε(ν) !!!	[ἐλύσ-α-το] ➤	ἐλύσατο
[ἐλύσ-α-μεν] ➤	ἐλύσαμεν	[ἐλυσ-ά-μεθα] ➤	ἐλυσάμεθα
[ἐλύσ-α-τε] ➤	ἐλύσατε	[ἐλύσ-α-σθε] ➤	ἐλύσασθε
[ἔλυσ-α-ν] ➤	ἔλυσαν	[ἐλύσ-α-ντο] ➤	ἐλύσαντο

The "no problem" Verbs of Assembly Line "A"

Several verbs we have learned add sigma-alpha (σα) **very easily** to the verb Root when forming the 3rd Principal Part.

1st PrinPart (Dictionary Entry)	Translation	Verb Root	**3rd PrinPart (Aor/Act/Ind/1s)**	Translation	Comments
λύω	*I am destroying*	[λυ]	ἔλυσα	*I destroyed*	Perfectly regular and obvious
ἀκούω	*I am hearing*	[ακου]	ἤκουσα	*I heard*	Perfectly regular and obvious
πιστεύω	*I am believing*	[πιστευ]	ἐπίστευσα	*I believed*	Perfectly regular and obvious

Short vowels at the end of a verb root are lengthened as the sigma is added: α to η; ε to η; and ο to ω.

1st PrinPart (Dictionary Entry)	Translation	Verb Root	3rd PrinPart (Aor/Act/Ind/1s)	Translation	Comments
ἀγαπάω	I am loving	[ἀγαπα]	ἠγάπησα	I loved	Perfectly regular and obvious
ζάω	I am living	[ζα]	ἔζησα	I lived	Perfectly regular and obvious
τιμάω	I am honoring	[τιμα]	ἐτίμησα	I honored	Perfectly regular and obvious
ἀκολουθέω	I am following	[ἀκολουθε]	ἠκολούθησα	I followed	Perfectly regular and obvious
ζητέω	I am seeking	[ζητε]	ἐζήτησα	I sought	Perfectly regular and obvious
καλέω	I am calling	[καλε]	ἐκάλεσα	I called	Epsilon does not lengthen!
ποιέω	I am making	[ποιε]	ἐποίησα	I made	Perfectly regular and obvious
δηλόω	I am showing	[δηλο]	ἐδήλωσα	I showed	Perfectly regular and obvious
ἵστημι	I am setting	[στα]	ἔστησα	I set (placed)	This μι verb chooses this company!

The "some-problem" Verbs of Assembly Line "A"   (adding σ to Verb Roots ending in mutes [π, β, φ, κ, γ, χ, τ, δ, θ])

If a verb root ends in a "mute" consonant, that consonant will amalgamate with the sigma in forming the 3rd Principal Part. Yet even after the contraction has take place, the "s" sound can easily be heard, signaling the Aorist. The contraction pattern is:

	Mute Final Consonant of Verb Root				**2nd PrinPrt Suffix**		**Result**	
	Voiceless	Voiced	Asperate					
Labial (lips)	π	β	φ	+	σ	=	ψ	(labial + σ = ψ)
Velar (throat)	κ	γ	χ	+	σ	=	ξ	(velar + σ = ξ)
Dental (teeth)	τ	δ	θ	+	σ	=	σ	(dental + σ = σ)

1st PrinPart (Dictionary Entry)	Translation	Verb Root	3rd PrinPart (Aor/Act/Ind/1s)	Translation	Comments
βλέπω	*I am seeing*	[βλεπ]	ἔβλεψα	*I saw*	Regular contraction, see above.
γράφω	*I am writing*	[γραφ]	ἔγραψα	*I wrote*	Regular contraction, see above.
δείκνυμι	*I am showing*	[δεικ]	ἔδειξα	*I showed*	Regular contraction, see above.
διδάσκω	*I am teaching*	[δακ]	ἐδίδαξα	*I taught*	Regular contraction, see above.
κηρύσσω	*I am preaching*	[κηρυγ]	ἐκήρυξα	*I preached*	Regular contraction, see above.
σῴζω	*I am saving*	[σωδ]	ἔσωσα	*I saved*	Regular contraction, see above.

Assembly Line "B"

Two of our verbs travel down Assembly Line "B," adding **kappa** (κ) to the **Root**. As you see from the factory diagram, this Assembly line also uses **alpha** as its connecting vowel. You might notice that two of these verbs (below) are μι verbs, though not all such verbs will travel down this Assembly Line. This fact should help remind us of a general principle throughout our study of Greek verbs: there will be may "patterns" to be observed in how verbs form their Principal Parts and combine various elements to create finished forms…. but….there are many unpredictable outcomes. For example, we might have expected ἵστημι to join its μι verb partners in traveling down Assembly Line B, *but it hasn't*!

1st PrinPart (Dictionary Entry)	Translation	Verb Root	3rd PrinPart (Aor/Act/Ind/1s)	Translation	Comments
δίδωμι	*I am giving*	[δο]	ἔδωκα	*I gave*	Perfectly regular and obvious
τίθημι	*I am placing*	[θε]	ἔθηκα	*I placed*	Perfectly regular and obvious

Assembly Line "C"

Several of our "liquid" verbs travel down Assembly Line "C," adding **no consonant** to the root, but using an **alpha** connector.

1st PrinPart (Dictionary Entry)	Translation	Verb Root	3rd PrinPart (Aor/Act/Ind/1s)	Translation	Comments
αἴρω	I am lifting up	[αρ]	ἦρα	I lifted up	Regular Liquid.
ἐγείρω	I am raising	[εγερ]	ἤγειρα !!!	I raised	Root vowel becomes a diphthong.
κρίνω	I am judging	[κριν]	ἔκρινα	I judged	Regular Liquid.
μένω	I am staying	[μεν]	ἔμεινα !!!	I stayed	Root vowel becomes a diphthong.
ἀποστέλλω	I am sending	[-στελ]	ἀπέστειλα !!!	I sent	Root vowel becomes a diphthong.
ἀποκρίνομαι	I am answering	[-κριν]	ἀπεκρινάμην	I answered	Deponent

Assembly Line "D"

Several of our verbs travel down Assembly Line "D," adding **no consonant** to the root, but using the ο/ε variable connecting vowel. Traditionally they are called **"Second" Aorists**, though this formational strategy was chronologically "first." Note carefully that the presence of the augment, the ο/ε variable connecting vowels, and the Secondary Endings will make some of these verbs look much like their **Imperfect** counterparts. But the distinction between them remains, since the Aorist is formed from the 3rd Principal Part, whereas the Imperfect is formed from the 1st.

1st PrinPart (Dictionary Entry)	Translation	Verb Root	3rd PrinPart (Aor/Act/Ind/1s)	Translation	Comments
ἄγω	I am leading	[αγ]	ἤγαγον	I led	(See #1 below)
βάλλω	I am throwing	[βαλ]	ἔβαλον	I threw	straight forward
εὑρίσκω	I am finding	[ευρ]	εὗρον	I found	(See #2 below)
ἔχω	I am having	[σεχ]	ἔσχον	I had	(See #3 below)
λαμβάνω	I am receiving	[λαβ]	ἔλαβον	I received	straight forward

1) This verb has undergone "Attic reduplication." The whole root (αγ) has been doubled (αγαγ), then augmented.

2) The initial diphthong appears not to have been lengthened in augmentation.

3) The internal vowel (ε) of the root (σεχ) has been "zeroed out."

Comparison of Imperfect and 2nd Aorist Forms

For several of the verbs above, the appearance of the **2nd *Aorist*** differs significantly from that of the ***Imperfect*** because of the obvious difference in appearance between the 1st and 3rd Principal Parts [***Imperfect:*** ἐλάμβανον vs. **2nd *Aorist:*** ἔλαβον]. But when the difference between the 1st and 3rd Principal Parts is ***subtle***, then the forms of the Imperfect and 2nd Aorist are nearly identical. Consider the forms below as a test bed for clarifying the issue at hand:

Internal Aspect: 1st Principal Part   **External Aspect: 3rd Principal Part**

[-βαλλ-]   [-βαλ-]

Imperfect Active Indicative	
ἔβαλλον	"I was throwing"
ἔβαλλεϛßß	"you were throwing"
ἔβαλλε(ν)	"he/she/it was throwing"
ἐβάλλομεν	"we were throwing"
ἐβάλλετε	"y'all were throwing"
ἔβαλλον	"they were throwing"

2nd Aorist Active Indicative	
ἔβαλον	"I threw"
ἔβαλες	"you threw"
ἔβαλε(ν)	"he/she/it threw"
ἐβάλομεν	"we threw"
ἐβάλετε	"y'all threw"
ἔβαλον	"they threw"

Imperfect Mid/Pass Indicative	
ἐβαλλόμην	"I was being thrown"
ἐβάλλουßß	"you were being thrown"
ἐβάλλετο	"he/she/it was being thrown"
ἐβαλλόμεθα	"we were being thrown"
ἐβάλλεσθε	"y'all were being thrown"
ἐβάλλοντο	"they were being thrown"

2nd Aorist Middle Indicative	
ἐβαλόμην	"I myself threw"
ἐβάλου	"you yourself threw"
ἐβάλετο	"he/she/it [him]self threw"
ἐβαλόμεθα	"we ourselves threw"
ἐβάλεσθε	"y'all yourselves threw"
ἐβάλοντο	"they themselves threw"

Suppletives: Salvage Yard Verbs

Most of the Suppletive verbs we have studied happen to take a 2nd Aorist approach when forming the 3rd Principal Part. That is, they move the verb Root (often a Root completely unrelated to the Root from which the 1st Principal Part was formed) down Assembly Line "D", using the variable vowels (ο/ε) to connect Personal Endings. Examine each of our Suppletives below, continuing to familiarize yourself with these awkward combinations of Roots.

1st PrinPar	Root	2nd PrinPart	Root	3rd PrinPart	Root	Comments
λέγω	[λεγ]	ἐρῶ	[ερ]	εἶπον	[επ}	New Root in 3rd PrinPart
ὁράω	[ορα]	ὄψομαι	[οπ]	εἶδον	[ιδ]	New Root in 3rd PrinPart
ἐσθίω	[εσθ]	φάγομαι	[φαγ]	ἔφαγον	[φαγ]	Same Root as in 2nd PrinPart
ἔρχομαι	[ερχ]	ἐλεύσομαι	[ελευθ]	ἦλθον	[ελευθ]	Same Root as in 2nd PrinPart [Root diphthong is "zeroed out."]

The fifth of our Suppletive verbs (φέρω) introduces a new Root in the 3rd Principal Part, but does not send it down Assembly Line "D." Rather, it travels Line "C," adding only alpha (α) to create the Aorist Indicative. The kappa (κ) is not the machinery of Assembly Line "B," but is simply part of the new Root itself.

1st PrinPar	Root	2nd PrinPart	Root	3rd PrinPart	Root	Comments
φέρω	[φερ]	οἴσω	[οι]	ἤνεγκα	[ενεγκ]	This 3rd Root is actually generated in a complex way from ενεκ.

Assembly Line "E"

Finally, two of our verbs travel down Assembly Line "E," the simplest of all formative strategies! To the verb Root is added **absolutely nothing**, except Personal Endings. It should be noted that **no connecting vowel** of any kind (ο, ε, or α) is being used, and that the vowel immediately preceding the Personal Ending is simply the (lengthened) final letter of the verb Root itself.

1st PrinPart (Dictionary Entry)	Translation	Verb Root	3rd PrinPart (Aor/Act/Ind/1s)	Translation	Comments
βαίνω	*I am going*	[βα]	ἔβην	*I went*	straight forward
γινώσκω	*I am knowing*	[γνο]	ἔγνων	*I knew*	straight forward

The appearance of these forms may seem odd (since they have no connecting vowels) until you can "see" the Secondary Personal Endings for what they are, and "see" the underline verb root (with its lengthened vowel stem) for what it is:

*This 3rd plural Personal Ending (σαν) is used in a set of peculiar circumstances we don't need to know right now.

ἔγνων	"I knew"	ἔγνωμεν	"We knew"
ἔγνωςßß	"you knew"	ἔγνωτε	"you knew"
ἔγνω	"he/she/it knew"	ἔγνωσαν*	"they knew"

The Formation of the Aorist Passive

It is clear from the chart (see page 162) that the **Aorist Passive Tenses** (down the entire External-Aspect column) are formed from the 6th Principal Part. We have already learned (in our study of the Future Passive in Chapter Eleven) how this Principal Part is formed. We need make only a few comments to adapt what we know about the Future Passive in order to make the **_Aorist Passive Indicative_**. Examine its forms (ἐλύθην etc.) below:

Aorist Active Indicative [3rd PrinPrt]		Aorist Middle Indicative [3rd PrinPrt]		Aorist Passive Indicative [6th PrinPrt]	
ἔλυσα	"I destroyed"	ἐλυσάμην	"I myself destroyed"	ἐλύθην	"I was destroyed"
ἔλυσαςßß	"you destroyed"	ἐλύσω	"you yourself destroyed"	ἐλύθης	"you were destroyed"
ἔλυσε(ν)	"he/she/it destroyed"	ἐλύσατο	"he/she/it [him]self destroyed"	ἐλύθη	"he/she/it was destroyed"
ἐλύσαμεν	"we destroyed"	ἐλυσάμεθα	"we ourselves destroyed"	ἐλύθημεν	"we were destroyed"
ἐλύσατε	"y'all destroyed"	ἐλύσασθε	"y'all yourselves destroyed"	ἐλύθητε	"y'all were destroyed"
ἔλυσαν	"they destroyed"	ἐλύσαντο	"they themselves destroyed"	ἐλύθη	"they were destroyed"

As presented in grammars, lexicons and vocabulary lists, the **6th Principal Part** is already "dressed" in the form of the <u>Aorist Passive Indicative, 1st singular</u>, as with the example of λύω below:

First Pr. Prt.	Second Pr. Prt.	Third Pr. Prt.	Fourth Pr. Prt.	Fifth Pr. Prt.	Sixth Pr. Prt.
λύω	λύσω	ἔλυσα	λέλυκα	λέλυμαι	ἐλύθην

As you can see, the remaining forms of the **Aorist Passive Indicative** are created simply by adding the other **Secondary Active Personal Endings** to the 6th Principal Part. The only oddity from your perspective is that the 3rd Plural Personal Ending is σαν, instead of ν (as appears in the Aorist Active).

Interpretive Meaning of the Aorist Indicative

In the **Indicative** Mood, the Aorist usually indicates that an action took place in **past time**, relative to the speaker.

But in **every Mood and Mode** (Indicative, Subjunctive, Imperative, Optative, Infinitive, Participle), the Aorist Tense commonly views actions (events, processes, or states) in one of three (3) ways:

The **Constative** Aorist:

The vast majority of Aorists simply view an event from a simple, external vantage point, without any interest in its internal progression or duration. The simple English past tense is often the most appropriate translation: "we sang," "we studied," "she swam," "they worked," etc. [Notice how these English expressions give no indication of duration, no "inside view" of progression or of stages.]

The **Ingressive** Aorist:

Sometimes the meaning of the verb itself, combined with the context in which it appears, suggests that the Aorist Tense is encouraging us to view the **onset** of the activity, not really its entirety. If an Aorist verb can effectively be translated into English with a **"began to"** introductory expression, then we may classify the usage as the **Ingressive** Aorist. "And they _began to_ follow him…"

The **Consummative** Aorist:

Sometimes the meaning of the verb itself, combined with the context in which it appears, suggests that the Aorist Tense is encouraging us to view the **completion** of the activity, not really the whole process leading up to the completion. Because no formulaic English translation exists which can convey this notion in every situation, we will need to experiment with various English paraphrases to communicate how an action may be viewed from its "finished" perspective.

A Review of the Ten Parts of Speech

As you have already learned, Greek may be analyzed as having a **total of ten (10)** different kinds of words. Every single Greek word you encounter in the GNT will fit into one of these word classes! Review the <u>names</u>, <u>roles</u>, <u>examples</u>, and <u>codes</u> (in Mounce) of the ten (10) "Parts of Speech" as listed below:

	<u>Part of Speech</u>	<u>Typical Role</u>	<u>English Example</u>	<u>Interlinear Code</u> (in Mounce)	
1)	verb	sets in motion an action or state	I *saw* the president.	v	(**v**erb)
2)	noun	person, place, "thing"	I saw the **president**.	n	(**n**oun)
3)	article	particularizes a noun	I saw **the** president.	d	(**d**efinite article)
4)	adverb	modifies a verb	I saw the president **yesterday**.	adv	(**adv**erb)
5)	adjective	modifies a noun	I saw the **former** president yesterday.	a	(**a**djective)
6)	conjunction	adds things together	I saw the president **and** the first lady.	cj	(**c**on**j**unction)
7)	pronoun	replaces a noun	I saw **them** yesterday.	r	(p**r**onoun)
8)	preposition	relates a noun to the sentence	I saw them **_in_** the deli yesterday.	p	(**p**reposition)
9)	interjection	attention-getting device	**Hey**! I saw them yesterday!	j	(inter**j**ection)
10)	particle	adds tone or nuance to a sentence	I **indeed** saw them yesterday.	pl	(**p**artic**l**e)

But Mounce isn't quite satisfied with these ten (10) categories, and has decided to treat the two verb Modes [*Infinitives* and *Participles*] as two additional categories of analysis. (Technically, these are simply *verbs*, and could be parsed accordingly.) So for purposes of working in Mounce's Interlinear, we'll need to add two more "classes" of words to the ten we already have:

	<u>Part of Speech</u>	<u>Typical Role</u>	<u>English Example</u>	<u>Interlinear Code</u> (in Mounce)	
11)	infinitive	a verbal noun	*To meet* the president is an honor.	f	(in**f**initive)
12)	participle	a verbal adjective	The *sitting* president lives in D.C.	pt	(**p**ar**t**iciple)

A Limited Comment on Infinitives and Participles

We are not able, in this first semester of Greek, to tackle the formation and use of Greek Infinitives and Participles. Yet it is possible to make brief mention of them, and offer English examples to illustrate their essential character.

The Infinitive is a hybrid, the combination of **verb and noun**. Notice in the examples below how an Infinitive can sometimes be substituted for a noun in a given sentence. [English Infinitives often take the form of "to 'blank.'"]

Sentence with a <u>Noun</u>:	I love <u>ice cream</u>.	<u>Jessica</u> is human.
Sentence with an <u>Infinitive</u>:	I love <u>to eat</u>.	<u>To err</u> is human.

The Participle likewise is a hybrid, the combination of **verb and adjective**. Notice in the examples below how a Participle can sometimes be substituted for an adjective in a given sentence: [English Participles can take the form of "blank-ing."]

Sentence with an <u>Adjective</u>:	The <u>yellow</u> boat might be smashed against the rocks.
Sentence with a <u>Participle</u>:	The <u>drifting</u> boat might be smashed against the rocks.

New Testament Exploration

1 Cor 15:11	Whether then it was I or they, οὕτως κηρύσσομεν καὶ οὕτως ἐπιστεύσατε.
Matt 4:25	καὶ ἠκολούθησαν αὐτῷ ὄχλοι πολλοὶ ἀπὸ τῆς Γαλιλαίας and Decapolis and Jerusalem and Judea and beyond the Jordan. (πολλοὶ = *many*; Γαλιλαίας = *Galilee*)

Mark 5:23–24	He asked him urgently, "My little daughter is near death. Come and lay your hands on her so that she may be healed and live." καὶ ἀπῆλθεν μετ' αὐτοῦ. καὶ ἠκολούθει αὐτῷ ὄχλος πολὺς καὶ συνέθλιβον αὐτόν. (πολὺς = *many*; συνέθλιβον = *they were crowding*)
Matt 8:32	And he said to them, "You all go!" Then they came out and entered the pigs, and the herd rushed down the steep slope into the lake καὶ ἀπέθανον ἐν τοῖς ὕδασιν. (ὕδασιν = *waters*)
John 8:20–21	These things he spoke in the treasury while he was teaching in the Temple. No one seized him because his hour had not yet come. Εἶπεν οὖν πάλιν αὐτοῖς· ἐγὼ ὑπάγω καὶ ζητήσετέ με, καὶ ἐν τῇ ἁμαρτίᾳ ὑμῶν ἀποθανεῖσθε· ὅπου ἐγὼ ὑπάγω ὑμεῖς οὐ δύνασθε ἐλθεῖν. (ὑπάγω = *I am going away*; ὅπου = *where*; δύνασθε ἐλθεῖν = *able to go*)

Digging Deeper into the New Testament Text

1) Find **John 2:12-22**, the story of the cleansing of the temple, in your GNT, and read these verses aloud. <u>Make mental notes to yourself as you recognize such things as pronouns, preposition, articles, conjunctions, adverbs, etc.</u> You may also be able to make out as much as a third of the vocabulary.

2) Now find the same verses in the Greek <u>Interlinear</u>. Almost 200 items are individually parsed by Mounce in these eleven verses. Your job? Construct a chart, tallying the number of occurrences of each **Part of Speech** represented. In other words, you should be able to show **how many** nouns, how many verbs, how many pronouns (etc., etc.) are found here in **John 2:12-22**. [It would be wise to review the codes that Mounce has devised to identify each Part of Speech.] [There is no need to write out the Greek words here. Simply tallying the count for each Part of Speech is adequate.] <u>What observations do you have regarding the frequencies of</u>

the Parts of Speech? <u>What Insights might this data suggest regarding the business of learning NT Greek?</u> How far have we come?

What abuses in interpreting the Aorist must likely have been taking place in previous (and present?) generations of scholars?

3)   In Mounce's Interlinear code, the **Aorist Tense** is identified by an "**a**" immediately after the Part-of-Speech identification (v = verb). As an example of an Aorist Indicative, see John 2:15 and the following verb within it:

In this circumstance, the code should be interpreted as follows:

"drove out"

ἐξέβαλεν

v . aai . 3s

Part of Speech	Tense	Voice	Mood	Person	Number
v	f	p	i	3	s
Verb	*aorist*	active	Indicative	3rd	singular

Now make a search to find **every Aorist Indicative** in this passage (**John 2:12-22**). The Code for such should read:

v.a?i.?? [You should find **about 20**.] <u>Record the verse numbers in which these **all** are found. Then choose and copy **any 8** of these forms, *identifying the various features* of each form which would help you recognize them as Aorist Indicatives.</u>

4)   In your Interlinear at **John 2:15** you will find the English word "whip," with the Greek noun φραγέλλιον beneath it. By using its vocabulary code (5848), you can find it in Appendix B of the Interlinear, and then find its entry in **BDAG**. Examine this entry in **BDAG**, noticing the comments made in this (and the next) entry. What interesting (parenthetical) comment near the end of the entry significantly "tones down" the action of Jesus as describe here in John 2?

5)   In Wallace's Intermediate Grammar *The Basics of NT Syntax* find pages 239-43 [*Greek Grammar Beyond the Basics*, pages 554–565]. Read these pages carefully, and follow closely the various nuances (subtle senses) of the **Aorist** described here. [No need to make this overly complicated. We've covered these uses in our treatment above.] <u>What do you make of the special "essays"</u> ["Thawing Out the Aorist" and "The Abused Aorist"]?

Chapter Twelve Vocabulary

We are adding no truly new vocabulary. The Suppletives and their roots are here shown together:

	1st PrinPart	Root	2nd PrinPart	Root	3rd PrinPart	Root
"say"	λέγω	λεγ	ἐρῶ	ερ	εἶπον	επ
"see"	ὁράω	ορα	ὄψομαι	οπ	εἶδον	ιδ
"eat"	ἐσθίω	εσθ	φάγομαι	φαγ	ἔφαγον	φαγ
"come"	ἔρχομαι	ερχ	ἐλεύσομαι	ελευθ	ἦλθον	ελευθ
"carry"	φέρω	φερ	οἴσω	οι	ἤνεγκα	ενεγκ

Exercises

I. Short Answer

1) What time (past, present or future) does the Greek Aorist Tense signify in the Indicative Mood?

2) What aspect (internal/continuous, external/undefined, or perfect) do Aorist Tenses (in every Mood) signify?

3) How would you express (in English) the notions of *time* and *aspect* (of the Aorist Indicative) with the verb "run" in the first person singular, active voice?

4) From which Principal Part is the Greek Aorist Tense (active and middle voices) built (in all Moods)?

5) From which Principal Part is the Greek Aorist Tense (passive voice) built?

6) With what set of personal endings is the Greek Aorist Tense built?

7) Does an augment appear with Greek verbs in the *Aorist Indicative*?

8) Does an augment appear with Greek verbs in non-Indicative *Aorist* Tenses?

9) How many different strategies (Assembly Lines) might be used to create the *3rd Principal Part* from a verb *Root*?

10) What are the three uses of the Aorist Tense, broadly speaking? Explain each.

11) An Infinitive combines what two Parts of Speech?

12) A Participle combines what two Parts of Speech?

13) What ten (10) Parts of Speech are represented by each of the following abbreviations from Mounce's Interlinear?

      v   n   d   adj   a   cj   r   p   j   pl

14) What two (2) verb Modes are represented by the following abbreviations from Mounce's Interlinear?

      f   pt

Solutions to Exercise I

1) past
2) external, viewed as a simple whole
3) I ran (notice: past time; external/simple aspect)
4) the 3rd Principal Part
5) the 6th Principal Part
6) secondary personal endings; [Aorist Active: secondary active; Aorist Middle: secondary middle; Aorist Passive: secondary active]
7) yes [augments appear in the three past time tenses of the Indicative (Imperfect, Aorist, Pluperfect)]
8) no [augments signal past time, which occurs only in the Indicative Mood]
9) five
10) Constative: [viewing an event as a simple whole]; Ingressive: [viewing the onset of an event]; Consummative: [viewing the completion of an event]
11) verb and noun
12) verb and adjective
13) Verb, Noun, Article, Adjective, Adverb, Conjunction, Pronoun, Preposition, Interjection, Particle
14) Infinitive, Participle

II. Part 1 Drills with Present, Imperfect, Future and Aorist Verbs in the Indicative

1) Working with the verb: σῴζω

    a) σῴζω

    b) ἔσῳζον

    c) σώσωἔ

    d) σωσα

2) Working with the verb: διδάσκω

    a) διδάσκεις

    b) ἐδίδασκες

    c) διδάξεις

    d) ἐδίδαξας

3)   Working with the verb: γράφω

    a)   γράφει

    b)   ἔγραφε

    c)   γράψει

    d)   ἔγραψε

4)   Working with the verb: ἀγαπαω

    a)   ἀγαπῶμεν

    b)   ἠγαπῶμεν

    c)   ἀγαπήσομεν

    d)   ἠγαπήσαμεν

5)   Working with the verb: κρίνω

    a)   κρίνετε

    b)   ἐκρίνετε

    c)   κρινεῖτε

    d)   ἐκρίνατε

6)   Working with the verb: λύω

    a)   λύουσι

    b)   ἔλυον

    c)   λύσουσι

    d)   ἔλυσαν

Solutions to Exercise II Part 1

1)   a) σώζομαι I am being saved.   (Pres. M/P.Ind.1stSg)
    b) ἐσωζόμην I was being saved. (Imperf.M/P.Ind.1stSg)
    c) σωθήσομαι I will be saved. (Fut.P.Ind.1stSg)
    d) ἐσώθην I was saved. (Aor.P.Ind.1stSg)

2)   a) διδάσκη You are being taught. (Pres. M/P.Ind.2ndSg)
    b) ἐδιδάσκου You were being taught. (Imperf.M/P.Ind.2ndSg)
    c) διδαχθήση You will be taught. (Fut.P.Ind.2ndSg)
    d) ἐδιδάχθης You were taught. (Aor.P.Ind.2ndSg)

3)   a) γράφεται It is being written. (Pres. M/P.Ind.3rdSg)
    b) ἐγράφετο It was being written. (Imperf.M/P.Ind.3rdSg)
    c) γραφήσεται It will be written. (Fut.P.Ind.3rdSg)
    d) ἐγράφη It was written. (Aor.P.Ind.3rdSg)

4)   a) ἀγαπώμεθα We are being loved. (Pres. M/P.Ind.1st Pl)
    b) ἠγαπώμεθα We were being loved. (Imperf. M/P.Ind.1st Pl)
    c) ἀγαπηθησόμεθα We will be loved. (Fut.P.Ind.1st Pl)
    d) ἠγαπήθημεν We were loved. (Aor.P.Ind.1st Pl)

5)   a) κρίνεσθε You are being judged. (Pres. M/P.Ind.2nd Pl)
    b) ἐκρίνεσθε You were being judged. (Imperf.M/P.Ind.2nd Pl)
    c) κριθήσεσθε You will be judged. (Fut.P.Ind.2nd Pl)
    d) ἐκρίθητε You were judged. (Aor.P.Ind.2nd Pl)

6)   a) λύονται They are being destroyed. (Pres. M/P.Ind.3rd Pl)
    b) ἐλύοντο They were being destroyed. (Imperf.M/P.Ind.3rd Pl)
    c) λυθήσονται They will be destroyed. (Fut.P.Ind.3rd Pl)
    d) ἐλύθησαν They were destroyed. (Aor.P.Ind.3rd Pl)

II. Part 2 Drills with Passive Forms: Present, Imperfect, Future, Aorist

1)   Working with the Verb: ἐσώθην

    a)   σώζομαι

    b)   ἐσωζόμην

    c)   σωθήσομαι

    d)   ἐσώθην

2) Working with the verb: διδάσκω

   a) διδάσκη

   b) ἐδιδάσκου

   c) διδαχθήσῃ

   d) ἐδιδάχθης

3) Working with the verb: γράφω

   a) γράφεται

   b) ἐγράφετο

   c) γραφήσεται

   d) ἐγράφη

4) Working with the verb: ἀγαπῶ

   a) ἀγαπώμεθα

   b) ἠγαπώμεθα

   c) ἀγαπηθησόμεθα

   d) ἠγαπήθημεν

5) Working with the verb: κρίνω

   a) κρίνεσθε

   b) ἐκρίνεσθε

   c) κριθήσεσθε

   d) ἐκρίθητε

6) Working with the verb: λύο

   a) λύονται

   b) ἐλύοντο

   c) λυθήσονται

   d) ἐλύθησαν

Solutions to Exercise II Part 2

1) a) σῴζομαι I am being saved (**Pres.** M/P.Ind.1stSg)
   b) ἐσῳζόμην I was being saved (**Imperf.**M/P.Ind.1stSg)
   c) σωθήσομαι I will be saved (**Fut.**P.Ind.1stSg)
   d) ἐσώθην I was saved (**Aor.**P.Ind.1stSg)
2) a) διδάσκη You are being taught (**Pres.** M/P.Ind.2ndSg)
   b) ἐδιδάσκου You were being taught (**Imperf.**M/P.Ind.2ndSg)
   c) διδαχθήση You will be taught (**Fut.**P.Ind.2ndSg)
   d) ἐδιδάχθης You were taught (**Aor.**P.Ind.2ndSg)
3) a) γράφεται It is being written (**Pres.** M/P.Ind.3rdSg)
   b) ἐγράφετο It was being written (**Imperf.**M/P.Ind.3rdSg)
   c) γραφήσεται It will be written (**Fut.**P.Ind.3rdSg)
   d) ἐγράφη It was written (**Aor.**P.Ind.3rdSg)
4) a) ἀγαπώμεθα We are being loved (**Pres.** M/P.Ind.1st Pl)
   b) ἠγαπώμεθα We were being loved (**Imperf.** M/P.Ind.1st Pl)
   c) ἀγαπηθησόμεθα We will be loved (**Fut.**P.Ind.1st Pl)
   d) ἠγαπήθημεν We were loved (**Aor.**P.Ind.1st Pl)
5) a) κρίνεσθε You are being judged. (**Pres.** M/P.Ind.2nd Pl)
   b) ἐκρίνεσθε You were being judged. (**Imperf.**M/P.Ind.2nd Pl)
   c) κριθήσεσθε You will be judged. (**Fut.**P.Ind.2nd Pl)
   d) ἐκρίθητε You were judged. (**Aor.**P.Ind.2nd Pl)
6) a) λύονται They are being destroyed (**Pres.** M/P.Ind.3rd Pl)
   b) ἐλύοντο They were being destroyed (**Imperf.**M/P.Ind.3rd Pl)
   c) λυθήσονται They will be destroyed (**Fut.**P.Ind.3rd Pl)
   d) ἐλύθησαν They were destroyed (**Aor.**P.Ind.3rd Pl)

III. Synthetic Sentences

The sentences below gather together most of what we have learned so far, including vocabulary. As usual, **1)** parse verbs; **2)** identify the cases and their uses; **3)** note the position of adjectives; **4)** identify and explain pronouns; **5)** provide a smooth English translation; **6)** diagram each sentence, with special attention to positioning clauses appropriately; **7)** and write out in Greek at least two sentences.

1) ἡμεῖς πιστεύομεν ὅτι ὁ κύριος ἐν ἐκείνῃ τῇ ἡμέρᾳ ἠγέρθη, καὶ ἐν τῇ ὥρᾳ ταύτῃ ζῇ, καὶ ἐλεύσεται αὐτὸς πάλιν εἰς τὴν γῆν ταύτην ἐν τῇ ἐσχάτῃ ἡμέρᾳ.

2) ὁ ἡμῶν θεὸς τὰ τέκνα τῶν ἀνθρώπων καλέσει εἰς τὴν βασιλείαν, εἰ τὴν ἀλήθειαν τοῦ εὐαγγελίου ζητοῦσι καὶ τούτους τοὺς λόγους λαμβάνουσιν εἰς τὰς καρδίας αὐτῶν.

3) ἀμὴν ἀμὴν ὑμῖν λέγω ὅτι τὴν δόξαν τοῦ θεοῦ οἱ ὀφθαλμοὶ ὑμῶν ὄψονται, ὅτι ὑπὸ τοῦ θεοῦ ἐδιδάχθητε καὶ ἡ ψυχὴ ὑμῶν τὸν ἄρτον τῆς ζωῆς ἐφάγετο.

4) εἰ καὶ ἐκ τοῦ θανάτου εἰς τὴν τῆς δόξης βασιλείαν ἤγοντο οἱ ἀπόστολοι, ἰδού, τὰ παιδία αὐτῶν ἐν τῷ κυρίῳ οὐκ ἐπίστευσαν, ἀλλὰ παρὰ τὴν ἑτέραν ὁδὸν ἠκολούθησαν.

5) ὁ θεὸς αὐτὸς τοὺς τῆς δικαιοσύνης διδασκάλους ἐγερεῖ, καθὼς τὸν υἱὸν αὐτοῦ εἰς τὴν ζωὴν ἤγειρε καὶ αὐτῷ τὴν ἐξουσίαν ὑπὲρ τὴν γῆν ἔδωκε.

6) νῦν ἀγαπᾶτε τοὺς ὑμῶν ἀδελφοὺς ἐκ τῆς καρδίας, τὸ γὰρ ἅγιον δῶρον τῆς ἀγάπης ὑπὸ τοῦ θεοῦ ὑμῖν ἐδόθη, καὶ ἐν ὑμῖν ἔμεινε.

7) οἱ τοῦ θανάτου ἄγγελοι κατὰ τὸν νόμον τὸν ἅγιον κριθήσονται, ἐκ δὲ τῆς βίβλου τῆς βασιλείας βληθήσονται, τὸν γὰρ ἄρτον τῆς ζωῆς ἀπὸ τῶν ἰδίων τέκνων ἔλαβον.

8) ὁ κόσμος τὴν φωνὴν τῶν τοῦ θεοῦ δούλων ἤκουσε καὶ ἐσώθη, ὅτι μετ᾽ ἐξουσίας τὸ εὐαγγέλιον ἐκηρύχθη ὑπὸ τῶν ἀποστόλων κατὰ τῆς ἁμαρτίας.

9) ὑπὸ τὴν ἐξουσίαν τῆς ἁμαρτίας ἦμεν ἐν ἐκείναις ταῖς ἡμέραις, ἀλλὰ νῦν τὰ τέκνα τοῦ θεοῦ ἐσμέν, καὶ ἐν τῇ ἐσχάτῃ ἡμέρᾳ μετὰ τοῦ ὄχλου τῶν ἁγίων ἐσόμεθα.

10) ὁ υἱὸς τοῦ ἀνθρώπου τὰ νεκρὰ ἔργα ἡμῶν εἶδε διὰ τῶν ἰδίων ὀφθαλμῶν, ἀλλὰ πρὸς τὸν τόπον τοῦ θανάτου ὑπὲρ ἡμῶν ἦλθε, καὶ τὰς ἡμῶν ἁμαρτίας ἤνεγκε διὰ τὴν αὐτοῦ ἀγάπην.

Master Vocabulary List by Part of Speech

(Chapter numbers in parentheses)

Adjectives

ἀγαθός, ή, όν *good (5)*

ἅγιος, ία, ον *holy (5)*

ἄλλος, η, ο *other (5)*

ἔσχατος, η, ον *last (5)*

ἕτερος, α, ον *other (5)*

ἴδιος, ία, ον *one's own (5)*

καλός, ή ον *good (5)*

μόνος, η, ον *only (5)*

νεκρός, ά, όν *dead (5)*

ὅλος, η, ον *whole (5)*

πρῶτος, η, ον *first (5)*

Adverbs

ἐκεῖ *there (4)*

ἔτι *still, even now (4)*

εὐθύς *immediately (4)*

ἰδού or Ἴδε *Look! Notice! See! (4)*

κακῶς *poorly, badly, wickedly (4)*

καλῶς *well, rightly, fittingly (4)*

νῦν *now (4)*

οὐ, οὐκ, οὐχ *not (4)*

οὐκέτι *no longer (4)*

πάλιν *again (4)*

πάντοτε *always (4)*

ποῦ *where? (4)*

πῶς *how? (4)*

ὧδε *here (4)*

Conjunctions

ἀλλά *but (3, 8)*

γάρ *for (8)*

δέ *and, but (8)*

εἰ *if (8)*

εἰ καί *though (8)*

ἕως *while (8)*

ἤ *or (8)*

ἵνα *in order that, so (8)*

καθώς *as (8)*

καί *and (3, 8)*

ὅτε *when (8)*

ὅτι *because, that (8)*

οὗ *where (8)*

οὖν *therefore, then (8)*

ὡς *as (8)*

ὥστε *with the result that (8)*

Nouns

ἀγάπη, ης, ἡ *love (5)*

ἄγγελος, ὁ *angel (3)*

ἀδελφός, ὁ *brother (7)*

ἀλήθεια, ας, ἡ *truth (5)*

ἁμαρτία, ας, ἡ *sin (5)*

ἄνθρωπος, ὁ *man (7)*

ἀπόστολος, ὁ *apostle (3)*

ἄρτος, ὁ *bread (7)*

βασιλεία, ας, ἡ *kingdom (5)*

βίβλος, ἡ *book (3)*

γῆ, ῆς, ἡ *earth (5)*

διδάσκαλος, ὁ *teacher (3)*

δικαιωσύνη, ης, ἡ *righteousness (5)*

δόξα, ης, ἡ *glory (5)*

δοῦλος, ὁ *slave, servant (8)*

δῶρον, τό *gift (3)*

εἰρήνη, ης, ἡ *peace (5)*

ἐκκλησία, ας, ἡ *church (5)*

ἐξουσία, ας, ἡ *authority (5)*

ἔργον, τό *work (3)*

ἔρημος, ἡ *wilderness (3)*

εὐαγγέλιον, τό *gospel (3)*

ζωή, ῆς, ἡ *life (5)*

ἡμέρα, ας, ἡ *day (5)*

θάνατος, ὁ *death (3)*

θεός, ὁ *God (7)*

καρδία, ας, ἡ *heart (5)*

κόσμος, ὁ *world (8)*

κύριος, ὁ *Lord (7)*

λαός, ὁ *people (8)*

λόγος, ὁ *word (3)*

νόμος, ὁ *law (7)*

ὁδός, ἡ *road (3)*

οἰκία, ας, ἡ *house (5)*

οἶκος, ὁ *house (8)*

οὐρανός, ὁ *heaven (8)*

ὀφθαλμός, ὁ *eye (8)*

ὄχλος, ὁ *crowd (3)*

παιδίον, τό *child (3)*

στέφανος, ὁ *crown (3)*

τέκνον, τό *child (3)*

τόπος, ὁ *place (8)*

υἱός, ὁ *son (7)*

φωνή, ῆς, ἡ *voice (5)*

χρυσός, ὁ *gold (3)*

ψυχή, ῆς, ἡ *soul (5)*

ὥρα, ας, ἡ *hour (5)*

Particles

ἀμήν *amen, truly (8)*

μέν *on one hand (8)*

μή *not (8)*

οὐ *not (8)*

Prepositions

ἀνά (+ *accusative) in the midst of (6)*

ἀντί (+ *genitive) instead of, for (6)*

ἀπό (+ *genitive) from, away from (6)*

διά (+ *genitive) through (6)*

διά (+ *accusative) because of (6)*

εἰς (+ *accusative) to, into (6)*

ἐκ (+ *genitive) from, out from (6)*

ἐν (+ *dative) in, among (6)*

ἐπί (+ *genitive) on, near, toward (6)*

ἐπί (+ *dative) on, near, toward (6)*

ἐπί (+ *accusative) on, near, toward (6)*

κατά (+ *genitive) against (6)*

κατά (+ *accusative) according to (6)*

μετά (+ *genitive) with (6)*

μετά (+ *accusative) after, behind (6)*

παρά (+ *genitive) out from (6)*

παρά (+ *dative) beside (6)*

παρά (+ *accusative) along side (6)*

περί (+ *genitive) concerning (6)*

περί (+ *accusative) around (6)*

πρό (+ *genitive) before (6)*

πρός (+ *accusative) to, toward (6)*

σύν (+ *dative) along with (6)*

ὑπέρ (+ *genitive) in behalf of (6)*

ὑπέρ (+ *accusative) over (6)*

ὑπό (+ *genitive) by (6)*

ὑπό (+ *accusative) underneath (6)*

Pronouns

αὐτός he *(7)*

ἐγώ I *(7)*

ἐκεῖνος that, those *(7)*

οὗτος this, these *(7)*

σύ you *(7)*

Proper Nouns

Μάρθα, ας, ἡ *Martha (5)*

Μαρία, ας, ἡ *Mary (5)*

Verbs

ἀγαπάω [αγαπα] *I love* (10)

ἄγω [αγ] I *draw, lead* (9)

αἴρω [αρ] *I lift up, take away* (8)

ἀκολουθέω [ακολουθε] *I follow* (10)

ἀκούω [ἀκου] *I hear, obey* (2)

ἀναβαίνω [(ανα)βα] I go up (9)

ἀπέρχομαι [(απ)ερχ] *I go away* (9)

ἀποθνήσκω [--θαν] *I kill* (7)

ἀποκρίνομαι [κριν] *I answer* (9)

ἀποστέλλω [ἀποστελ] *I send (out, away)* (2)

--βαίνω [βα] I *go* (Always with a prefix) (9)

βάλλω [βαλ] *I throw* (7)

βλέπω [βλεπ] *I see* (2)

γεννάω [γεννα] *I beget, sire, give birth to* (10)

γίνομαι [γεν] *I am, become* (9)

γινώσκω [γνω] *I know* (2)

γράφω [γραφ] *I write* (2)

δείκνυμι [δεικ] *I show, explain* (2)

δηλόω [δηλο] *I show, explain* (2)

διδάσκω [δακ] *I teach, instruct* (7)

δίδωμι [δο] *I give* (2)

ἐγείρω [εγερ] *I rise* (7)

εἶδον [ιδ, *Aorist of* ὁράω] *I saw* (12)

εἰμί *I am* (5)

εἶπον [επ, *Aorist of* λέγω] *I said* (12)

εἰσέρχομαι [(εισ)ερχ] *I go into, enter* (9)

ἐλεύσομαι [ελευθ, *Future of* ἔρχομαι] *I will come* (11)

ἐξέρχομαι [(εξ)ερχ] *I go out* (9)

ἔρχομαι [ερχ] *I come, go* (9)

ἐρῶ [ερ, *Future of* λέγω] *I will say* (11)

ἐσθίω [εδ] *I eat* (7)

ἔσομαι [*Future of* εἰμί] *I will be* (11)

εὑρίσκω [ευρ] *I find, discover* (7)

ἔφαγον [φαγ, *Aorist of* ἐσθίω] *I ate* (12)

ἔχω [σεχ] *I have* (8)

ζάω [ζα] *I live, am alive* (10)

ζητέω [ζητε] *I seek* (10)

ἦλθον [ελευθ, *Aorist of* ἔρχομαι] *I came* (12)

ἤμην [*Imperfect of* εἰμί] *I was* (10)

ἤνεγκα [ενεγκ, *Aorist of* φέρω] *I carried* (12)

ἵστημι [στα] *I set, place, stand* (2)

καλέω [καλε] *I call* (10)

καταβαίνω [(κατα)βα] I go down (9)

κηρύσσω [κηρυγ] *I preach, proclaim* (2)

κρίνω [κριν] *I judge* (8)

λαλέω [λαλε] *I speak* (10)

λαμβάνω [λαβ] *I take, receive* (2)

λέγω [λεγ] *I say* (2)

λύω [λυ] *I destroy* (2)

μένω [μεν] *I remain* (8)

οἴσω [οι, *Future of* φέρω] *I will carry* (11)

ὁράω [ορα] *I see, perceive, experience* (10)

ὄψομαι [οπ, *Future of* ὁράω] *I will see* (11)

πίπτω [πτ] *I fall* (7)

πιστεύω [πιστευ] *I believe* (7)

ποιέω [ποιε] *I make, do* (2)

πορεύομαι [πορευ] *I go* (9)

σώζω [σωι] *I save* (8)

τίθημι [θε] *I put, place, lay* (2)

τιμάω [τιμα] *I honor* (2)

φάγομαι [φαγ, *Future of* ἐσθίω] *I will eat* (11)

φέρω [φερ] I *carry, bring, lead* (9)

φοβέομαι [φοβε] *I fear, dread* (9)

Master Vocabulary List Alphabetical

(Chapter numbers in parentheses)

α

ἀγαθός, ή, όν *good (5)*

ἀγαπάω [αγαπα] *I love (10)*

ἀγάπη, ης, ἡ *love (5)*

ἀ,γγελος, ὁ *angel (3)*

ἅγιος, ία, ον *holy (5)*

ἄγω [αγ] *draw, lead (9)*

ἀδελφός, ὁ *brother (7)*

αἴρω [αρ] *I lift up, take away (8)*

ἀκολουθέω [ακολουθε] *I follow (10)*

ἀκούω [ἀκου] *I hear, obey (2)*

ἀλήθεια, ας, ἡ *truth (5)*

ἀλλά *but (3, 8)*

ἄλλος, η, ο *other (5)*

ἁμαρτία, ας, ἡ *sin (5)*

ἀμήν *amen, truly (8)*

ἀνά (+ **accusative) in the midst of** *(6)*

ἀναβαίνω [(ανα)βα] I go up *(9)*

ἄνθρωπος, ὁ *man (7)*

ἀντί (+ **genitive) instead of, for** *(6)*

ἀπέρχομαι [(απ)ερχ] I go away *(9)*

ἀπό (+ **genitive) from, away from** *(6)*

ἀποθνήσκω [--θαν] *I kill (7)*

ἀποκρίνομαι [κριν] *I answer (9)*

ἀποστέλλω [(ἀπο)στελ] *I send (out, away) (2)*

ἀπόστολος, ὁ *apostle (3)*

ἄρτος, ὁ *bread (7)*

αὐτός *he (7)*

β

--βαίνω [βα] I go (Always with a prefix) *(9)*

βάλλω [βαλ] *I throw (7)*

βασιλεία, ας , ἡ *kingdom (5)*

βίβλος, ἡ *book (3)*

βλέπω [βλεπ] *I see (2)*

γ

γάρ *for (8)*

γεννάω [γεννα] *I beget, sire, give birth to (10)*

γῆ, ῆς, ἡ *earth (5)*

γίνομαι [γεν] *I am, become (9)*

γινώσκω [γνω] *I know (2)*

γράφω [γραφ] *I write (2)*

δ

δέ *and, but (8)*

δείκνυμι [δεικ] *I show, explain (2)*

δηλόω [δηλο] *I show, explain (2)*

διά (+ **genitive) through** *(6)*

διά (+ **accusative) because of** *(6)*

διδάσκαλος, ὁ *teacher (3)*

διδάσκω [δακ] *I teach, instruct (7)*

δίδωμι [δο] *I give (2)*

δικαιωσύνη, ης, ἡ *righteousness (5)*

δόξα, ης , ἡ *glory (5)*

δοῦλος, ὁ *slave, servant (8)*

δῶρον, τό *gift (3)*

ε

ἐγείρω [εγερ] *I rise (7)*

ἐγώ *I (7)*

εἰ *if (8)*

εἰ καί *though (8)*

εἶδον [ιδ] *I saw (12)*

εἶπον [επ] *I said (12)*

εἰρήνη, ης, ἡ *peace (5)*

εἰς (+ **accusative) to, into** *(6)*

εἰσέρχομαι [(εισ)ερχ] *I go into, enter (9)*

ἐκ (+ **genitive) from, out from** *(6)*

ἐκεῖ *there (4)*

ἐκεῖνος *that, those (7)*

ἐκκλησία, ας, ἡ *church (5)*

ἐλεύσομαι [ελευθ] *I will come (11)*

ἐν (+ **dative) in, among** *(6)*

ἐξέρχομαι [(εξ)ερχ] *I go out (9)*

ἐξουσία, ας , ἡ *authority (5)*

ἐπί (+ *genitive*) **on, near, toward** *(6)*

ἐπί (+ *dative*) **on, near, toward** *(6)*

ἐπί (+ *accusative*) **on, near, toward** *(6)*

ἔργον, τό *work (3)*

ἔρημος, ἡ *wilderness (3)*

ἔρχομαι [ερχ] *I come, go (9)*

ἐρῶ [ερ] *I will say (11)*

ἐσθίω [εδ] *I eat (7)*

ἔσχατος , η, ον *last (5)*

ἕτερος, α, ον *other (5)*

ἔτι *still, even now (4)*

εὐαγγέλιον, τό *gospel (3)*

εὐθύς *immediately (4)*

εὑρίσκω [ευρ] *I find, discover (7)*

ἔφαγον [φαγ] *I ate (12)*

ἔχω [σεχ] *I have (8)*

ἕως *while (8)*

ζ

ζάω [ζα] *I live, am alive (10)*

ζητέω [ζητε] *I seek (10)*

ζωή, ῆς, ἡ *life (5)*

η

ἤ *or (8)*

ἦλθον [ελευθ] *I came (12)*

ἡμέρα, ας , ἡ *day (5)*

ἤνεγκα [ενεγκ] *I carried (12)*

θ

θάνατος, ὁ *death (3)*

θεός, ὁ *God (7)*

ι

ἴδιος, ία, ον *one's own (5)*

ἰδού *or* Ι;δε *Look! Notice! See! (4)*

ἵνα *in order that, so (8)*

ἵστημι [στα] *I set, place, stand (2)*

κ

καθώς *as (8)*

καί *and (3, 8)*

κακῶς *poorly, badly, wickedly (4)*

καλέω [καλε] *I call (10)*

καλος., ή ον *good (5)*

καλῶς *well, rightly, fittingly (4)*

καρδία, ας, ἡ *heart (5)*

κατά (+ **genitive) against** *(6)*

κατά (+ **accusative) according to** *(6)*

καταβαίνω [(κατα)βα] *I go down (9)*

κηρύσσω [κηρυγ] *I preach, proclaim (2)*

κόσμος, ὅ *world (8)*

κρίνω [κριν] *I judge (8)*

κύριος, ὁ *Lord (7)*

λ

λαλέω [λαλε] *I speak (10)*

λαμβάνω [λαβ] *I take, receive (2)*

λάος, ὅ *people (8)*

λέγω [λεγ] *I say (2)*

λόγος, ὁ *word (3)*

λύω [λυ] *I destroy (2)*

μ

Μάρθα, ας, ἡ *Martha (5)*

Μαρία, ας, ἡ *Mary (5)*

μέν *on one hand (8)*

μένω [μεν] *I remain (8)*

μετά (+ **genitive) with** *(6)*

μετά (+ **accusative) after, behind** *(6)*

μή *not (8)*

μόνος, η, ον *only (5)*

ν

νεκρός, ά, όν *dead (5)*

νόμος, ὁ *law (7)*

νῦν *now (4)*

ο

ὅδος, ἡ *road (3)*

οἰκία, ας, ἡ *house (5)*

οἴκος, ὅ *house (8)*

οἴσω [οι] *I will carry (11)*

ὅλος, η, ον *whole (5)*

ὁράω [ορα] *I see, perceive, experience (10)*

ὅτε *when (8)*

ὅτι *because, that (8)*

οὗ *where (8)*

οὐ, οὐκ, οὐχ *not (4, 8)*

οὐκέτι *no longer (4)*

οὖν *therefore, then (8)*

οὐρανός, ὅ *heaven (8)*

οὗτος *this, these (7)*

ὀφθαλμός, ὅ *eye (8)*

ὄχλος, ὁ *crowd (3)*

ὄψομαι [οπ], *I will see (11)*

π

παιδίον, τό *child (3)*

πάλιν *again (4)*

πάντοτε *always (4)*

παρά (+ *genitive*) **out from** *(6)*

παρά (+ *dative*) **beside** *(6)*

παρά (+ *accusative*) **along side** *(6)*

περί (+ ***genitive***) ***concerning*** *(6)*

περί (+ ***accusative***) ***around*** *(6)*

πίπτω [πτ] *I fall (7)*

πιστεύω [πιστευ] *I believe (7)*

ποιέω [ποιε] *I make, do (2)*

πορεύομαι [πορευ] *I go (9)*

ποῦ *where? (4)*

πρό (+ ***genitive***) ***before*** *(6)*

πρός (+ ***accusative***) ***to, toward*** *(6)*

πρῶτος, η, ον *first (5)*

πῶς *how? (4)*

σ

στέφανος, ὁ *crown (3)*

σύ *you (7)*

σύν (+ ***dative***) ***along with*** *(6)*

σῴζω [σωι] *I save (8)*

τέκνον, τό *child (3)*

τίθημι [θε] *I put, place, lay (2)*

τιμάω [τιμα] *I honor (2)*

τόπος, ὁ *place (8)*

υ

υἱός, ὁ *son (7)*

ὑπέρ (+ ***genitive***) ***in behalf of*** *(6)*

ὑπέρ (+ ***accusative***) ***over*** *(6)*

ὑπό (+ ***genitive***) ***by*** *(6)*

ὑπό (+ ***accusative***) ***underneath*** *(6)*

φ

φάγομαι [φαγ] *I will eat (11)*

φέρω [φερ] *I carry, bring, lead (9)*

φοβέομαι [φοβε] *I fear, dread (9)*

φωνή, ῆς, ἡ *voice (5)*

χ

χρυσός, ὁ *gold (3)*

ψ

ψυχή, ῆς, ἡ *soul (5)*

ω

ὧδε *here (4)*

ὥρα, ας, ἡ *hour (5)*

ὡς *as (8)*

ὥστε *with the result that (8)*

Paradigms

First Declension

The 1st declension is classified as nouns having an α or η stem vowel. The following chart contains the 1st declension endings with stem vowels:

	Singular				Plural
	Feminine			Masculine	
Stem Ending In	εα, ια, ρα	α¹	η		
Nominative	−α	−α	−η	−ης	−αι
Genitive	−ας	−ης	−ης	−ου	−ων
Dative	−ᾳ	−ῃ	−ῃ	−ῃ	−αις
Accusative	−αν	−αν	−ην	−ν	−ας
Vocative	−α	−α	−η	−α	−αι

¹ Stem ending in α and the preceding letter is not ε, ι, or ρ.

The declension of ὥρα, ἡ, stem ὡρα−, *an hour*, ἀλήθεια, ἡ, stem ἀληεια−, *truth*, δόξα, ἡ, stem δοξα−, *glory*, and γραφή, ἡ, stem γραφα−, *a writing, a Scripture*, is as follows:

	Singular				Plural			
Nominative	ὥρα	ἀλήθεια	δόξα	γραφή	ὧραι	ἀλήθειαι	δόξαι	γραφαί
Genitive	ὥρας	ἀληθείας	δόξης	γραφῆς	ὡρῶν	ἀληθειῶν	δοξῶν	γραφῶν
Dative	ὥρᾳ	ἀληθείᾳ	δόξῃ	γραφῇ	ὥραις	ἀληθείαις	δόξαις	γραφαῖς
Accusative	ὥραν	ἀλήθειαν	δόξαν	γραφήν	ὥρας	ἀληθείας	δόξας	γραφάς
Vocative	ὥρα	ἀλήθεια	δόξα	γραφή	ὧραι	ἀλήθειαι	δόξαι	γραφαί

The declension of προφήτης, ὁ, stem προφητα–, *a prophet*, and μαθητής, ὁ, stem μαθητα–, *a disciple*, is as follows:

	Singular		Plural	
Nominative	προφήτης	μαθητής	προφῆται	μαθηταί
Genitive	προφήτου	μαθητοῦ	προφητῶν	μαθητῶν
Dative	προφήτῃ	μαθητῇ	προφήταις	μαθηταῖς
Accusative	προφήτην	μαθητήν	προφήτας	μαθητάς
Vocative	προφῆτα	μαθητά	προφῆται	μαθηταί

Second Declension

The 2nd declension is classified as nouns having an O stem vowel. The following chart contains the 2nd declension endings with stem vowels:

	Singular			Plural		
	Masculine	Feminine	Neuter	Masculine	Feminine	Neuter
Nominative	–ος	–ος	–ον	–οι	–οι	–α
Genitive	–ου	–ου	–ου	–ων	–ων	–ων
Dative	–ῳ	–ῳ	–ῳ	–οις	–οις	–οις
Accusative	–ον	–ον	–ον	–ους	–ους	–α
Vocative	–ε	–ε	–ον	–οι	–οι	–α

The declension of λόγος, ὁ, stem λογο–, *a word*, ἄνθρωπος, ὁ, stem ἀνθρωπο–, *a man*, υἱός, ὁ, stem υἱο–, *a son*, and δοῦλος, ὁ, stem δουλο–, *a slave*, is as follows:

	Singular				Plural			
Nominative	λόγος	ἄνθρωπος	υἱός	δοῦλος	λόγοι	ἄνθρωποι	υἱοί	δοῦλοι
Genitive	λόγου	ἀνθρώπου	υἱοῦ	δούλου	λόγων	ἀνθρώπων	υἱῶν	δούλων
Dative	λόγῳ	ἀνθρώπῳ	υἱῷ	δούλῳ	λόγοις	ἀνθρώποις	υἱοῖς	δούλοις
Accusative	λόγον	ἄνθρωπον	υἱόν	δοῦλον	λόγους	ἀνθρώπους	υἱούς	δούλους
Vocative	λόγε	ἄνθρωπε	υἱέ	δοῦλε	λόγοι	ἄνθρωποι	υἱοί	δοῦλοι

The declension of δῶρον, τό, stem δωρο–, *a gift*, is as follows:

	Singular	Plural
Nominative	δῶρον	δῶρα
Genitive	δώρου	δώρων
Dative	δώρῳ	δώροις
Accusative	δῶρον	δῶρα
Vocative	δῶρον	δῶρα

Third Declension

The 3rd declension is classified as nouns ending in a consonant, thus not containing a stem vowel. The following chart contains the 3rd declension endings:

	Singular			Plural		
	Masculine	Feminine	Neuter	Masculine	Feminine	Neuter
Nominative	–ς / –	–ς / –	–	–ες	–ες	–α
Genitive	–ος	–ος	–ος	–ων	–ων	–ων
Dative	–ι	–ι	–ι	–σι(ν)	–σι(ν)	–σι(ν)
Accusative	–α / –ν	–α / –ν	–	–ας / –ες	–ας / –ες	–α
Vocative	–ς / –	–ς / –	–	–ες	–ες	–α

The declension of νύξ, ἡ, stem νυκτ–, *a night*, σάρξ, ἡ, stem σαρκ–, *flesh*, ἄρχων, ὁ, stem ἀρχοντ–, *a ruler*, is as follows:

	Singular			Plural		
Nominative	νύξ	σάρξ	ἄρχων	νύκτες	σάρκες	ἄρχοντες
Genitive	νυκτός	σαρκός	ἄρχοντος	νυκτῶν	σαρκῶν	ἀρχόντων
Dative	νυκτί	σαρκί	ἄρχοντι	νυξί(ν)	σαρξί(ν)	ἄρχουσι(ν)
Accusative	νύκτα	σάρκα	ἄρχοντα	νύκτας	σάρκας	ἄρχοντας
Vocative	νύξ	σάρξ	ἄρχων	νύκτες	σάρκες	ἄρχοντες

The declension of ἐλπίς, ἡ, stem ἐλπιδ–, *hope*, and χάρις, ἡ, stem χαριτ–, *grace*, is as follows:

	Singular		Plural	
Nominative	ἐλπίς	χάρις	ἐλπίδες	χάριτες
Genitive	ἐλπίδος	χάριτος	ἐλπίδων	χαρίτων
Dative	ἐλπίδι	χάριτι	ἐλπίσι(ν)	χάρισι(ν)
Accusative	ἐλπίδα	χάριν	ἐλπίδας	χάριτας
Vocative	ἐλπί	χάρις	ἐλπίδες	χάριτες

The declension of ὄνομα, τό, stem ὀνοματ–, *a name*, is as follows:

	Singular	Plural
Nominative	ὄνομα	ὀνόματα
Genitive	ὀνόματος	ὀναμάτων
Dative	ὀνόματι	ὀνόμασι(ν)
Accusative	ὄνομα	ὀνόματα
Vocative	ὄνομα	ὀνόματα

The declension of γένος, τό, stem γενεσ–, *a race*, is as follows:

	Singular	Plural
Nominative	γένος	γένη
Genitive	γένους	γενῶν
Dative	γένει	γένεσι(ν)
Accusative	γένος	γένη
Vocative	γένος	γένη

The declension of πόλις, ἡ, stem πολι–, *a city*, is as follows:

	Singular	Plural
Nominative	πόλις	πόλεις
Genitive	πόλεως	πόλεων
Dative	πόλει	πόλεσι(ν)
Accusative	πόλιν	πόλεις
Vocative	πόλι	πόλεις

The declension of βασιλεύς, ὁ, stem βασιλευ–, *a king*, is as follows:

	Singular	Plural
Nominative	βασιλεύς	βασιλεῖς
Genitive	βασιλέως	βασιλέων
Dative	βασιλεῖ	βασιλεῦσι(ν)
Accusative	βασιλέα	βασιλεῖς
Vocative	βασιλεῦ	βασιλεῖς

The declension of πατήρ, ὁ, stem πατερ–, *a father*, ἀνήρ, ὁ, stem ἀνερ–, *a man*, and μήτηρ, ἡ, stem μητερ–, *a mother*, is as follows:

	Singular			Plural		
Nominative	πατήρ	ἀνήρ	μήτηρ	πατέρες	ἄνδρες	μητέρες
Genitive	πατρός	ἀνδρός	μητρός	πατέρων	ἀνδρῶν	μητέρων
Dative	πατρί	ἀνδρί	μητρί	πατράσι(ν)	ἀνδράσι(ν)	μητράσι(ν)
Accusative	πατέρα	ἄνδρα	μητέρα	πατέρας	ἄνδρας	μητέρας
Vocative	πάτερ	ἄνερ	μῆτερ	πατέρες	ἄνδρες	μητέρες

The declension of χείρ, ἡ, *a hand*, and γυνή, ἡ, *a woman*, is as follows:

	Singular		Plural	
Nominative	χείρ	γυνή	χεῖρες	γυναῖκες
Genitive	χειρός	γυναικός	χειρῶν	γυναικῶν
Dative	χειρί	γυναικί	χερσί(ν)	γυνειξί(ν)
Accusative	χεῖρα	γυναῖκα	χεῖρας	γυναῖκας
Vocative	χείρ	γύναι	χεῖρες	γυναῖκες

The Article

The declension of the article, ὁ, ἡ, τό, *the*, is as follows:

	Singular			Plural		
	Masculine	Feminine	Neuter	Masculine	Feminine	Neuter
Nominative	ὁ	ἡ	τό	οἱ	αἱ	τά
Genitive	τοῦ	τῆς	τοῦ	τῶν	τῶν	τῶν
Dative	τῷ	τῇ	τῷ	τοῖς	ταῖς	τοῖς
Accusative	τόν	τήν	τό	τούς	τάς	τά

Adjectives

The declension of ἀγαθός, ή, όν, *good*, is as follows:

	Singular			Plural		
	Masculine	Feminine	Neuter	Masculine	Feminine	Neuter
Nominative	ἀγαθός	ἀγαθή	ἀγαθόν	ἀγαθοί	ἀγαθαί	ἀγαθά
Genitive	ἀγαθοῦ	ἀγαθῆς	ἀγαθοῦ	ἀγαθῶν	ἀγαθῶν	ἀγαθῶν
Dative	ἀγαθῷ	ἀγαθῇ	ἀγαθῷ	ἀγαθοῖς	ἀγαθαῖς	ἀγαθοῖς
Accusative	ἀγαθόν	ἀγαθήν	ἀγαθόν	ἀγαθούς	ἀγαθάς	ἀγαθά
Vocative	ἀγαθέ	ἀγαθή	ἀγαθόν	ἀγαθοί	ἀγαθαί	ἀγαθά

The declension of μικρός, ά, όν, *small*, is as follows;

	Singular			Plural		
	Masculine	Feminine	Neuter	Masculine	Feminine	Neuter
Nominative	μικρός	μικρά	μικρόν	μικροί	μικραί	μικρά
Genitive	μικροῦ	μικρᾶς	μικροῦ	μικρῶν	μικρῶν	μικρῶν
Dative	μικρῷ	μικρᾷ	μικρῷ	μικροῖς	μικραῖς	μικροῖς
Accusative	μικρόν	μικράν	μικρόν	μικρούς	μικρᾶς	μικρά
Vocative	μικρέ	μικρά	μικρόν	μικροί	μικραί	μικρά

The declension of δίκαιος, α, ον, *righteous*, is as follows:

	Singular			Plural		
	Masculine	Feminine	Neuter	Masculine	Feminine	Neuter
Nominative	δίκαιος	δικαία	δίκαιον	δίκαιοι	δίκαιαι	δίκαια
Genitive	δικαίου	δικαίας	δικαίου	δικαίων	δικαίων	δικαίων
Dative	δικαίῳ	δικαίᾳ	δικαίῳ	δικαίοις	δικαίαις	δικαίοις
Accusative	δίκαιον	δικαίαν	δίκαιον	δικαίους	δικαίας	δίκαια
Vocative	δίκαιε	δικαία	δίκαιον	δίκαιοι	δίκαιαι	δίκαια

The declension of the comparative adjective μείζων, μεῖζον, *greater*, is as follows: (Note that there are sometimes two forms for the same case)

	Singular			Plural		
	Masculine	Feminine	Neuter	Masculine	Feminine	Neuter
Nominative	μείζων	μείζων	μεῖζον	μείζονες / μείζους	μείζονες / μείζους	μείζονα / μείζω
Genitive	μείζονος	μείζονος	μείζονος	μειζόνων	μειζόνων	μειζόνων
Dative	μείζονι	μείζονι	μείζονι	μείζοσι(ν)	μείζοσι(ν)	μείζοσι(ν)
Accusative	μείζονα / μείζω	μείζονα / μείζω	μεῖζον	μείζονας / μείζους	μείζονας / μείζους	μείζονα / μείζω

The declension of ἀληθής, ές, *true*, is as follows:

	Singular			Plural		
	Masculine	Feminine	Neuter	Masculine	Feminine	Neuter
Nominative	ἀληθής	ἀληθής	ἀληθές	ἀληθεῖς	ἀληθεῖς	ἀληθῆ
Genitive	ἀληθοῦς	ἀληθοῦς	ἀληθοῦς	ἀληθῶν	ἀληθῶν	ἀληθῶν
Dative	ἀληθεῖ	ἀληθεῖ	ἀληθεῖ	ἀληθέσι(ν)	ἀληθέσι(ν)	ἀληθέσι(ν)
Accusative	ἀληθῆ	ἀληθῆ	ἀληθές	ἀληθεῖς	ἀληθεῖς	ἀληθῆ
Vocative	ἀληθές	ἀληθές	ἀληθές	ἀληθεῖς	ἀληθεῖς	ἀληθῆ

The declension of πᾶς, πᾶσα, πᾶν, *all*, is as follows:

	Singular			Plural		
	Masculine	Feminine	Neuter	Masculine	Feminine	Neuter
Nominative	πᾶς	πᾶσα	πᾶν	πάντες	πᾶσαι	πάντα
Genitive	παντός	πάσης	παντός	πάντων	πασῶν	πάντων
Dative	παντί	πάσῃ	παντί	πᾶσι(ν)	πάσαις	πᾶσι(ν)
Accusative	πάντα	πᾶσαν	πᾶν	πάντας	πάσας	πάντα

The declension of πολύς, πολλή, πολύ, *much*, is as follows:

	Singular			Plural		
	Masculine	Feminine	Neuter	Masculine	Feminine	Neuter
Nominative	πολύς	πολλή	πολύ	πολλοί	πολλαί	πολλά
Genitive	πολλοῦ	πολλῆς	πολλοῦ	πολλῶν	πολλῶν	πολλῶν
Dative	πολλῷ	πολλῇ	πολλῷ	πολλοῖς	πολλαῖς	πολλοῖς
Accusative	πολύν	πολλήν	πολύ	πολλούς	πολλάς	πολλά

The declension of μέγας, μεγάλη, μέγα, *great*, is as follows:

	Singular			Plural		
	Masculine	Feminine	Neuter	Masculine	Feminine	Neuter
Nominative	μέγας	μεγάλη	μέγα	μεγάλοι	μεγάλαι	μεγάλα
Genitive	μεγάλου	μεγάλης	μεγάλου	μεγάλων	μεγάλων	μεγάλων
Dative	μεγάλῳ	μεγάλη	μεγάλῳ	μεγάλοις	μεγάλαις	μεγάλοις
Accusative	μέγαν	μεγάλην	μέγα	μεγάλους	μεγάλας	μεγάλοις
Vocative	μεγάλε	μεγάλη	μέγα	μεγάλοι	μεγάλαι	μεγάλα

Participles

The declension of λύων, λύουσα, λῦον, *destroying*, the present active participle of λύω, is as follows:

	Singular			Plural		
	Masculine	Feminine	Neuter	Masculine	Feminine	Neuter
Nominative	λύων	λύουσα	λῦον	λύοντες	λύουσαι	λύοντα
Genitive	λύοντος	λυούσης	λύοντος	λυόντων	λυουσῶν	λυόντων
Dative	λύοντι	λυούση	λύοντι	λύουσι(ν)	λυούσαις	λύουσι(ν)
Accusative	λύοντα	λύουσαν	λῦον	λύοντας	λυούσας	λύοντα

The declension of λυόμενος, λυομένη, λυόμενον, *being destroyed*, the present middle/passive participle of λύω, is as follows:

	Singular			Plural		
	Masculine	Feminine	Neuter	Masculine	Feminine	Neuter
Nominative	λυόμενος	λυομένη	λυόμενον	λυόμενοι	λυόμεναι	λυόμενα
Genitive	λυομένου	λυομένης	λυομένου	λυομένων	λυομένων	λυομένων
Dative	λυομένῳ	λυομένη	λυομένῳ	λυομένοις	λυομέναις	λυομένοις
Accusative	λυόμενον	λυομένην	λυόμενον	λυομένους	λυομένας	λυόμενα

The declension of λύσας, λύσασα, λῦσαν, *having destroyed*, the aorist active participle of λύω, is as follows:

	Singular			Plural		
	Masculine	Feminine	Neuter	Masculine	Feminine	Neuter
Nominative	λύσας	λύσασα	λῦσαν	λύσαντες	λύσασαι	λύσαντα
Genitive	λύσαντος	λυσάσης	λύσαντος	λυσάντων	λυσασῶν	λυσάντων
Dative	λύσαντι	λυσάση	λύσαντι	λύσασι(ν)	λυσάσαις	λύσασι(ν)
Accusative	λύσαντα	λύσασαν	λῦσαν	λύσαντας	λυσάσας	λύσαντα

The declension of λυσάμενος, λυσαμένη, λυσάμενον, *myself having destroyed*, the aorist middle participle of λύω, is as follows:

	Singular			Plural		
	Masculine	Feminine	Neuter	Masculine	Feminine	Neuter
Nominative	λυσάμενος	λυσαμένη	λυσάμενον	λυσάμενοι	λυσάμεναι	λυσάμενα
Genitive	λυσαμένου	λυσαμένης	λυσαμένου	λυσαμένων	λυσαμένων	λυσαμένων
Dative	λυσαμένῳ	λυσαμένη	λυσαμένῳ	λυσαμένοις	λυσαμέναις	λυσαμένοις
Accusative	λυσάμενον	λθσαμένην	λυσάμενον	λυσαμένους	λυσαμένας	λυσάμενα

The declension of λυθείς, λυθεῖσα, λυθέν, *having been destroyed*, the aorist passive participle of λύω, is as follows:

	Singular			Plural		
	Masculine	Feminine	Neuter	Masculine	Feminine	Neuter
Nominative	λυθείς	λυθεῖσα	λυθέν	λυθέντες	λυθεῖσαι	λυθέντα
Genitive	λυθέντος	λυθείσης	λυθέντος	λυθέντων	λυθεισῶν	λυθέντων
Dative	λυθέντι	λυθείσῃ	λυθέντι	λυθεῖσι(ν)	λυθείσαις	λυθεῖσι(ν)
Accusative	λυθέντα	λυθεῖσαν	λυθέν	λυθέντας	λυθείσας	λυθέντα

The declension of λελυκώς, λελυκυῖα, λελυκός, *having destroyed*, the perfect active participle of λύω, is as follows:

	Singular			Plural		
	Masculine	Feminine	Neuter	Masculine	Feminine	Neuter
Nominative	λελυκώς	λελυκυῖα	λελυκός	λελυκότες	λελυκυῖαι	λελυκότα
Genitive	λελυκότος	λελυκυίας	λελυκότος	λελυκότων	λελυκυιῶν	λελυκότων
Dative	λελυκότι	λελυκυίᾳ	λελυκότι	λελυκόσι(ν)	λελυκυίαις	λελυκόσι(ν)
Accusative	λελυκότα	λελυκυῖαν	λελυκός	λελυκότας	λελυκυίας	λελυκότα

The declension of λελυμένος, λελυμένη, λελυμένον, *having been destroyed*, the perfect middle/passive participle of λύω, is as follows:

	Singular			Plural		
	Masculine	Feminine	Neuter	Masculine	Feminine	Neuter
Nominative	λελυμένος	λελυμένη	λελυμένον	λελυμένοι	λελυμέναι	λελυμένα
Genitive	λελυμένου	λελυμένης	λελυμένου	λελυμένων	λελυμένων	λελυμένων
Dative	λελυμένῳ	λελυμένῃ	λελυμένῳ	λελυμένοις	λελυμέναις	λελυμένοις
Accusative	λελυμένον	λελυμένην	λελυμένον	λελυμένους	λελυμένας	λελυμένα

The declension of ὤν, οὖσα, ὄν, *being*, the present participle of εἰμί, is as follows:

	Singular			Plural		
	Masculine	Feminine	Neuter	Masculine	Feminine	Neuter
Nominative	ὤν	οὖσα	ὄν	ὄντες	οὖσαι	ὄντα
Genitive	ὄντος	οὔσης	ὄντος	ὄντων	οὐσῶν	ὄντων
Dative	ὄντι	οὔσῃ	ὄντι	οὖσι(ν)	οὔσαις	οὖσι(ν)
Accusative	ὄντα	οὖσαν	ὄν	ὄντας	οὔσας	ὄντα

Pronouns

The declensions of the first and second personal pronouns, ἐγώ, *I*, and σύ, *you*, are as follows: (Note that an emphatic ε may be present on the singular forms of ἐγώ)

	Singular		Plural	
Nominative	ἐγώ	σύ	ἡμεῖς	ὑμεῖς
Genitive	ἐμοῦ / μου	σοῦ	ἡμῶν	ὑμῶν
Dative	ἐμοί / μοι	σοί	ἡμῖν	ὑμῖν
Accusative	ἐμί / με	σέ	ἡμᾶς	ὑμᾶς

The declension of the third personal pronoun, αὐτός, ή, ό, *he, she, it,* is as follows:

	Singular			Plural		
	Masculine	Feminine	Neuter	Masculine	Feminine	Neuter
Nominative	αὐτός	αὐτή	αὐτό	αὐτοί	αὐταί	αὐτά
Genitive	αὐτοῦ	αὐτῆς	αὐτοῦ	αὐτῶν	αὐτῶν	αὐτῶν
Dative	αὐτῷ	αὐτῇ	αὐτῷ	αὐτοῖς	αὐταῖς	αὐτοῖς
Accusative	αὐτόν	αὐτήν	αὐτό	αὐτούς	αὐτάς	αὐτά

The declension of οὗτος, αὕτη, τοῦτο, *this*, is as follows:

	Singular			Plural		
	Masculine	Feminine	Neuter	Masculine	Feminine	Neuter
Nominative	οὗτος	αὕτη	τοῦτο	οὗτοι	αὗται	ταῦτα
Genitive	τούτου	ταύτης	τούτου	τούτων	τούτων	τούτων
Dative	τούτῳ	ταύτῃ	τούτῳ	τούτοις	ταύταις	τούτοις
Accusative	τοῦτον	ταύτην	τοῦτο	τούτους	ταύτας	ταῦτα

The declension of ἐκεῖνος, ἐκείνη, ἐκεῖνο, *that*, is as follows:

	Singular			Plural		
	Masculine	Feminine	Neuter	Masculine	Feminine	Neuter
Nominative	ἐκεῖνος	ἐκείνη	ἐκεῖνο	ἐκεῖνοι	ἐκεῖναι	ἐκεῖνα
Genitive	ἐκείνου	ἐκείνης	ἐκείνου	ἐκείνων	ἐκείνων	ἐκείνων
Dative	ἐκείνῳ	ἐκείνῃ	ἐκείνῳ	ἐκείνοις	ἐκείναις	ἐκείνοις
Accusative	ἐκεῖνον	ἐκείνην	ἐκεῖνο	ἐκείνους	ἐκείνας	ἐκεῖνα

The declension of the relative pronoun, ὅς, ἥ, ὅ, *who, which, what,* is as follows:

	Singular			Plural		
	Masculine	Feminine	Neuter	Masculine	Feminine	Neuter
Nominative	ὅς	ἥ	ὅ	οἵ	αἵ	ἅ
Genitive	οὗ	ἧς	οὗ	ὧν	ὧν	ὧν
Dative	ᾧ	ᾗ	ᾧ	οἷς	αἷς	οἷς
Accusative	ὅν	ἥν	ὅ	οὕς	ἅς	ἅ

The declension of the indefinite relative pronoun, ὅστις, ἥτις, ὅ τι, *whoever, whichever, everyone who*, is as follows:

	Singular			Plural		
	Masculine	Feminine	Neuter	Masculine	Feminine	Neuter
Nominative	ὅστις	ἥτις	ὅ τι / ὅτι	οἵτινες	αἵτινες	ἅτινα
Genitive	οὗτινος	ἧστινος	οὗτινος	ὧντινων	ὧντινων	ὧντινων
Dative	ᾧτινι	ᾗτινι	ᾧτινι	οἷστισι(ν)	αἷστισι(ν)	οἷστισι(ν)
Accusative	ὅντινα	ἥντινα	ὅ τι / ὅτι	οὕστινας	ἅστινας	ἅτινα

The declension of the interrogative pronoun, τίς, τί, *who? which? what?*, is as follows:

	Singular			Plural		
	Masculine	Feminine	Neuter	Masculine	Feminine	Neuter
Nominative	τίς	τίς	τί	τίνες	τίνες	τίνα
Genitive	τίνος	τίνος	τίνος	τίνων	τίνων	τίνων
Dative	τίνι	τίνι	τίνι	τίσι(ν)	τίσι(ν)	τίσι(ν)
Accusative	τίνα	τίνα	τί	τίνας	τίνας	τίνα

The declension of the indefinite pronoun, τις, τι, *someone, something*, is as follows:

	Singular			Plural		
	Masculine	Feminine	Neuter	Masculine	Feminine	Neuter
Nominative	τις	τις	τι	τινές	τινές	τινά
Genitive	τινός	τινός	τινός	τινῶν	τινῶν	τινῶν
Dative	τινί	τινί	τινί	τισί(ν)	τισί(ν)	τισί(ν)
Accusative	τινά	τινά	τι	τινάς	τινάς	τινά

The declension of the reflexing pronouns, ἐμαυτοῦ, ῆς, *of myself*, σεαυτοῦ, ῆς, *of yourself*, and ἑαυτοῦ, ῆς, οὖ, *of himself, of herself, of itself*, is as follows:

		1st Person		2nd Person		3rd Person		
		Masculine	Feminine	Masculine	Feminine	Masculine	Feminine	Neuter
Singular	Genitive	ἐμαυτοῦ	ἐμαυτῆς	σεαυτοῦ	σεαυτῆς	ἑαυτοῦ	ἑαυτῆς	ἑαυτοῦ
	Dative	ἐμαυτῷ	ἐμαυτῇ	σεαυτῷ	σεαυτῇ	ἑαυτῷ	ἑαυτῇ	ἑαυτῷ
	Accusative	ἐμαυτόν	ἐμαυτήν	σεαυτόν	σεαυτήν	ἑαυτόν	ἑαυτήν	ἑαυτό
Plural	Genitive	ἑαυτῶν	ἑαυτῶν	ἑαυτῶν	ἑαυτῶν	ἑαυτῶν	ἑαυτῶν	ἑαυτῶν
	Dative	ἑαυτοῖς	ἑαυταῖς	ἑαυτοῖς	ἑαυταῖς	ἑαυτοῖς	ἑαυταῖς	ἑαυτοῖς
	Accusative	ἑαυτούς	ἑαυτάς	ἑαυτούς	ἑαυτάς	ἑαυτούς	ἑαυτάς	ἑαυτά

The declension of the reciprocal pronouns, ἀλλήλων, *one another*, is as follows:

	Plural
Genitive	ἀλλήλων
Dative	ἀλλήλοις
Accusative	ἀλλήλους

Verbs

The athematic (μι) or common/pure personal endings are as follows:

	Primary Tense Endings				Secondary/Historical Tense Endings			
	Active		Middle/Passive		Active		Middle/Passive	
	Singular	Plural	Singular	Plural	Singular	Plural	Singular	Plural
1st	–μι	–μεν	–μαι	–μεθα	–ν	–μεν	–μην	–μεθα
2nd	–σι[1]	–τε	–σαι	–σθε	–ς	–τε	–σο	–σθε
3rd	–τι[2]	–ντι[3]	–ται	–νται	–	–ν	–το	–ντο

[1] Will appear as ς   [2] Will appear as σι(ν)   [3] Will appear as ασι(ν)

The thematic (ω) or personal endings combined with connecting vowels are as follows:

	Primary Tense Endings				Secondary/Historical Tense Endings			
	Active		Middle/Passive		Active		Middle/Passive	
	Singular	Plural	Singular	Plural	Singular	Plural	Singular	Plural
1st	–ω	–ομεν	–ομαι	–ομεθα	–ον	–ομεν	–ομην	–ομεθα
2nd	–εις	–ετε	–η	–εσθε	–ες	–ετε	–ου	–εσθε
3rd	–ει	–ουσι(ν)	–εται	–ονται	–[1]	–ον	–ετο	–οντο

[1] May appear as ε

The first principal part of the conjugation of λύω, *I destroy*, root λυ–, is as follows:

		λυ–							
		Present Active		Present Middle/Passive		Imperfect Active		Imperfect Middle/Passive	
		Singular	Plural	Singular	Plural	Singular	Plural	Singular	Plural
Indicative Mood	1st	λύω	λύομεν	λύομαι	λυόμεθα	ἔλυον	ἐλύομεν	ἐλυόμην	ἐλυόμεθα
	2nd	λύεις	λύετε	λύῃ	λύεσθε	ἔλυες	ἐλύετε	ἐλύου	ἐλύεσθε
	3rd	λύει	λύουσι(ν)	λύεται	λύονται	ἔλυε(ν)	ἔλυον	ἐλύετο	ἐλύοντο
Subjunctive Mood	1st	λύω	λύωμεν	λύωμαι	λυώμεθα				
	2nd	λύῃς	λύητε	λύῃ	λύησθε				
	3rd	λύῃ	λύωσι(ν)	λύηται	λύωνται				
Imperative Mood	2nd	λῦε	λύετε	λύου	λύεσθε				
	3rd	λυέτω	λυέτωσαν	λυέσθω	λυέσθωσαν				
Infinitive Mode		λύειν		λύεσθαι					
Participle Mode (Nom. Sg. Form)	Masculine	λύων		λυόμενος					
	Feminine	λύουσα		λυομένη					
	Neuter	λῦον		λυόμενον					

The second and third principle parts of the conjugation of λύω, *I destroy*, root λυ–, is as follows:

		λυσ–				λυσα-			
		Future Active		Future Middle		Aorist Active		Aorist Middle	
		Singular	Plural	Singular	Plural	Singular	Plural	Singular	Plural
Indicative Mood	1st	λύσω	λύσομεν	λύσομαι	λυσόμεθα	ἔλυσα	ἐλύσαμεν	ἐλυσάμην	ἐλυσάμεθα
	2nd	λύσεις	λύσετε	λύσῃ	λύσεσθε	ἔλυσας	ἐλύσατε	ἐλύσω	ἐλύσασθε
	3rd	λύσει	λύσουσι(ν)	λύσεται	λύσονται	ἔλυσε(ν)	ἔλυσαν	ἐλύσατο	ἐλύσαντο
Subjunctive Mood	1st					λύσω	λύσωμεν	λύσωμαι	λυσώμεθα
	2nd					λύσῃς	λύσητε	λύσῃ	λύσησθε
	3rd					λύσῃ	λύσωσι(ν)	λύσηται	λύσωντα
Imperative Mood	2nd					λῦσον	λύσατε	λῦσαι	λύσασθε
	3rd					λυσάτω	λυσάτωσαν	λυσάσθω	λυσάσθωσαν
Infinitive Mode						λῦσαι		λύσασθαι	
Participle Mode (Nom. Sg. Form)	Masculine					λύσας		λυσάμενος	
	Feminine					λύσασα		λυσαμένη	
	Neuter					λῦσαν		λυσάμενον	

The fourth and fifth principle parts of the conjugation of λύω, *I destroy*, root λυ–, is as follows:

		λελυκα–				λελυ–	
		Perfect Active		Pluperfect Active		Perfect Middle/Passive	
		Singular	Plural	Singular	Plural	Singular	Plural
Indicative Mood	1st	λέλυκα	λελύκαμεν	(ἐ)λελύκειν	(ἐ)λελύκειμεν	λέλυμαι	λελύμεθα
	2nd	λέλυκας	λελύκατε	(ἐ)λελύκεις	(ἐ)λελύκειτε	λέλυσαι	λέλυσθα
	3rd	λέλυκε(ν)	λελύκασι(ν) or λέλυκαν	(ἐ)λελύκει	(ἐ) λελύκεισαν	λέλυται	λέλυνται
Infinitive Mode		λελυκέναι				λελύσθαι	
Participle Mode (Nom. Sg. Form)	Masculine	λελυκώς				λελυμένος	
	Feminine	λελυκυῖα				λελυμένη	
	Neuter	λελυκός				λελυμένον	

The sixth principle part of the conjugation of λύω, *I destroy*, root λυ–, is as follows:

		λυθη–			
		Aorist Passive		Future Passive	
		Singular	Plural	Singular	Plural
Indicative Mood	1st	ἐλύθην	ἐλύθημεν	λυθήσομαι	λυθησόμεθα
	2nd	ἐλύθης	ἐλύθητε	λυθήσῃ	λυθήσεσθε
	3rd	ἐλύθη	ἐλύθησαν	λυθήσεται	λυθήσονται
Subjunctive Mood	1st	λυθῶ	λυθῶμεν		
	2nd	λυθῇς	λυθῆτε		
	3rd	λυθῇ	λυθῶσι(ν)		
Imperative Mood	2nd	λύθητι	λυθήτε		
	3rd	λυθήτω	λυθήτωσαν		
Infinitive Mode		λυθῆναι			
Participle Mode (Nom. Sg. Form)	Masculine	λυθείς			
	Feminine	λυθεῖσα			
	Neuter	λυθέν			

The first principle part of the conjugation of τιμάω, *I honor*, root τιμα–, is as follows:

		Present Active		Present Middle/Passive		Imperfect Active		Imperfect Middle/Passive	
		Singular	Plural	Singular	Plural	Singular	Plural	Singular	Plural
Indicative Mood	1st	(τιμάω) τιμῶ	(τιμάομεν) τιμῶμεν	(τιμάομαι) τιμῶμαι	(τιμαόμεθα) τιμώμεθα	(ἐτίμαον) ἐτίμων	(ἐτιμάομεν) ἐτιμῶμεν	(ἐτιμαόμην) ἐτιμώμην	(ἐτιμαόμεθα) ἐτιμώμεθα
	2nd	(τιμάεις) τιμᾷς	(τιμάετε) τιμᾶτε	(τιμάῃ) τιμᾷ	(τιμάεσθε) τιμᾶσθε	(ἐτίμαες) ἐτίμας	(ἐτιμάετε) ἐτιμᾶτε	(ἐτιμάου) ἐτιμῶ	(ἐτιμάεσθε) ἐτιμᾶσθε
	3rd	(τιμάει) τιμᾷ	(τιμάουσι(ν)) τιμῶσι(ν)	(τιμάεται) τιμᾶται	(τιμάονται) τιμῶνται	(ἐτίμαε) ἐτίμα	(ἐτίμαον) ἐτίμων	(ἐτιμάετο) ἐτιμᾶτο	(ἐτιμάοντο) ἐτιμῶντο
Subjunctive Mood	1st	(τιμάω) τιμῶ	(τιμάωμεν) τιμῶμεν	(τιμάωμαι) τιμῶμαι	(τιμαώμεθα) τιμώμεθα				
	2nd	(τιμάῃς) τιμᾷς	(τιμάητε) τιμᾶτε	(τιμάῃ) τιμᾷ	(τιμάησθε) τιμᾶσθε				
	3rd	(τιμάῃ) τιμᾷ	(τιμάωσι(ν)) τιμῶσι(ν)	(τιμάηται) τιμᾶται	(τιμάωνται) τιμῶνται				
Imperative Mood	2nd	(τίμαε) τίμα	(τιμάετε) τιμᾶτε	(τιμάου) τιμῶ	(τιμάεσθε) τιμᾶσθε				
	3rd	(τιμαέτω) τιμάτω	(τιμαέτωσαν) τιμάτωσαν	(τιμαέσθω) τιμάσθω	(τιμαέσθωσαν) τιμάσθωσαν				
Infinitive Mode		(τιμάειν) τιμᾶν		(τιμάεσθαι) τιμᾶσθαι					
Participle Mode (Nom. Sg. Form)	Masculine	(τιμάων) τιμῶν		(τιμαόμενος) τιμώμενος					
	Feminine	(τιμάουσα) τιμῶσα		(τιμαομένη) τιμωμένη					
	Neuter	(τιμάον) τιμῶν		(τιμαόμενον) τιμώμενον					

The first principle part of the conjugation of φιλέω, *I love*, root φιλε–, is as follows:

φιλε–

		Present Active Singular	Present Active Plural	Imperfect Active Singular	Imperfect Active Plural	Present Middle/Passive Singular	Present Middle/Passive Plural	Imperfect Middle/Passive Singular	Imperfect Middle/Passive Plural
Indicative Mood	1st	φιλῶ (φιλέω)	φιλοῦμεν (φιλέομεν)	ἐφίλουν (ἐφίλεον)	ἐφιλοῦμεν (ἐφιλέομεν)	φιλοῦμαι (φιλέομαι)	φιλούμεθα (φιλεόμεθα)	ἐφιλούμην (ἐφιλεόμην)	ἐφιλούμεθα (ἐφιλεόμεθα)
	2nd	φιλεῖς (φιλέεις)	φιλεῖτε (φιλέετε)	ἐφίλεις (ἐφίλεες)	ἐφιλεῖτε (ἐφιλέετε)	φιλῇ (φιλέῃ)	φιλεῖσθε (φιλέεσθε)	ἐφιλοῦ (ἐφιλέου)	ἐφιλεῖσθε (ἐφιλέεσθε)
	3rd	φιλεῖ (φιλέει)	φιλοῦσι(ν) (φιλέουσι(ν))	ἐφίλει (ἐφίλεε)	ἐφίλουν (ἐφίλεον)	φιλεῖται (φιλέεται)	φιλοῦνται (φιλέονται)	ἐφιλεῖτο (ἐφιλέετο)	ἐφιλοῦντο (ἐφιλέοντο)
Subjunctive Mood	1st	φιλῶ (φιλέω)	φιλῶμεν (φιλέωμεν)			φιλῶμαι (φιλέωμαι)	φιλώμεθα (φιλεώμεθα)		
	2nd	φιλῇς (φιλέῃς)	φιλῆτε (φιλέητε)			φιλῇ (φιλέῃ)	φιλῆσθε (φιλέησθε)		
	3rd	φιλῇ (φιλέῃ)	φιλῶσι(ν) (φιλέωσι(ν))			φιλῆται (φιλέηται)	φιλῶνται (φιλέωνται)		
Imperative Mood	2nd	φίλει (φίλεε)	φιλεῖτε (φιλέετε)			φιλοῦ (φιλέου)	φιλεῖσθε (φιλέεσθε)		
	3rd	φιλείτω (φιλεέτω)	φιλείτωσαν (φιλεέτωσαν)			φιλείσθω (φιλεέσθω)	φιλείσθωσαν (φιλεέσθωσαν)		

		Active	Middle/Passive
Infinitive Mode		φιλεῖν (φιλέειν)	φιλεῖσθαι (φιλέεσθαι)
Participle Mode (Nom. Sg. Form)	Masculine	φιλῶν (φιλέων)	φιλούμενος (φιλεόμενος)
	Feminine	φιλοῦσα (φιλέουσα)	φιλουμένη (φιλεομένη)
	Neuter	φιλοῦν (φιλέον)	φιλούμενον (φιλεόμενον)

The first principle part of the conjugation of δηλόω, *I make,* root δηλο–, is as follows:

δηλο–									
		Present Active		**Present Middle/Passive**		**Imperfect Active**		**Imperfect Middle/Passive**	
		Singular	Plural	Singular	Plural	Singular	Plural	Singular	Plural
Indicative Mood	1st	(δηλόω) δηλῶ	(δηλόομεν) δηλοῦμεν	(δηλόομαι) δηλοῦμαι	(δηλοόμεθα) δηλούμεθα	(ἐδήλοον) ἐδήλουν	(ἐδηλόομεν) ἐδηλοῦμεν	(ἐδηλοόμην) ἐδηλούμην	(ἐδηλοόμεθα) ἐδηλούμεθα
	2nd	(δηλόεις) δηλοῖς	(δηλόετε) δηλοῦτε	(δηλόῃ) δηλοῖ	(δηλόεσθε) δηλοῦσθε	(ἐδήλοες) ἐδήλους	(ἐδηλόετε) ἐδηλοῦτε	(ἐδηλόου) ἐδηλοῦ	(ἐδηλόεσθε) ἐδηλοῦσθε
	3rd	(δηλόει) δηλοῖ	(δηλόουσι(ν)) δηλοῦσι(ν)	(δηλόεται) δηλοῦται	(δηλόονται) δηλοῦνται	(ἐδήλοε) ἐδήλου	(ἐδήλοον) ἐδήλουν	(ἐδηλόετο) ἐδηλοῦτο	(ἐδηλόοντο) ἐδηλοῦντο
Subjunctive Mood	1st	(δηλόω) δηλῶ	(δηλόωμεν) δηλῶμεν	(δηλόωμαι) δηλῶμαι	(δηλοώμεθα) δηλώμεθα				
	2nd	(δηλόῃς) δηλοῖς	(δηλόητε) δηλῶτε	(δηλόῃ) δηλοῖ	(δηλόησθε) δηλῶσθε				
	3rd	(δηλόῃ) δηλοῖ	(δηλόωσι(ν)) δηλῶσι(ν)	(δηλόηται) δηλῶται)	(δηλόωνται) δηλῶνται				
Imperative Mood	2nd	(δήλοε) δήλου	(δηλόετε) δηλοῦτε	(δηλόου) δηλοῦ	(δηλόεσθε) δηλοῦσθε				
	3rd	(δηλοέτω) δηλούτω	(δηλοέτωσαν) δηλούτωσαν	(δηλοέσθω) δηλούσθω	(δηλοέσθωσαν) δηλούσθωσαν				
Infinitive Mode		(δηλόειν) δηλοῦν		(δηλόεσθαι) δηλοῦσθαι					
Participle Mode (Nom. Sg. Form)	Masculine	(δηλόων) δηλῶν		(δηλοόμενος) δηλούμενος					
	Feminine	(δηλόουσα) δυλοῦσα		(δηλοομένη) δηλουμένη					
	Neuter	(δηλόον) δηλοῦν		(δηλοόμενον) δηλούμενον					

Verbs: Second Aorist Active and Middle Voice

The third principle part of λείπω, *I leave*, root λιπ–, is as follows:

		ἐλιπ–			
		Aorist Active		Aorist Middle	
		Singular	Plural	Singular	Plural
Indicative Mood	1st	ἔλιπον	ἐλίπομεν	ἐλιπόμην	ἐλιπόμεθα
	2nd	ἔλιπες	ἐλίπετε	ἐλίπου	ἐλίπεσθε
	3rd	ἔλιπε(ν)	ἔλιπον	ἐλίπετο	ἐλίποντο
Subjunctive Mood	1st	λίπω	λίπωμεν	λίπωμαι	λιπώμεθα
	2nd	λίπῃς	λίπητε	λίπῃ	λίπησθε
	3rd	λίπῃ	λίπωσι(ν)	λίπηται	λίπωνται
Imperative Mood	2nd	λίπε	λίπετε	λιπου	λίπεσθε
	3rd	λιπέτω	λιπέτωσαν	λιπέσθω	λιπέσθωσαν
Infinitive Mode		λιπεῖν		λιπέσθαι	
Participle Mode (Nom. Sg. Form)	Masculine	λιπών		λιπόμενος	
	Feminine	λιποῦσα		λιπομένη	
	Neuter	λιπόν		λιπόμενον	

Verbs: Future and Aorist of Liquid Verbs

The second and third principle parts of κρίνω, *I judge*, root κριν–, is as follows:

		κρινεσ–				κρινα-			
		Future Active		Future Middle		Aorist Active		Aorist Middle	
		Singular	Plural	Singular	Plural	Singular	Plural	Singular	Plural
Indicative Mood	1st	κρινῶ	κρινοῦμεν	κρινοῦμαι	κρινούμεθα	ἔκρινα	ἐκίναμεν	ἐκρινάμην	ἐκρινάμεθα
	2nd	κρινεῖς	κρινεῖτε	κρινῇ	κρινεῖσθε	ἔκρινας	ἐκρίνατε	ἐκρίνω	ἐκρίνασθε
	3rd	κρινεῖ	κρινοῦσι(ν)	κρινεῖται	κρινοῦνται	ἔκρινε(ν)	ἔκριναν	ἐκρίνατο	ἐκρίναντο
Subjunctive Mood	1st					κρίνω	κρίνωμεν	κρίνωμαι	κρίνωμεθα
	2nd					κρίνῃς	κρίνητε	κρίνῃ	κρίνησθε
	3rd					κρίνῃ	κρίνωσι(ν)	κρίνηται	κρίνωνται
Imperative Mood	2nd					κρῖνον	κρίνατε	κρῖναι	κρίνασθε
	3rd					κρινάτω	κρινάτωσαν	κρινάσθω	κρινάσθωσαν
Infinitive Mode						κρῖναι		κρίνασθαι	
Participle Mode (Nom. Sg. Form)	Masculine					κρίνας		κρινάμενος	
	Feminine					κρίνασα		κριναμένη	
	Neuter					κρῖναν		κρινάμενον	

Verbs: μι conjugation

The first principle part of δίδωμι, *I give*, root δο–, is as follows:

δίδο–								
		Present Active		Present Middle/Passive		Imperfect Active		Imperfect Middle/Passive	
		Singular	Plural	Singular	Plural	Singular	Plural	Singular	Plural
Indicative Mood	1st	δίδωμι	δίδομεν	δίδομαι	διδόμεθα	ἐδίδουν	ἐδίδομεν	ἐδιδόμην	ἐδιδόμεθα
	2nd	δίδως	δίδοτε	δίδοσαι	δίδοσθε	ἐδίδους	ἐδίδοτε	ἐδίδοσο	ἐδίδοσθε
	3rd	δίδωσι(ν)	διδόασι(ν)	δίδοται	δίδονται	ἐδίδου	ἐδίδοσαν	ἐδίδοτο	ἐδίδοντο

		Present Active		Present Middle/Passive			
		Singular	Plural	Singular	Plural		
Subjunctive Mood	1st	διδῶ	διδῶμεν	διδῶμαι	διδώμεθα		
	2nd	διδῷς	διδῶτε	διδῷ	διδῶσθε		
	3rd	διδῷ	διδῶσι(ν)	διδῶται	διδῶνται		
Imperative Mood	2nd	δίδου	δίδοτε	δίδοσο	δίδοσθε		
	3rd	διδότω	διδότωσαν	διδόσθω	διδόσθωσαν		

Infinitive Mode		διδόναι		διδόσθαι	

Participle Mode (Nom. Sg. Form)	Masculine	διδούς		διδόμενος	
	Feminine	διδοῦσα		διδομένη	
	Neuter	διδόν		διδόμενον	

The third principle part of δίδωμι, *I give*, root δο–, is as follows:

		δωκα–			
		Aorist Active		Aorist Middle	
		Singular	Plural	Singular	Plural
Indicative Mood	1st	ἔδωκα	ἐδώκαμεν	ἐδόμην	ἐδόμεθα
	2nd	ἔδωκας	ἐδώκατε	ἔδου	ἔδοσθε
	3rd	ἔδωκε(ν)	ἔδωκαν	ἔδοτο	ἔδοντο
Subjunctive Mood	1st	δῶ	δῶμεν	δῶμαι	δώμεθα
	2nd	δῷς	δῶτε	δῷ	δῶσθε
	3rd	δῷ	δῶσι(ν)	δῶται	δῶνται
Imperative Mood	2nd	δός	δότε	δοῦ	δόσθε
	3rd	δότω	δότωσαν	δόσθω	δόσθωσαν
Infinitive Mode		δοῦναι		δόσθαι	
Participle Mode (Nom. Sg. Form)	Masculine	δούς		δόμενος	
	Feminine	δοῦσα		δομένη	
	Neuter	δόν		δόμενον	

The first principle part of τίθημι, *I place*, root θε–, is as follows:

τίθε–

		Present Active		Present Middle/Passive		Imperfect Active		Imperfect Middle/Passive	
		Singular	Plural	Singular	Plural	Singular	Plural	Singular	Plural
Indicative Mood	1st	τίθημι	τίθεμεν	τίθεμαι	τιθέμεθα	ἐτίθην	ἐτίθεμεν	ἐτιθέμην	ἐτιθέμεθα
	2nd	τίθης	τίθετε	τίθεσαι	τίθεσθε	ἐτίθεις	ἐτίθετε	ἐτίθεσο	ἐτίθεσθε
	3rd	τίθησι(ν)	τιθέασι(ν)	τίθεται	τίθενται	ἐτίθει	ἐτίθεσαν	ἐτίθετο	ἐτίθεντο
Subjunctive Mood	1st	τιθῶ	τιθῶμεν	τιθῶμαι	τιθώμεθα				
	2nd	τιθῇς	τιθῆτε	τιθῇ	τιθῆσθε				
	3rd	τιθῇ	τιθῶσι(ν)	τιθῆται	τιθῶνται				
Imperative Mood	2nd	τίθει	τίθετε	τίθεσο	τίθεσθε				
	3rd	τιθέτω	τιθέτωσαν	τιθέσθω	τιθέσθωσαν				
Infinitive Mode		τιθέναι		τίθεσθαι					
Participle Mode (Nom. Sg. Form)	Masculine	τιθείς		τιθέμενος					
	Feminine	τιθεῖσα		τιθεμένη					
	Neuter	τιθέν		τιθέμενον					

The third principle part of τίθημι, *I place*, root θε–, is as follows:

		θηκα–			
		Aorist Active		**Aorist Middle**	
		Singular	Plural	Singular	Plural
Indicative Mood	1st	ἔθηκα	ἐθήκαμεν	ἐθέμην	ἐθέμεθα
	2nd	ἔθηκας	ἐθήκατε	ἔθου	ἔθεσθε
	3rd	ἔθηκε(ν)	ἔθηκαν	ἔθετο	ἔθεντπ
Subjunctive Mood	1st	θῶ	θῶμεν	θῶμαι	θώμεθα
	2nd	θῇς	θῆτε	θῇ	θῆστε
	3rd	θῇ	θῶσι(ν)	θῆται	θῶνται
Imperative Mood	2nd	θές	θέτε	θοῦ	θέσθε
	3rd	θέτω	θέτωσαν	θέσθω	θέσθωσαν
Infinitive Mode		θεῖναι		θέσθαι	
Participle Mode	Masculine	θείς		θέμενος	
	Feminine	θεῖσα		θεμένη	
(Nom. Sg. Form)	Neuter	θέν		θέμενον	

The first principle part of ἵστημι, I stand, root στα–, is as follows:

ἵστα–

		Present Active		Present Middle/Passive		Imperfect Active		Imperfect Middle/Passive	
		Singular	Plural	Singular	Plural	Singular	Plural	Singular	Plural
Indicative Mood	1st	ἵστημι	ἵσταμεν	ἵσταμαι	ἱστάμεθα	ἵστην	ἵσταμεν	ἱστάμην	ἱστάμεθα
	2nd	ἵστης	ἵστατε	ἵστασαι	ἵστασθε	ἵστης	ἵστατε	ἵστασο	ἵστασθε
	3rd	ἵστησι(ν)	ἱστᾶσι(ν)	ἵσταται	ἵστανται	ἵστη	ἵστασαν	ἵστατο	ἵσταντο

		Present Active		Present Middle/Passive	
		Singular	Plural	Singular	Plural
Subjunctive Mood	1st	ἱστῶ	ἱστῶμεν	ἱστῶμαι	ἱστώμεθα
	2nd	ἱστῇς	ἱστῆτε	ἱστῇ	ἱστῆσθε
	3rd	ἱστῇ	ἱστῶσι(ν)	ἱστῆται	ἱστῶνται
Imperative Mood	2nd	ἵστη	ἵστατε	ἵστασο	ἵστασθε
	3rd	ἱστάτω	ἱστάντων	ἱστάσθω	ἱστάσθων

Infinitive Mode	ἱστάναι	ἵστασθαι

Participle Mode (Nom. Sg. Form)	Masculine	ἱστάς	ἱστάμενος
	Feminine	ἱστᾶσα	ἱσταμένη
	Neuter	ἱστάν	ἱστάμενον

The third principle part of ἵστημι, *I stand*, root στα–, and γινώσκω, *I know*, root γνω–, is as follows: (Note that ἵστημι sometimes occurs as a second or root aroist, as this paradigm shows.)

		στη–		γνω–	
		Aorist Active		**Aorist Middle**	
		Singular	Plural	Singular	Plural
Indicative Mood	1st	ἔστην	ἔστημεν	ἔγνων	ἔγνωμεν
	2nd	ἔστης	ἔστητε	ἔγνως	ἔγνωτε
	3rd	ἔστη	ἔστησαν	ἔγνω	ἔγνωσαν
Subjunctive Mood	1st	στῶ	στῶμεν	γνῶ	γνῶμεν
	2nd	στῇς	στῆτε	γνῷς	γνῶτε
	3rd	στῇ	στῶσι(ν)	γνῷ / γνοῖ	γνῶσι(ν)
Imperative Mood	2nd	στῆθι	στῆτε	γνῶθι	γνῶτε
	3rd	στήτω	στήτωσαν	γνώτω	γνώτωσαν
Infinitive Mode		στῆναι		γνῶναι	
Participle Mode	Masculine	στάς		γνούς	
	Feminine	στᾶσα		γνοῦσα	
(Nom. Sg. Form)	Neuter	στάν		γνόν	

The conjugation of εἰμί, *I am*, root εσ-, is as follows:

εἰμί						
		Present		Imperfect		Future	
		Singular	Plural	Singular	Plural	Singular	Plural
Indicative Mood	1st	εἰμί	ἐσμέν	ἤμην	ἦμεν	ἔσομαι	ἐσόμεθα
	2nd	εἶ	ἐστέ	ἦς	ἦτε	ἔσῃ	ἔσεσθε
	3rd	ἐστί(ν)	εἰσί(ν)	ἦν	ἦσαν	ἔσται	ἔσονται
Subjunctive Mood	1st	ὦ	ὦμεν				
	2nd	ᾖς	ἦτε				
	3rd	ᾖ	ὦσι(ν)				
Imperative Mood	2nd	ἴσθι	ἔστε				
	3rd	ἔστω	ἔστωσαν				
Optative Mood	1st	εἴην	εἶμεν / εἴημεν				
	2nd	εἴης	εἶτε / εἴητε				
	3rd	εἴη	εἶεν / εἴησαν				
Infinitive Mode		εἶναι					
Participle Mode (Nom. Sg. Form)	Masculine	ὤν					
	Feminine	οὖσα					
	Neuter	ὄν					

Verbs: Conjugation of οἶδα

The conjugation of οἶδα, *I know*, root οἰδ–, is as follows:

		Perfect Active		Pluperfect Active	
		Singular	Plural	Singular	Plural
Indicative Mood	1st	οἶδα	οἴδαμεν	ᾔδειν	ᾔδειμεν
	2nd	οἶδας	οἴδατε	ᾔδεις	ᾔδειτε
	3rd	οἶδε(ν)	οἴδασι(ν)	ᾔδει	ᾔδεισαν
Subjunctive Mood	1st	εἰδῶ	εἰδῶμεν		
	2nd	εἰδῇς	εἰδῆτε		
	3rd	εἰδῇ	εἰδῶσι(ν)		
Imperative Mood	2nd	ἴσθι	ἴστε		
	3rd	ἴστω	ἴστωσαν		
Infinitive Mode		εἰδέναι			
Participle Mode (Nom. Sg. Form)	Masculine	εἰδώς			
	Feminine	εἰδυῖα			
	Neuter	εἰδός			

7127849R00133